600942

769.207 NEL

D1356466

WITHDRAWN FROM LIBRARY STOCK

THE DESIGN WAY

THE DESIGN WAY

Intentional Change in an Unpredictable World

Second Edition

Harold G. Nelson and Erik Stolterman

The MIT Press
Cambridge, Massachusetts
London, England

© 2012 Harold G. Nelson and Erik Stolterman

All rights reserved. No part of this book may be reproduced in any form by any electronic or mechanical means (including photocopying, recording, or information storage and retrieval) without permission in writing from the publisher.

MIT Press books may be purchased at special quantity discounts for business or sales promotional use. For information, please email special_sales@mitpress.mit.edu or write to Special Sales Department, The MIT Press, 55 Hayward Street, Cambridge, MA 02142.

This book was set in Stone Sans and Stone Serif by Toppan Best-set Premedia Limited. Printed and bound in the United States of America.

Library of Congress Cataloging-in-Publication Data

Nelson, Harold G.
The design way : intentional change in an unpredictable world / Harold G. Nelson and Erik Stolterman.—Second edition.
    p.   cm.
Includes bibliographical references and index.
ISBN 978-0-262-01817-3 (hardcover : alk. paper)
1. Design—Philosophy. 2. System design. 3. Design—Study and teaching.
I. Stolterman, Erik. II. Title.
NK1505.N43   2012
745.401—dc23
2011053205

10 9 8 7 6 5 4 3 2 1

This book is dedicated to:
Anne, Autumn, Erikka, Evelyn
Adam, Ludvig

Contents

Preface to the Second Edition

It was with mixed feelings of excitement and hesitancy that we approached the opportunity and concomitant responsibility for developing a second edition of this book. The excitement came from the opportunity both to refine some of the ideas introduced in the first edition and to add many of the new ideas that we have been working with over the last few years. The hesitation came from the realization that we might easily make changes and additions that would not necessarily be seen as improvements over what was accomplished in the first edition.

The responses we received from readers of the first edition convinced us that there indeed had been a need for the kind of book about design we wrote. Based on feedback from an astonishingly broad spectrum of readers we realized that there are people from all around the globe who are deeply engaged in advancing design scholarship. We found that there are many design practitioners who devote a significant amount of time and effort to the development of both their understanding of design as well as their improved practice of design. We also discovered that there are an immense number of people, new to the game of design, who are interested in becoming designers in newly emerging fields and professions that were just beginning to appear when we published the first edition. In addition, the growing interest in adapting design thinking to established fields, domains, or professions became apparent from the diversity of backgrounds of the readers making contact with us.

It is with amazement and satisfaction that we have followed the development over the last few years of the increasing general interest among a broad set of stakeholders in design thinking, design theory, and even in the philosophy of design. We started our work on the first edition in the early 1990s, finalizing the writing about ten years later. During that time we had little idea that design learning, design thinking, and design practice would become such a recognized part of not only academia, but the realms of business and government as well.

The ever-growing interest in design as an important and essential approach to intentional change made it compelling to further develop our ideas from the first edition of this book. However, even if awareness and interest in design have grown, there is still a need for further advancing and championing the "big" ideas introduced in the first edition. We are still pushing to make a case for the recognition of design as its own intellectual and practical tradition of human inquiry and action on equal footing with science, art, and the humanities. Today it is even more important to make the case for an intellectually viable and well-grounded scholarly approach to design.

We see the second edition of our book as a continuation of the first edition's support for the development of a widespread design culture and a philosophy of design that is stable and true to the "nature" of design. Our intention is that this new edition will be even more supportive of the individual designer learning how to think and act with increasing competence in a designerly way.

This second edition has gone through both large and small revisions. Every chapter has been refined and modified. We have revisited our use of core concepts and terms with the purpose of being more consistent. We have added, updated, or removed references where it was important to do so.

We have also changed our approach to graphics in the second edition. We have introduced the notion of *schema* as the primary means for representing holistic concepts, ideas, and fundamental knowledge in visual form. This means that there is an increased importance vested in the graphics—that is, the schemas—to expand and complement the text in revealing or reflecting deeper understandings of design.

Among the bigger changes that appear in the second edition are two rewritten chapters—chapter 3, formerly "Systems," is now "Systemics" and chapter 10, "Production and Caretaking," is now "Craft and Material." We have completely removed the last part of the first edition—Character and Competence—and added a new part V—A Drawing Together—with two new chapters—chapter 14, "Becoming a Designer," and chapter 15, "Being a Designer." We have added an epilogue—"The Way Forward"— where we invite the readers to take a look into the future of design and their own design futures.

We are extremely grateful to all the students and colleagues who have commented on and critiqued the book over the years. This includes nonacademic colleagues and interested individuals as well who have provided us a tremendous amount of support and encouragement. The critiques, both positive and negative, have been very helpful and are appreciated. They have helped us to understand how we can further develop and communicate our ideas—to make them more available and relevant to our readers.

We would like to thank our colleagues and students at Carnegie Mellon University; The Naval Postgraduate School; Indiana University Bloomington; and Umeå University, Sweden. We thank the School of Computer Science at the University of Montana for their support. We also thank Anne Nelson for her continued invaluable assistance in crafting the draft document. We are very appreciative of Robert Sandusky's reviews of earlier drafts and his invaluable suggestions for their improvement.

We are particularly grateful to Doug Sery and the MIT Press for giving us this opportunity to publish the second edition of *The Design Way*.

Harold G. Nelson
Erik Stolterman

Acknowledgments from First Edition

Many people have helped us in developing both the content of this book and its form. We owe them a great deal and would like to give them our thanks for their friendship, support, and professionalism. We have had the chance to work with a number of colleagues in different design fields over the years. Their questions, thoughts, and ideas have greatly helped us to formulate our own composition. But, since our work on the book has been going on for quite some time, we know that we cannot acknowledge all of you, who in one way or another contributed to this final version of the book. So, to all of you: Thanks!

We are deeply thankful to our students, both in the United States and in Sweden, who have helped us by reading earlier versions, asking questions, and being honestly critical of ideas, but especially for encouraging us to go on with our work.

We want to thank the following individuals and organizations specifically. We would like to thank our colleague and friend Bob Sandusky, cofounder and officer in the Advanced Design Institute. We send our thanks to Elizabeth Heffron as well, for her invaluable insights, guidance, and support in crafting the final text. We also thank Torbjörn Nordström, Anna Croon Fors, Kristo Ivanov, Jonas Löwgren, and Lawrence Lipsitz for their willingness to read, reflect, and comment on earlier versions of this text. In addition, we would like to thank Anne Nelson for her assistance with the early drafts as well as the final drafting of our manuscript. Her energy and support were the constants we came to depend on. Finally, we would like to thank those who read and commented on our final draft of the manuscript: Russell Ackoff, Tom Fisher, Russell Osguthorpe, Jim Platts, and Gordon Rowland.

We also want to express our gratitude to the Swedish research funds, The Bank of Sweden Tercentenary Foundation and The Swedish Research

Council, for their financial support; without their assistance this work would never have been possible.

Most important, we want to thank our families for their unconditional support and encouragement.

Harold G. Nelson, Seattle
Erik Stolterman, Djäkneböle

Prelude

Genesis is ongoing. As human beings, we continuously create things that help reshape the reality and essence of the world as we know it. When we create new things—technologies, organizations, processes, environments, ways of thinking, or systems—we engage in design. To come up with an idea of what we think would be an ideal addition to the world, and to give real existence—form, structure, and shape—to that idea, is at the core of design as a human activity. This book is about that activity.

Design is a natural and ancient human ability—the first tradition among many traditions of human inquiry and action. Everyone is designing most of the time—whether they are conscious of it, or not. Framing our understanding of design in this way, we define, and promote, a new philosophical look at this seminal human tradition through a reconstituted culture of inquiry and action. We identify that culture as The Design Way— manifested as a schema of the first tradition. This approach applies to an infinite variety of design domains including those fields that are traditionally thought of when we consider the concept of design, such as architectural and interior design, industrial design, engineering design, graphic design, urban design, information systems design, software design, interaction design, fashion design, and other forms of material and immaterial design. But our approach also allows us to include nontraditional design areas, such as organizational design, social systems design, educational systems design, workplace design, and healthcare design. Such a design approach can even be applied to significant social institutions such as governance, including the design of democratic constitutions (Sunstein 2001).

In the struggle to understand and interact in an ever more complex and dynamic reality, we believe the current traditions of inquiry and action prevalent in our society do not give us the support we need—as designers and leaders—to meet the emergent challenges that now confront us and will continue to confront us in the future. The world is changing rapidly, sometimes with intent, but too often by accident. The world has proven to be unpredictable, despite the best attempts of science and technology to bring predictability and control to worldly affairs. The laws of nature may be universal, but the complex interactions of everyday events, whether provoked by accident or fate, result in unpredictable outcomes. The one thing that makes this state of affairs tolerable is the inchoate knowledge that change—desired change—can be wrought by human intention. Human intention, made visible and concrete through the instrumentality of design, enables us to create conditions, systems, and artifacts that facilitate the unfolding of human potential through designed evolution in contrast to an evolution based on chance and necessity—a highly unpredictable process.

In our attempts to design the world to be what we would like it to be, we find that the intellectual traditions at hand cannot fully support that task. Science, art, spirituality, economics, and technology are all important traditions of inquiry in their own right. However, they do not embody the unique attributes and competencies of the design tradition, with its corresponding approach to scholarship and praxis. Each of the prevailing traditions has developed a depth of knowledge and insight that is impressive, but it is often focused on only one aspect or dimension of our human experience—one that is necessary but not solely sufficient in the management of human affairs.

We believe the culture of inquiry and action that infuses design thinking is an essential part of the variety of human traditions of being in the world—of "human being." Even though other outstanding scholars (Schön 1983; Margolin and Buchanan 1995; Banathy 1996; Cross 2001; Krippendorff 2006) have investigated the concept of a design tradition, design has remained surprisingly invisible and unrecognized in the world at large. This book is an attempt to change this, making the case for design as its own tradition by formulating its fundamental core of ideas. *The Design Way* does not present a ready-made recipe on how to think about or engage in design. This is not a detailed hands-on book about design praxis (which is a topic that deserves several books of its own). It is not exclusively something for professional designers or design academics. It is a way to approach the reality of the human condition by intentionally embracing the richness of possibilities; the complexity of choices and the overwhelming challenges of getting it right—in short, a book on how to understand design.

Our ultimate desire is to encourage and promote a design culture. For any tradition to flourish, that tradition requires a nurturing environment, a protective container within which its frontiers and prospects are defined and protected. A viable design tradition requires the enabling presence of a design culture, one that defines conceptual expanses and boundaries, and provides a context for setting particular limits on any design project. Such a design culture acts as a catalyst in the formation of social crucibles essential for sustaining the intensity of design action. It is a protective environment that provides the space and freedom necessary to foster a process that is both powerful and vulnerable at the same time.

What is presented in this book is a composition of what we believe a broad and deep understanding of design—as a tradition of inquiry and action—should include. This composition is, in itself, a design. It is not an attempt to present a scientifically true or accurate description of a design culture. Nor is it an attempt to answer all questions that might emerge concerning what a design culture might, should, or ought to, be. It is our understanding of design, as its own tradition and not merely a variant of science, or art, or technology, or spirituality. It is an effort to build a deeper understanding of design, based on ideas we believe must be present in the development and implementation of a design culture—the necessary ingredients for the release of design's full potential and promise for generative human agency.

What we have set out to do was to write a book about the philosophy of design in distinction to a book about the philosophy of science, the philosophy of the science of design, or the philosophy of design science. Those were all candidates but we very carefully attempted to look at design as its own tradition and not as a specific or special form of science, art, or any other existing approach.

It follows that we did not attempt to make our case using evidence-supported design (a Lockean analysis), or theorizing about design, (a Leibnizian analysis), or as a dialectic approach focused on design issues (a Hegelian analysis). Instead, we want to make our case using a design approach to inquiry. We do not ignore or reject science, art, and other traditions of inquiry—we sweep them in as part of design inquiry. This does not mean that we have just "made things up," however, any more than an artist just "makes up" a painting or a composer "makes up" a symphony. We have used the same design foundations and fundamentals we write about as touchstones for crafting the book. What we hope readers will do is to look at the ideas presented here from the stance of a designer.

The book is not a scientific treatise or a manifesto. It is a composition of ideas. We are not basing our concept on a body of data or a consensus of agreement among experts as would be rightly expected in a science-based dissertation. It is true that there are habits of thinking that will be challenged in the way the book has been composed and in the ideas forming the color and texture of the overall composition. We hope that the book will be read from the design tradition rather than regarded from a science or arts and humanities tradition.

The Design Way is an introduction to many ideas that deserve a composition of their own. We feel that it is important, however, to present them here as a whole, as part of our composition. We are not proposing a particular theory, or a set of theorems, or axioms. Instead, we have chosen to use a schema of *foundations*, *fundamentals*, and *metaphysics* as the unifying elements of the book. The foundations are equivalent to the first principles or causes of other traditions such as science. The fundamentals we identify as those core concepts of the design approach that can be learned and improved on through practice and reflection. The metaphysics arises as a consequence of the interaction of the foundations and fundamentals of the design tradition, with one another and with the larger domains of human existence.

This structure of foundations, fundamentals, and metaphysics best reflects the level of our intention in making a case for a design culture. Over the years, we have found that these are emergent patterns that have continually informed the integration of our ideas as a whole. We find that it is possible to make a composition from this tripartite relationship; one that reflects, in different ways, what we see as the core of a design approach —a design way. The concluding part V titled A Drawing Together brings the foundational, fundamental, and metaphysical issues discussed in the book to bear on two integrative discussions concerning what is entailed in becoming a designer and what one must understand in order to practice as a designer. These two design dialogues form distinct compositional depictions of what a design culture might look like from a learner's perspective and from a practitioner's perspective.

The idea of a design culture is one that promotes an understanding of design as transcendent of particular contexts, specific disciplines, or single concepts. For instance, it is commonly believed that design is simply a form of creativity. Creativity is thought of as the activity that gives design its special qualities even though creativity is equally important in the arts and sciences. But, even though creativity is seminal to design, design is larger and more comprehensive than that. Design is inclusive not only of creative thinking but innovative, productive, and compositional activities as well. Innovation and production differ from creativity in that they are oriented to taking action in the real world whereas creativity can be done for its own sake. Design is realized through the manifestation and integration of ideal, if not always creative, concepts into the real world. Design is a compound of rational, ideal, and pragmatic inquiry. Design is constituted of reflective and critical thinking, productive action, and responsible follow through. Therefore, a single concept, such as creativity, does not capture the full richness of the design tradition.

A design culture needs to be broad in its scope and deep in its meaning and utility. Thinking about design in this way, we hope to define a firm platform from which designers, in any field, can bring this new appreciation for the potential of design into action. With this in mind, we will often use the term "design" to stand for this broader meaning of a design culture.

The process of design is always the most effective and efficient means of getting organizations and individuals to new places. Design is therefore about leadership—and leadership is therefore an essential element of any design culture. Leadership today demands action and the ability to act, based on an overwhelming amount of insufficient information within restrictive limits of resources and time. These demands cannot be met primarily from within the traditions of science, art, or pragmatic technology. These demands require leaders to imagine, implement, and communicate adequate responses that are sustainable—in all their implications. This is a task that calls for good judgment—not problem solving. It calls for compelling compositions and effective creations—not true solutions. We argue therefore that *The Design Way* is not only for designers, but for leaders as well. We believe that leaders and designers are often one and the same, and that it is important for leaders to recognize that their challenge is that of a designer—to determine direction and destination via the design tradition.

The Design Way is based on the notion of reflections and substance. We hope that the book, as a composition, will evoke an appreciation for what design is all about in both its form and substance. Each chapter is an attempt to reflect that substance and give it some form. Each reflection reveals an image of one aspect of design, which obviously is not enough on its own to reveal the bigger picture of design. We do believe, though, that by moving among these different reflective images, recognition and understanding of the substance itself (i.e., what design is all about) and its compound form will emerge. This means we encourage readers to choose to read those reflections (or chapters) that seem most interesting or suitable

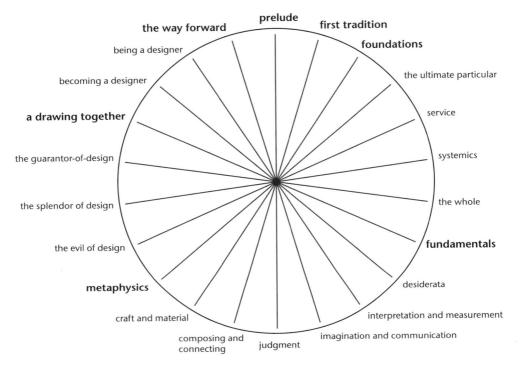

Figure P.1
The Design Way hyperlogue

to them. Even if the book is designed as a composition with an overarching structure, it is possible to read the chapters independently, as parts of a *hyperlogue* (see figure P.1). In a hyperlogue one can start on any topic and move to another in no particular order, other than interest, with the assurance that a pattern of interests will emerge and that all topics will be interconnected at the end.

Our hope is that each reflection or image of design, each chapter, will intrigue the reader to delve further, eventually creating a more comprehensive understanding of the substance of design. This is also true of the individual graphics found throughout the text. The graphics are not meant merely to illustrate the text, as the text is not meant merely to explain the graphics. The graphics in many cases are meant to momentarily arrest the progress of the acquiring eye in order to give the reflective eye time and space to provoke questions and elicit understandings and insights that are relevant to the reader's own experiences and understanding. In this way the author's ideas can be translated into the reader's own ideas.

The graphics or illustrations in this book should be understood and read as design *schemas*. Schemas can be divided into two different categories—ontological (inquiry into the nature of real things) and epistemological (inquiry into how we learn and know about things). *Ontological schemas* are cognitive models, or mental models, that humans create for themselves to help make sense of complex real-world experiences. *Design schemas* are epistemological models utilized in design inquiry. They are compositionally ordered or organized cognitive schematics used to support design inquiry and action, just as scientific schemas—hypothesis and theories, for example—are structured to assist in predicting the behavior and nature of things in the real world:

As Immanuel Kant put it, more than 200 years ago, scientific theories are *schemas*: they "enable the understanding to apply its categories and unify experience." In other words, the grand strategy of research is not just to trace out itineraries of cause and effect: it is to *represent* "schematically" those aspects of nature that can be grasped in principle and/or used in practice.

Thus, the conceptual culture of science includes a number of characteristic schemas. Of these, the simplest and most widely used is the notion of a *system*. (Ziman 2000)

Unlike scientific schemas, which represent true things, design schemas are used to form particular representations or aspects of ideal things out of a cloud of possibilities, in support of a divergent or expansive process of inquiry. It is a process that brings things into existence and whose outcomes are not predetermined but are the consequence of human volition and judgment.

A design schema is insufficient as a sole guide to design inquiry, since it offers only a singular perspective, among multiple possible perspectives, of phenomena or concepts too complex to be captured from a single station point. A schema's value is determined by its advantage in use. There are no true or false design schemas, as in the case of scientific schemas, but only ones that turn out to be very effective or else prove to be unhelpful. Specific design schemas may work better for some designers than other designers.

We have chosen to use design schemas as a means throughout the book to visualize, conceptualize, and structure our understanding of design inquiry. These schemas do not have the same epistemological purpose as scientific schemas, that is, they do not take on the intention of representing a true description of reality. Design schemas instead are strategies or tactics for design inquiry that can be characterized as:

• Organized patterns of thinking, that is, models of design inquiry.
• Ordered clusters of ideas for guiding design inquiry.

• Strategies for gaining design knowledge with the purpose of taking action.

• Knowledge structures or cognitive representations of design thinking.

• Cognitive frameworks representing a means for managing systemic inquiry formulated around specific design issues.

• Insights into how to give form to infinitely complex information and sense data.

• Cognitive structures that organize subjective, objective, and imaginative design-thinking processes.

Design schemas are the product of creative insights into how to engage in design inquiry in the same way that breakthrough thinking—the "ah-ha!" moments in creative endeavors—are representations of possible solutions for particular design outcomes. They share the same underlying processes of subconscious judgment making that unify immensely complex inputs of information and design reasoning into singular images. The ability to create and use high-value schemas is at the heart of design scholarship, just as the ability to creatively posit well-formed hypotheses and test their validity is at the heart of scientific scholarship. We therefore hope that the reader will take the needed time to pause, examine, and reflect on the (often graphical) schemas we present. In line with the saying "a picture is worth a thousand words" we believe that a good schema has the same quality as a great photo. Great schemas invite close readings, offer many ways to be interpreted, and inspire different meanings and understandings.

We also hope that reading *The Design Way* will sway others to participate in the creation of a design culture as a consequence of the influences of a revitalized and reconstituted tradition of design. This means the book is not only for designers, or for those who hope to become designers: it is for everyone. Each person, in his or her own way, can become responsible for the creation of a design culture. With such a design culture in place, designers will find themselves encouraged to safely pursue their design intentions in an open and supportive environment on behalf of those they serve.

In our attempts to present a broad understanding of design, we have been pragmatic in our relation to other sources. We have drawn from many intellectual traditions, and we have used philosophers and design thinkers in ways not always obvious from a standard perspective. When we make a reference to a specific philosopher, or thinker, this does not imply that we endorse the entirety of his or her work.

To make the design tradition visibly distinct from other intellectual traditions, we sometimes portray those traditions in ways that may not do them full justice. To make these traditions visible, we sometimes use an idealized and simplified understanding of their essential nature. This may seem offensive to some readers, who are led to believe our purpose is to diminish the richness of the other traditions in order to make the design tradition appear more valuable. This is not our intention, however, but merely an artifact of our pedagogical approach.

When it comes to our own ideas, we have tried to be congruent with the design tradition we are trying to explore and develop. It is the composition of our thoughts—as a whole—that carries the primary message. This means that when we discuss specific concepts—such as judgment, composition, contracting, communication, or character—we do this from within the design tradition. We do not try to provide universal definitions of these concepts that would apply across other traditions of inquiry and action. These concepts are defined through use in pragmatic design ways, with the specific purpose of revealing our grasp of design as a whole.

1 THE FIRST TRADITION

Humans did not discover fire—they designed it. The wheel was not something our ancestors merely stumbled over in a stroke of good luck; it, too, was designed. The habit of labeling significant human achievements as "discoveries," rather than "designs," discloses a critical bias in our Western tradition whereby observation dominates imagination. Absent from the conflicting descriptions of Leonardo da Vinci, as either scientist or artist, is the missing insight into his essential nature as a designer. His practical, purpose-driven and integrative approach to the world—an archetypal designer's approach—is primarily what made him so distinct in his own time, as well as our own. Through his imaginative genius, augmentations to the real world were made manifest. This has been the contribution of all designers throughout human history. Outside of nature, they are the prime creators of our experienced reality.

Carefully designed artifacts accompany the remains of our earliest ancestors. Designed implements have been found that predate the earliest human fossil remains discovered so far. In fact, it is evidence of design ability, and activity, which allows an archeologist to distinguish between a species that is not quite human and one that is. So, it appears that it is our very ability to design that determines our humanness.

Design is a *tertium quid*—a third way—distinct from the arts and sciences. In support of this argument we make a case for the reconstitution of *sophia*—the integration of *thought* and *action* through design. We make a case for design as its own tradition, one that reintegrates sophia rather than following the historical Western split between science and craft or, more recently, between science and the humanities. A similar split can be found in everyday language between thinking and doing, theory and practice, white collar and blue collar, and so on. A great deal of argument and discussion about this split has come about in the aftermath of the famous formulation by C. P. Snow (1959) of the humanities and sciences as two cultures that would not or could not be reconciled.

In the same way that confusion often arises whether architecture is a midpoint between science and art, the nature of design, too, is misrepresented. However, design is not a midpoint between the applied arts and sciences. Design is a third culture with its own founding postulates and axioms, with its own approach to learning and inquiry. Design is inclusive of things found in science such as reason and in the arts such as creativity. But just as science is inclusive of creativity it does not follow that science is the same as art or that art is subsumed under science. They are different ways of approaching and being in the world. This is also the case for design.

Design is the ability to imagine that-which-does-not-yet-exist, to make it appear in concrete form as a new, purposeful addition to the real world. Design is the *first tradition* among the many traditions of inquiry and action developed over time, including art, religion, science, and technology. We design our cosmologies, our homes, our businesses, and our lives, as well as our material artifacts. As such, design touches nearly every aspect of our experienced world. It is an important capacity, not only for those who wish to be designers, but also for those who are served in the design relationship as well. Things that really count, and are highly valued, come from design, when not directly from nature.

Possessing the ability to engage so powerfully in the world is the essence of human potential. But it is also true that humans are fallible. Design activities can do, and have done, great service for humanity. But design has done great harm as well. We cannot know for certain, that what we design is what ought to be designed. We cannot know what the unintended consequences of a design will be, and we cannot know, ahead of time, the full, systemic effects of a design implementation. We can be godlike in the cocreation of the world, yet we cannot be godlike in our guarantee that the design will be only what we intended it to be, for the reasons we intended, even with a full understanding of the necessity of the design in the first place. We will always be startled by the appearance of unintended consequences and unpleasant surprises.

An archetypal designer is represented in the Greek pantheon of gods in the persona of Hephaistos—the lame god whose counterparts appear in African and Middle Eastern mythology as well. Depending on the particular story you read, the reasons for Hephaistos's lameness vary. However, as a consequence of his condition, he was required to create tools and devices—designed artifacts, if you will—which enabled him to overcome his handicap, setting him apart from the other, more perfect gods. His great

- survive
- improve
- develop and grow
- thrive
- evolve
- serve others
- make something of lasting quality
- create something of real consequence
- participate in the never-ending genesis

Figure I.1
Purpose of designing

creativity and craftsmanship attracted the attention of the others, who contracted for his services for the creation of jewelry, homes, armor, and other godly necessities.

Hephaistos had the full potential of the other gods, but did not have their full capacity. This lack of capacity required him to bring things into existence to overcome his imperfection. With the aid of his own creations, he became the archetypal designer allowing him to fulfill his potential and claim his birthright. In the process, he began to improve the experienced realities of the other, uncompromised deities. Human designers share Hephaistos's challenge. We are lame gods in the service of prosthetic gods. We must design, because we are not perfect. Yet even though we lack this capacity for perfection, we share the potential of our creator gods to do great good, or immense harm, as we have continually demonstrated to others and ourselves over time.

As shown in the figures that follow, the question of why we design does not lend itself to a simple answer (see figure I.1). Like Hephaistos, we have to design because we want to survive, but humans also seem to have a will for continuous improvement and development that aims way beyond survival. Different psychological theories tell us that we have other purposes; for instance, we want to make a difference in the world. At the highest level, it might be that we want to participate in the "creation." In effect, we want to make the world our world.

We also display varying levels of motivation (see figure I.2). At the most basic level, we as human beings are compelled to design—it is our calling as agents of free will, who through design intelligence, can act with *design will*. As humans with design will, we are impelled to create new meaning, new forms, and new realities. The source of our free will and the compelling nature of our design will remains a mystery of human nature. Joseph

- to gain power
- to control
- from necessity
- bring order
- give meaning
- a calling
- design will
- for enlightenment
- wisdom
- lack of wholeness
- to be of service

Figure I.2
Motivation for designing

Campbell's (1968) description of the "hero's quest," a common theme in most mythologies, begins with the "call" for a hero or heroine to step out of his or her normal and comfortable life into a dangerous but necessary quest for life-enhancing wisdom. The call can be ignored, but not without consequences. The call, when answered, initiates a process leading to a life-affirming boon for the hero and his or her society—motivated by the desire to be in service to others. But that is not our only motivation. We also have the desire to be in more control of as much of our lives as possible.

On yet another level, we are drawn to design because we may feel a lack of wholeness—we do not find the world in a condition that is satisfying or fulfilling for us. And, ultimately, we are motivated to design because it is an accessible means to enlightenment, bringing order and giving meaning to our lives. It is a way for us, as it was for Hephaistos, to become what we are capable of being, but do not have the full capacity to be without our creations to aid us: what Sigmund Freud called being "prosthetic gods."

Design, as a unique way of thinking and acting, does not have a long, well-developed scholarly history. Other intellectual traditions, such as science and art, have enjoyed thousands of years of considered thought. But, in the Western tradition at the time of Socrates, Plato, and Aristotle, design, as a focus of philosophic reflection, was divided. The word "philosophy" is a compound of two Greek root terms: *philo* and *sophia*. Philo is love and sophia is wisdom; thus the term philosophy means the love of wisdom. During the pre-Socratic period in Greece, the defined understanding of wisdom or sophia, was the *knowing hand*. Sophia was an integration of thinking and action, as well as reflection and production: "For sophia originally means the skill of the craftsman, the carpenter (Iliad XV.412), the seafarer (Hesiod, Works 651), the sculptor (Aristotle, Nic. Eth. Vi.1141a). Sophia originates in and refers to the aesthetic hands of Daedalus and of Hephaistos" (Hillman 1992).

However, during the time of these philosophers, sophia was divided. In the philosophic writings of Aristotle, wisdom (sophia) became primarily the concern for first principles and causes—thus cleaving it from practical wisdom and productive action. Sophia was further divided into knowledge of ideals (the abstract) and the capacity for practical actions (the concrete). As McEwen explained:

> For Plato, episteme and sophia no longer had anything do with skill. Daedalean episteme, the uncertain, elusive knowledge of experiences, was subsumed to, absorbed by the certainty of knowledge as seeing, eidenai, with the eidos, the things seen, fixed and eternal, as its ultimate object and source. . . . The earlier understanding that sophia-as-skill, the complement of a techne that allowed kosmos to appear, was itself the very revelation of the divine in experience, had been lost. (McEwen 1993)

Sophia was not only divided into separate parts, but the resulting components were also placed at the extremes of a hierarchy. In Plato's Republic, those who *thought* about things were elevated to the pinnacle of society, while those who *made* things were positioned at the bottom of the social hierarchy. This hierarchy can be seen continued in today's world. Polarities between people, such as white-collar and blue-collar workers, management and labor, thinkers and doers, continue to play out this division of sophia. The split widens further in the polarization of ideas, like rigor versus relevance, emotion versus intellect, thinking versus doing, or abstract versus concrete. This split has proven detrimental to any formation of an inclusive and developed understanding of design as a human activity dependent on the integration of both sides.

Design's historical roots were further frayed when Aristotle's four causes—material cause (substance), instrumental cause (means), formal cause (forms), final cause (ends)—that he used to describe and explain the world were reduced in the Middle Ages to just two causes: material cause and instrumental cause (i.e., pure science and applied science). The original understanding of sophia—design—in the pre-Socratic era not only included Aristotle's full complement of causes, but also required the addition of other causes that focused on making and production—in distinction to just description and explanation.

These historical polarizations and separations have influenced the way in which we today understand and justify taking any collective action.

1. understand problem
2. gather information
3. analyze information
4. generate solutions
5. assess the solutions
6. implement
7. test
8. modify

Figure I.3
Solving tame problems (Rittel 1972)

Without an intellectual understanding of the tradition of design in place—
in its pre-Socratic form—we have looked to other traditions of inquiry for
insight into the nature of, justification for, and management of change.

The dominant trigger for initiating change in human affairs is, today,
primarily based on the existence of a clear and immediate understanding
of a particular problem or set of problems. Political action, professional
performance, economic decisions, social planning, and business choices
are almost entirely justified on the grounds that life is a set of problems
requiring practical, efficient, and effective solutions. Much of formal education or training is based on preparing students to better identify and
solve problems creatively, quickly, fairly, rationally, and prudently. This
essentially reactive mode, applied to every realm of life, is reinforced and
supported by well-developed procedures for problem solving. Horst Rittel
(1972) has identified such problems as "tame" (see figure I.3).

Tame problems are appropriate for simple or trivial concerns, but more
important or significant issues are better characterized, according to Rittel,
as "wicked" problems (see figure I.4). The characteristics of wicked problems do not lend themselves to simple procedures, or even easy characterizations. If taken seriously, the wicked nature of these types of problems
leads to paralysis. This paralysis is most often skirted by the assumption
that wicked problems can be simplified and recast as tame problems. This,
of course, exacerbates the original wicked problem situation and creates
an even greater mess.

The characteristics of a wicked problem are not descriptive of the
process for determining solutions to such problems, but are merely explanative of the nature of wicked problems. These characteristics are the result
of the limits and paradoxes of reason when applied to real-world situations in human affairs that are unique, contingent, unpredictable, and
complex.

- cannot be exhaustively formulated
- every formulation is a statement of a solution
- no stopping rule
- no true or false
- no exhaustive list of operations
- many explanations for the same problem
- every problem is a symptom of another problem
- no immediate or ultimate test
- one-shot solutions
- every problem is essentially unique
- problem solver has no right to be wrong

Figure I.4
Characteristics of wicked problems (Rittel 1972)

By treating a wicked problem as a tame problem, energy and resources are misdirected, resulting in solutions that not only are ineffective, but also can create more difficulty because the approach used is an intervention that is, by necessity, inappropriately conceptualized. Most of our significant everyday encounters with a problematic reality have the characteristics of wicked problems. Very few everyday situations of any importance can be described as tame problems. For instance, there is never only one best solution to such problems. There are only solutions that are good or bad. There is no one correct approach or methodology for solving these problems, and it is not possible to formulate one comprehensive and accurate description of a problematic situation from the beginning. Tame and wicked problems are not governed by the same logic. The strategies developed to deal with tame problems are not only different in degree, but also different in kind from those required for dealing with the complexity, ambiguity, and epistemological uniqueness of wicked problems.

The focus on problems, whether wicked or tame, as the primary justifiable trigger for taking action in human affairs has limited our ability to frame change as an outcome of intention and purpose. It means that wise action, or wisdom, is starved of its potential (Nelson 1994). Wisdom—specifically that which we call design wisdom—is a much richer concept than problem solving, because it shifts one's thoughts from focusing only on avoiding undesirable states, to focusing on intentional actions that lead to states of reality which are desirable and appropriate.

As only the intellectual or reflective components of the pre-Socratic concept of wisdom (i.e., the wisdom of reason) remain present in Western thought, wisdom is most often treated as simply the summation of data, translated into information, which is then transformed into knowledge.

On the rare occasions that wisdom is discussed in practical settings, the challenge is how to make and maintain the linkages between the rational components of wisdom, while accommodating the challenges of unique particular design situations.

The wisdom of the knowing hand—that of making, producing, and acting—must be connected to the wisdom of reason. But, wisdom in the realm of design requires that we take a step back. Design wisdom requires the reconstitution of sophia. Design wisdom is an integration of reason with observation, reflection, imagination, action, and production or making.

Another demand that design wisdom makes on us is to reintroduce the analog into a world long dominated by the digital and the analytic. The digital and analytic perspectives have heavily influenced Western traditions of thought for centuries. For instance, the division of the day into hours, minutes, and seconds that are indifferent to the particular qualities of any one day is an example of the digital. The division of land into grids indifferent to terrain or social habitation is another example. The division of sound or light waves into electronic pulses is another form of digital translation. The digital approach divides information into packets that are stable and congruent but detached from the qualities of the substance or event itself.

The division of all academic reality into disciplines of the sciences or the humanities, and further into narrow disciplines, is an example of the analytic. The analytic is an approach that divides things into constituent parts or categories of similarity using ordering systems. The division of professional services into areas of expertise is another example of the analytic. This approach has allowed us to make significant advances in technology and related scientific endeavors. Unfortunately, concurrent with this, the analog has become conspicuous in its absence in contemporary technical societies. This absence is a natural consequence of societies divided and separated by specialization, by taxonomies and categorizations, by social hierarchies and by administrative conveniences.

Individuals struggle to comprehend their experience of life as an analog reality—an integrated, complex whole that is not cleaved into clear, distinct, and separate taxonomies or categories. The digital and analytic approach to making sense of this undifferentiated experience helps to facilitate intentional change by reducing the overwhelming complexity of any particular situation and by providing instrumental distinctions that can become elements in new design compositions. Design wisdom has the ability to shift from an analog experience of life, to a digital or analytic perspective of the world and *back again*. This is done by means of a design process that begins initially with a complex, undifferentiated situation, which then transitions through a process of discernment and distinction and ultimately terminates with the integration of innovative designs into a desired seamless reality for those being served directly or affected incidentally. Therefore, one of the most vital aspects of design is that the outcome of any practical digital and analytic intervention must be transformed back into the analog. This is to assure that, with each new design addition, life continues to be experienced as a whole.

One more factor in design wisdom concerns the nature of change. Change is an oft-evoked concept in politics, planning, management, and other forms of intervention, but it is often not clearly articulated. In the tradition of scientific thinking, change is a consequence of either chance or necessity. Probability theory and statistical analysis are examples of approaches to change as a result of chance. In human affairs, chance is often experienced as luck, or fate, whereas scientific principles, or laws, and rules of behavior are examples of how we react when necessity (or certainty) is the cause of change.

Design wisdom—as a first tradition—provides an escape from this limited state of affairs. Change, as a consequence of design cause and intention, is an approach available to us, as a third option (Nelson 1987). In order to develop a robust tradition of design thinking, this concept of intention needs to be added as an agent of change to the ones already existing. The concept of change needs to be deepened as well in this context. Change—in relationship to design wisdom—has multiple levels of meaning, significance, and consequence (see figure I.5).

The challenge to cultures, or societies, on how to deal with change at these multiple levels was formulated by Arnold J. Toynbee (1948), and presented in mythic terms in the work of Joseph Campbell (1968) (see figure I.6). According to Toynbee's findings, based on his research into the behavior of past civilizations, social systems historically evoke four types of responses when confronted by change. The only cultures that seem successfully to move through major challenges, or crises, are those that engage in change in a radical and proactive manner that is consistent with design wisdom and leads to transformational change.

Of course, cultures, civilizations, nations, and other forms of large-scale social systems can escape major change over extended periods of time. But, when the pressures for change build internally or externally, accidentally or intentionally, successful survival and improvement seem to come only as consequences of an approach that can radically transform the existing

- change
  is
  difference

- change of difference
  is
  process

- change of process
  is
  evolution

- change of evolution
  is
  design

Figure I.5
Hierarchy of change

A. "return" to the good old days
B. "hang-on-to" the present
C. "reach" for a utopia
D. radically "transform" the existing

Figure I.6
Toynbee's reactive social change strategies

order of things as per Toynbee's model. Such an approach is a design approach.

Change is a vital part of our everyday experience of life. We often feel pushed into design because of the perceived pace of change in contemporary human affairs. We are pushed again by the explosion of information we are challenged to gather, understand, and utilize. We are pushed still further by the immense increase in Western technologic development, with its fallout of incomprehensible numbers of distinct tools, machines, products, and all manner of designed artifacts. Thus, we are confronted with more varieties of what can be done, than with what we know we want done.

But it is also true that we are pulled into design because it allows us to initiate intentional action out of strength, hope, passion, desire, and love. It is a form of action that generates more energy than it consumes. It is innovative inquiry that creates more resources—of greater variety and potential—than are used. In this way design action is distinct from problem-based reaction, which is triggered by need, fear, weakness, hate, and pain.

A desire for change is often assumed to imply a need for comprehensive analysis, and rational decision making, leading to a clear choice for action. The reality is that analysis often leads to ever-greater numbers of choices, which then require more analysis. The consequence is that decisions cannot, and are not, made rationally—at least not in the rational tradition of scientific comprehensiveness. The real world is much too complex to be dealt with comprehensively.

Design—as an alternative to this limit on rationality—uses a process of composing and connecting, which pulls a variety of elements into relationships with one another that are then formed into functional assemblies. These teleological systems serve the purposes, and intentions, of diverse populations of human beings. For example, any human activity system is an example of this, including transportation systems, governance systems, economics systems, health systems, and education systems. Whenever such systems are created or modified, a design approach is used. We also use the same process when we create new material goods and services. In addition, the compositional assembly process creates emergent qualities that become accessible when the designs are experienced as wholes in their intended environments. These emergent qualities transcend a design's simple functional qualities, often serving deeper, more significant needs and desires.

So, to summarize a bit, the design tradition's thread of continuity frayed, and finally broke, over the centuries, as the Western world poured its resources on the development of analytic and reductive thinking to the detriment of synthetic and integrative design thinking. Yet, to be able to successfully deal with change in the twenty-first century, it is now critical that we pick up those frayed design threads, and weave them back into new patterns, integrating their wisdom into a more holistic fabric of life.

How do we go about doing this? We believe that for a design tradition to flourish it is necessary to create a design culture. That is, a culture that embraces a social, economic, political, and personal environment into which designing, and designers, are not only invited, but also welcomed. It is equally important to populate this culture with competent designers who have the education, experience, and desire to practice design from a broader perspective than the traditional practices of material design.

Is it possible to present the essential qualities of such a culture in a book? We believe that it is, and this book is our attempt. Of course, a culture can never be created by merely writing a book, but we hope to initiate a reflective dialogue on what a design culture might look like—

at least in the beginning stages of its development, joining with others with similar interests.

We believe the first step in establishing a design culture is to conceptualize design as a unique way of looking at the human condition with the purpose to create change. To that end, we need to develop and use design wisdom as a frame of reference grounded in its own unique tradition. It is, in effect, our first tradition, as was discussed earlier. The remainder of this book deals with considering the character and consequences of this idea more fully.

In any particular design, there are specific dimensions of art, technology, and science, but in the totality of that design, in its inclusiveness of generalized aspects of the experienced world, it has a commonality with all applications of design. Herbert Simon (1969), speaking from an engineering background, made a seminal contribution to the development of a broader understanding of design by introducing the concept of the science of the artificial—design. There has been a continuation and expansion of this idea, in more recent work, among others by Schön (1983, 1987), Banathy (1996), Boland and Collopy (2004), Krippendorff (2006), and Cross (2011).

That design thinkers hail from a variety of backgrounds should not come as a surprise. Designers from any design field, formally defined or not, can relate to other designers because they all are striving toward the same goal; they are hoping to add to, or change, the real world. They do this through their service-related creativity and innovation, in both particular and universal ways.

Culture is never a natural occurrence. Cultures can be created by design, however. Cultures are a living tension between tradition and innovation, between stability and change. This type of social structure and process can be changed, developed, deepened, misunderstood, or misinterpreted. Working to develop a conscious design tradition, it must be remembered that any change to a cultural tradition can easily be blocked by unseen habits or forces not easily understood. A social culture often consists of ideas, norms, and a "common sense" understanding that are taken for granted, often without questioning their origin or benefit. This means that it is imperative to maintain both open and critical minds in the creation of a design culture within the milieu of established social cultures.

Evan as we focus on the cultural similarities among different kinds of designers, we do so based on a recognition and acceptance of their differences. It is important to acknowledge that every formally recognized professional designer has a specific field of design expertise—a range of specific crafts, skills, and knowledge) forming professional domains such as: industrial design, architecture, information design, software design, urban design, organizational design, educational design, instructional design, and so on. It is equally important to remember that every informally recognized designer has a similar field of expertise. Every designer's competence relies on his or her knowledge and skills, concerning materials, tools, methods, languages, traditions, styles, and so on, found in his or her specific design field.

This book is not centered on those specialized competencies. Instead it concentrates on the characteristics and qualities of the cultural tradition within which all designers practice. We argue that, to be a thoughtful and responsible designer, any general understanding of what design is ultimately about has to be critically appraised, by you—the individual designer, client, stakeholder—or anyone else affected by design. In addition, any understanding of design should be the result of reflective practice, intellectual apperception, and intentional choice. This book is meant to be a resource in the facilitation of such an individualized understanding of design.

II FOUNDATIONS

Although it is common to assume that any new way of thinking must be defined by a new paradigm (Kuhn 1962), it is equally important to uncover the conceptual foundations upon which a new culture of inquiry plans to stand. The design hypostasis we present in the following four chapters acts as the supporting platform for the design approach.

We believe these chapters cover the seminal ideas supportive of a design culture. When studied, these foundational concepts will help any designer— or champion of design—develop an understanding of the conditions necessary for real design inquiry and action to flourish.

In these chapters, we will focus on the particular, service, systemics, and the whole, and explore each of these foundational precepts in detail.

1 The Ultimate Particular

As we noted earlier scientists tend to label ancient human designs, such as fire or the wheel, as "discoveries" because of their bias toward observation away from imagination. This penchant is an extension of the traditional approach to labeling scientific phenomena. When a researcher first becomes aware of something in the physical realm—something that has existed since time immemorial but has only now come to this researcher's consciousness—he or she is said to have "discovered" that phenomenon. We accept that scientists have "discovered" gravity, evolution, entropy, and other seminal natural laws, through careful observation and critical evaluation—revealing that which is true. In design, we are equally interested in that which *universal* and true *and* that which is an *ultimate particular* and real.

In the theoretical world of science, we do not think about natural laws or truths as being designed. But, in the real world—the present environment that surrounds all of us—we understand that we "create" as well as "discover" this reality. This is because the real world has many facets of an artificial world and is very much a designed world. In fact scientists have begun to label the present epoch as the *Anthropocene* era because of the dominant effect human activity has had on global systems, making them ever more unnatural and artificial. Based on this, scientists describing and explaining the world can be understood more as design critics than natural scientists.

We do not talk about our cities as if they were strange things that appeared to pop up out of nowhere, or about our cars and houses as discoveries, or about our social organizations as natural artifacts suddenly brought to light through carefully executed empirical studies. We see them as created. We see them as true, in the sense that they exist. We do not see them as true in the same way a scientific law is universally true. They are not, deterministically, the only possible and necessary city, car, house, or organization. Nor are they great accidents of time and chance. They are not abstractions of particular examples but realities in and of themselves. They are unique and singular in their temporal existence.

We know, in our experience of everyday life, that we have the power to decide what we would like to have become a part of our real world. We can design the real world in almost any form imaginable. And, we are quite certain that there is little chance of some day discovering the "right" answers to the question of what kind of world we ought to have created. Although there are people who claim they have access to the truth—that is, that they are able to discern what should, or should not, be regarded as an appropriate addition to our real world—most of us know that the way the world is designed is a result of a series of human judgments and interventions. We understand that we ought to do the best we can to create a world of quality, beauty, and fulfillment—although we're aware that not everyone will use the power of design for the same ends.

There are basic truths, however, that help guide us in making good design judgments. For example, we know, nowadays, about the fragility of our natural environment. We understand the importance of being concerned about water and air. Almost all of us are convinced (this may not be a truth yet, but only a hope) that we have to take care of all forms of life on the planet, if we want our own species to survive. We have learned how to design and make products that are safer for ourselves and the environment while at the same time we have learned how to manipulate the needs, desires, and behaviors of others in relationship to products in general. Unfortunately, to take in and integrate all of these understandings into a concrete single design situation is often too complex a task for us. No matter how much we want to take into account all possible truths, in a design situation, we will find that some of them appear to be contradictory, unclear, or not yet fully revealed. We will find that all these truths do not provide us with one clear and correct choice.

This means we will never be able to ground design on the idea that the "right" design is out there, embedded in reality, just waiting to be discovered. To the contrary, design will always be about creating something that does not yet exist. It is not about finding something already in existence. Science can help us in our design process by providing knowledge about structures, laws, and processes that reveal the natural world. But the primary thing this kind of knowledge gives us is a description, or explanation, of already existing things. Science cannot provide insight into what should be brought into existence, through intention, imagination, and innovation. It can only confirm potentiality and assist realization.

Designers want to be able to make good design judgments that will, at the very least, make a company efficient, a nonprofit effective, or a governmental agency politically popular. They want to make designs that lead to better products, services, organizational behavior, or global sustainability. They also want to be seen as designers worth the compensation, prestige, and trust they desire, or receive.

Leaders and managers, as well, are facing ever-increasing demands on their design judgment skills. The market overflows with workshops and training sessions that promise to provide the right sequence of learning experiences leading to easily accessible, and cost-effective problem-solving skills. The underlying promise is that these skills will consistently provide ready-made, transferable solutions to the complex problems facing leaders today. Design and creative problem-solving processes for business have been commoditized into branded approaches for delivering expected outcomes. The challenge and mystery of designing, as pointed out by Roger Martin (2009), have been tamed by recipes that disappoint more often than not. His recommendation is that designers need to return to unscripted approaches to design. "Design thinking," for example, has been transformed into rule-based algorithms fashioned out of heuristics that seemed to have worked within limitations in the real world (see figure 1.1).

A desire for consistency and certainty has been part of the human condition for as long as recorded time. The earliest cosmologies, with their associated rites and rituals, were all meant to give structure to chaos and mystery. But, even with a cosmology in place, there has always been less predictability than desired, and more unpredictability than tolerable.

algorithms *routine expertise*	methods and training	rule-based
heuristics *adaptive expertise*	experiential learning	trial and error
designing *design expertise*	design learning	intention

Figure 1.1
Approaches to inquiry for action

Ancient Greek decision makers would go to great effort to ask the Oracle at Delphi for a simple answer to their straightforward question, only to be given responses that, by necessity, required deeper thinking on the questioner's side. The early Christians found that their leader spoke only in parables, leaving centuries of interpretation as to what the "true" answers were. Despite the popularity of these traditional sources of wisdom, decision makers have continued to look for other means of inquiry that will provide information that is more accessible, straightforward, accurate, and consistent over time.

In the Western tradition, the right answer was soon identified as an outcome of rational thought, using the protocols of the scientific method. This approach worked so well for gaining a better understanding of the natural world, and for the creation of sophisticated technology, that it was only natural that managers, administrators, and even designers would begin to depend heavily on this particular form of inquiry as well. However, this scientific approach, with some exceptions, has not provided the kind of guarantee of outcomes one would imagine possible. This comes from confusion between what is true and what is real. Science deals only with what is true, but leaders or managers—and definitely designers—must deal with what is real, in addition to what is true.

When something is true, it has to be true in all cases and situations. We do not accept as a scientific truth a statement that sometimes is true, and sometimes not. Science deals with what is general and universal. There are extensive discussions concerning whether some of the newer scientific methods used in social science, such as case studies, interpretative studies, or qualitative methods, have the ability to create any kind of universal, or generalizable, truths. If a rational method leads only to an understanding of a specific case, and not to some universal truth, then it is not really considered to be a scientific method. Based on this kind of thinking, modern social science is often accused by other researchers of being the same thing as journalism or even creative writing. However, it is still the case that all research strives for trustworthiness, which can be understood as a measure of truth. Research, in all fashions, aim at producing knowledge that is trustworthy and thereby has a higher degree of universality than other forms of knowledge.

In science, we strive to reason from ultimate particulars to universal principles and laws. This is done by the method of *induction*. Through science, we can also explain something quite particular with the help of the universal, by the method of *deduction*. But, the process for creating the *ultimate particular* is not based on scientific induction or scientific deduction. There is no scientific approach for creating an ultimate particular because science is a process of discerning abstractions that apply across categories or taxonomies of phenomena, while the ultimate particular is a singular and unique composition or assembly. Creating that which is unique and thus particular, therefore, cannot be accomplished using a scientific approach.

An action taken by an individual at a specific time and place is an example of something that is an ultimate particular. The outcome of a specific design process, such as a chair, a curriculum, or a policy, is an ultimate particular. It is something unique. It is not the universal chair, the universal curriculum, or the universal policy. We create a particular, which when taken together with other particulars makes up the whole of our experienced reality. Even when products are designed in great numbers, with wide distribution, they still have the quality of being particular and not universal, since they do not represent the only possibility for accomplishing the same end or serving the same purpose and in situ they are truly unique and an ultimate particular.

Design is a process of moving from the universal, general, and particular to the ultimate particular—the specific design (see figure 1.2) (a related

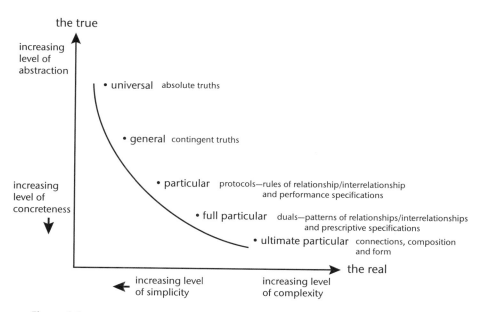

Figure 1.2
Universal to ultimate particular

concept called *full particular* is developed in Sunstein 2001). The way this is done is by making design judgments. What we desire to come into existence is a matter of judgment—based on design *will* (volition) and *intention* (aim)—and can never be found in explanations, descriptions, or predictions. Design will and design intentions are the means for initiating and directing change based on human agency. It is design will and design intention, guided by design judgment, that transform the abstractness of relevant scientific knowledge and other forms of knowledge into a final unique design, the ultimate particular. The ultimate particular is that which "appears" in the world.

In design, we are not dealing with a universal or contingent truth—we are dealing with the particular; as well as with that which is real. Distinctions between what is true (e.g., universal or general) and what is real (e.g., particular, full particular, and ultimate particular) can be made in the following ways. A painting by Cézanne is real; the atomic weight of copper is true. An experience is real; a scientific theory is true. An organization is real; a proven principle or law is true. An individual's perspective is real; a predictable trend is true. The true, on the one hand, comes from patterns of accurate descriptions, and explanations, through controlled observation, such as William James's "tough-minded" empiricism. The true can also come from careful abstract reasoning, and logic, as in William James's "tender-minded" rationalism (James 1975). The real, on the other hand, is the result of particular actions, taken through specific judgments, and formed by distinct intentions.

Right decisions and appropriate actions in human activities do not and cannot arise from what is true only. When this fact is not appreciated, it leads both designers and decision makers into dead-end states of *analysis paralysis* and *value paralysis*. Decisions, and actions, must be based on what is real, and ideal, in addition to what is true. The real and the true are, of course, not exclusive. When dealing with the real, we often benefit from the instrumental support given to us by scientific knowledge, which is essential to any designer. There needs to be a symmetry between the real and the true, and not polarity. We need to find the unity between the two, rather than a compromise.

Over time, many different ways of conducting inquiry into what can confidently be considered to be true have been "designed" as opposed to being inherently obvious. These differing forms of inquiry have been sufficiently successful—in the right context, and at certain moments in history—to be championed as superior forms of inquiry, regardless of the situation or need. This is especially true of inquiry based on the scientific method. The hegemony of science and scientific thought, in the developed world over the last century, is an indicator of the winner of the most recent battle for dominance among systems of inquiry. A belief in the scientific method, as the only and superior valid method of inquiry for describing, explaining, and interceding in the world, is a hallmark of our technological age. Science, as an activity of disciplined inquiry, has often been called the new religion of the contemporary age.

C. West Churchman introduced the idea of designing systems of rational inquiry by contrasting, and comparing, historical forms of inquiry (Churchman 1971). The basic types of rational inquiry Churchman discussed are fact nets, consensus, representation, dialectic, progress, mechanism, teleology, and probability. Churchman used the thought processes of famous philosophers as examples of the designs of inquiry he presented. All the approaches he discussed are constructed in the tradition of the true—the scientific search for knowledge. They are all based on the idea of a rational approach that is guided by strict rules on how to go about finding knowledge. In today's world of design, we can find modern approaches resembling all of these various scientific traditions. A designer can greatly benefit from having a basic knowledge of traditional systems of inquiry. Such knowledge can help in evaluating the constant flow of "new" approaches but also as a tool for critical examination and reflection on one's own approach.

The design tradition, however, requires that we follow a different path. The choice a designer makes, as to how to acquire knowledge, deeply affects how his or her design work is done. If the designer chooses a scientific approach, the whole design process will have strong similarities to a research process. This will limit or eliminate not only what is considered to be the preconditions of the design, but also what is possible, what is needed, what is desired, and what the eventual outcome will be. It will no longer be a design process.

In some cultures, the most dominant form of inquiry is the spiritual. In the spiritual tradition, knowledge is not necessarily something we have to gain for ourselves, or discover in the world. It is instead handed down to us, through different channels, from some divine or spiritual source. The work of a designer, who builds on this tradition, will be radically different from designs based on scientific methods of inquiry. It is not uncommon, even in today's technological world, to find designs inspired by and even argued to be "given" to humans from a higher source.

Another form of inquiry, over which there is a great deal of disagreement, is defined as intuition. Intuition is a form of unconscious knowing.

designs of inquiry	outcomes
real	ultimate particulars
true	facts
ideal	desiderata

Figure 1.3
Components of design inquiry

A basic version of intuition is instinct. When we find animals engaging in design-like activity (creating tools for instance) we do not ascribe any advanced forms of inquiry to their behavior. Instead, we define their behavior as instinctive and not based on reflective reasoning at all. In the same way, it is possible to understand some of our human design behaviors as more a result of instinct, rather than reason and reflection. At a much higher level, intuition is an unconscious knowing gained through a unification of complex sense data, resulting in an integrated understanding of real-time experience.

There are many types of relationships that develop between these varying forms of inquiry. Most often, the relationship is defined as either a polarity or a continuum. One of the more enduring relationships is the polarity that is seen as existing between the two cultures of inquiry as identified by C. P. Snow (1959); that of science and the humanities. An equally enduring example of a continuum relationship is the one defined between art and science. On this continuum, as we have discussed earlier, architecture commonly has been placed at the midpoint. In similar fashion, design of any type is often defined as occurring at the same midpoint. Design is also considered to be at a midpoint between intuition and logic, or imagination and reason. These different ideas of midpoints are all too-simplistic understandings of any form of inquiry in practice. However, every chosen form of inquiry—intuitive, artistic, scientific, logical, or composite thereof—will lead to a specific body of knowledge. The chosen form of inquiry influences both what constitutes knowledge and how knowledge is gained. Each particular approach is based on some fundamental assumptions concerning what it means to create knowledge.

We suggest that design, as presented in this book, is based on a compound form of inquiry, composed of true, ideal, and real approaches to gaining knowledge (see figure 1.3). As we've said, there is a broad spectrum of inquiry systems that have been designed over the course of human history. Some are long forgotten, while others still form the armature upon which we base particular ways of asking, and answering, questions—questions ultimately intended to expose the essence of the human condition. In our contemporary world, there are several common forms of inquiry in use at any one time.

Among these is the *ideal*. The notion of the ideal refers to the kind of inquiry devoted to the realm of norms and values. Sometimes it is focused on knowledge that says something about how the world "ought" to be in respect to some higher order, spiritual constitution, or idealistic system. In design the ideal represents what is considered to be desirable as an outcome. What is ideally found to be desired or desirable cannot realistically be made into a concrete reality; however, good approximations can be realized. Design is a process of making close approximations, the closest possible, to these idealistic desires.

Inquiry into what is *true* is the most common form of expected outcome of inquiry and is found in artistic and religious thinking as much as it is in scientific thinking. Inquiry into the true and inquiry into the ideal—in relationships to religious and utopian contexts—are well-formed modalities with long traditions of development, suitable vocabularies, historically defined frames of reference, and well-known instruments of thought. For example, for centuries the scientific method has been used to determine the true. Enlightenment, through reflection, contemplation, meditation, or prayer, has been used to access insights into visionary forms of the ideal. However, extensive scholarly attention and historical intellectual development have not occurred in the case of inquiry into the intentional forms of the ideal and the concrete forms of the real. As a consequence, there is no time-tested body of knowledge from past experience to count on.

Inquiry into the ideal is not only a form of reflective, abstract, or conceptual inquiry, but is also action oriented. Its focus, when used for design purposes, is on production and innovation. The ideal, as a focus of inquiry into what is desirable, is essential to the ultimate design goal of creating the not-yet-existing. It is about helping to operationalize the creation of the not-yet-real and the particular as defined earlier.

When we compare the three forms of inquiry—the real, the true, and the ideal—some immediate differences and similarities are revealed (see figure 1.4). We will not go through this comparison in detail here (since it is covered in detail in the chapters that follow). We will simply mention that using an integrative model, such as the one preceding, is a good way

Designs of Inquiry and Action

foundations	the real	the true	the ideal
intention	reveal the particular	reason the universal	envision the desireable
purpose	survive and thrive	understand	progress
form	systemic	taxonomic	natural or created
unity	wholeness	comprehensive	oneness
fundamentals			
motivation	angst and awe	curiosity and wonder	desiderata and inspiration
understanding	meaning	fact	enlightenment
input	sensation	observation	inspiration and imagination
meaning making	relating	reason and logic	reflection and judgment
output	schema	description and explanation	approximation of perfection
process	being	knowing	composing and creating

Figure 1.4
Designs of inquiry: the real, the true, and the ideal

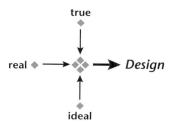

Figure 1.5
Design inquiry: an emergent compound

to reflect on these forms of inquiry and build a deeper appreciation for how they can be understood from a design perspective. An integrative model can also be helpful as an analytic tool, when your purpose is to determine the basis of the particular design that underlies a specific approach to inquiry. For example, using such a model enables one to examine various design approaches, and reveal the different assumptions that are built into their systems of inquiry and action.

Even though we have primarily focused on the notion that design inquiry and action reside in the domain of the ideal becoming real, design inquiry is, in actuality, an emergent, compound form of inquiry that is inclusive of the real, the true, and the ideal. All three of these forms of inquiry are essential to designers and their work. When used together, the resulting approach to knowledge acquisition is much more synergistic, comprehensive, and integrative than the individual approaches taken in summation (see figure 1.5). Therefore, design inquiry displays emergent qualities as a consequence of being a compound that would not be visible and accessible otherwise.

Concomitant with design inquiry is design action. Design action is both a journey and a destination. The journey has to do with change, and the destination with ends, or outcomes. "Change" is a term with many meanings. One of the most important definitions of change— which has considerable importance in a design context—is that which denotes the process of "coming into existence"—a birthing, genesis, or creation. This attribute of change is dramatically different from the more common use of the term, which states that change is a distinguishing difference in the already existing—that is, a change in "existence." We should note that change, as a difference in something, is also distinctly separate from a difference between things, which is essentially the definition of information.

Designs of Inquiry and Action

	the real	the true	the ideal
triggers for change	reaction and interaction	chance and necessity	intention

Figure 1.6
Triggers for change

Change is initiated or triggered differently depending on which form of inquiry is dominant in any situation (see figure 1.6). The triggers also vary depending on the type of change; whether it is part of a process of coming into existence, or whether it is transforming that which already is in existence.

As stated earlier, scientific inquiry focuses on change that is triggered by chance and necessity. Statistics and probability theories deal with change caused by chance, while laws, principles, and rules define change brought by necessity. Change that is triggered in response to the demanding norm of an idealized standard is often attributed to some form of sovereign or controlling authority that can range from the Word of God to mere peer pressure or expert opinion.

Change that is triggered by human intention is at the heart of design. It is a hallmark of design that human intention is essential and central to the instigation of change in the real world. Human intention is, therefore, a singularly important and consequential cause of change. The idea of cause is complex but key to understanding designed change. Cause is natural (as defined by science, through the conceptualization of chance and necessity). Design, therefore, must accommodate change brought about by natural causes; but the most challenging forms of cause are those that are rooted in human agency. These intentional forms of cause are diverse. The type of intentional cause that is of particular interest here is *design cause*. Design cause is the consequence of human volition and the capacity for humans to be proactive and purposeful in their interaction with the real world. Design cause is essential both for initiating change that brings new things into existence and for modifying those things that are already in existence.

The kinds of outcomes that result from inquiry for action vary widely, depending on the inquiry approach being used (see figure 1.7). Each form of inquiry has its own ends. The point of intentional change, triggered by design cause, is to bring about a specific, desired end.

Designs of Inquiry and Action

	the real	the true	the ideal
ends	that-which-is	that-which-can-be	that-which-is-desired-to-be
		that-which-needs-to-be	that-which-should-be
			that-which-ought-to-be

Figure 1.7

Outcomes of inquiry for action

- conscious knowing   — reason
- unconscious knowing   — intuition
- subconscious knowing   — imagination
- conscious not-knowing   — design thinking

Figure 1.8

Design knowing

The most obvious outcome of inquiry is knowledge. The type of knowledge, or knowing, is determined by the primary mode of inquiry (see figure 1.8). For example, a fundamental type of knowing is knowledge associated with judgment, which is different in kind from most forms of knowledge, because it is knowledge that is inseparable from the knower and is only made visible through action.

The interesting thing about one type of design knowledge is that it emerges from a *conscious not-knowing*. By this, we mean that design knowledge—while using reason (conscious knowledge), intuition (hardwired, unconscious knowledge), and imagination (subconscious knowledge) as constituent elements—requires an initial state of *intentional not-knowing*. This state is very much like the Taoist "empty mind" or the Buddhist "new mind." It is the quality of mind that is present during play, when it is important to be completely open to what is emergent in the moment, rather than being preoccupied with past experience, or anticipating a future event.

Design is about evoking, or creating, the ideal in the real. But design has to be grounded in what is already real, as well as what is actually true. Since the real is overwhelmingly complex and rich, we are unable to grasp the totality of that complexity and richness solely by using the systems of inquiry created to reveal what is true and factual. The reductive approaches made available to us through analytic science are not meant to handle inquiry from a holistic sense, but the real is a whole and therefore we need another approach. Any new design is something that is both real and whole. As such, that new design is, by definition, too complex and rich to be completely understood during the process of creation. We cannot predict with accuracy how any real design will serve the world and, in turn, how it will change it or be changed by it.

What we can do is to begin to understand that the real—as is manifested in both the particular and the ultimate particular—is a concept that distinguishes design from other traditions of inquiry and action. The real must be approached through judgment (see chapter 8) augmented by science-based tools and methods—the true. Design thinking, to be accepted in part as a legitimate decision-making process and foundation for leadership, needs to be grounded in scientific truths—but not to the exclusion of the strategy of judgment making based on subjective as well as objective influences, or to the exclusion of the desiderata of the ideal. To reiterate, there is a need to combine the true, ideal, and real into a balanced compound approach to inquiry.

2   Service

Design, as defined in this book, is different from other traditions of inquiry and action in that *service* is a defining element. Design is, by definition, a service relationship. All design activities are animated through dynamic relationships between those being served—clients, surrogate clients (those who act on behalf of clients), customers, and consumers or end users—and those in service, including the designers. Design ideally is about service on behalf of the other—not merely about changing someone's behavior for their own good or convincing them to buy products and services. This is not always obvious when observing the behavior of many of today's designers; neither is it adequately dealt with in the contemporary writings on design. When the primary focus for design is on consumers or customer behavior rather than client needs and desires it is less clear what service relationship, if any, is in place. It is also unclear in this case what the path of accountability and responsibility is between the designer's decisions and consequences in stakeholders' lives. It becomes a special case of design agency and service in general.

The presence of a binding service relationship in design contributes to a clear distinction between the tradition of design and the traditions of art or science. Science and art essentially are cultures of inquiry and action that are, in the best sense, *self-serving*. Scientists ideally are seen as motivated by their own curiosity and pursue their passion for knowing, in order to satisfy their curiosity objectively. Their gift is a subsequent knowledge that may be of use, somehow, at some point in human affairs. Artists, on the one hand, express their passions, feelings, understandings, and critique of the world out of their own need for self-expression. Their gift is that these insights are shared with audiences who can then make what they will of these personal glimpses into the human condition. Designers, on the other hand, are not self-serving, but *other-serving*. We should note that it is possible for designers to choose themselves as the client, the one to be served, but that is a special and maybe the most difficult case.

Being in service does not mean being a servant, or subservient. It does not mean acting as a mere facilitator on behalf of someone else's needs. Nor does service exclude self-expression. It just means that self-expression is not dominant in a design relationship, as it is in the traditions of science and art.

We should also point out that service is not about helping people create what they already know they want. The success of the design process can best be determined when those being served experience the *surprise of self-recognition.* This comes when that which emerges from a design process meets and exceeds the client's original expression of that which they (usually only dimly) perceived as desirable in the beginning. This original expression of what is desired is known as the client's *desiderata* (see chapter 5) The designer's role is to midwife that desiderata, which could not have been imagined fully from the beginning by either client or designer, and to provide end results in the form of an *expected unexpected* outcome.

What is meant by this paradoxical expression? We are saying that in contracting with a designer one has the double intention of wanting the expected and desired outcome, but also hoping to be surprised with an unexpected benefit that transcends original expectations. More specifically, the expected unexpected is about an unexpected result that is still recognizable as something that is in resonance with what is desired and anticipated yet adds something of significance. The client will, if the design is done in service to that client, understand that the outcome is something new, but at the same time, recognize it as something appropriate to the particular situation and the client's own interests.

A service relationship is a distinct, complex, and systemic relationship, with a particular focus on responsibility, accountability, and intention. Designed products, whether concrete or conceptual, only have value and meaning because of this intentional service relationship. Therefore, it is through the presence of a service relationship that intentional change, and the consequences of intentional change, can come to have meaning and give meaning to individual and collective lives. For a designer, the service relationship is the basic teleological cause, that is to say, the purpose of design.

There is a subtle distinction here between designs that are done *with* clients and those that are done *to* clients, like customers or consumers. In the latter case, which is not the service relationship as described earlier, need and desirability are discovered through persuasion or by the experience of change brought about through use. There is also intentional change that is done to people. Acts of terrorism or other forced changes in people's lives require that meaning be reconstructed in reaction to the intentionality being used against these people—the quintessential opposite of service. Unintentional change, such as accidents, natural catastrophes, or the death of a loved one, also requires that meaning be recovered, not because of intention, but in the absence of intention. An example in this last case is that humans have developed grieving processes as a way to secure meaning in the face of irretrievable loss.

It is important, at this juncture, to make a distinction between "finding meaning"—that is, adaptive expertise—in things that happen, and "making meaning"—design expertise—by causing things to happen. The former is reactive and adaptive, while the latter is proactive and intentional. To be in service is to be proactive. This means the designer cannot wait around for things to just fall into place. Clients may not fully know what is concretely desired in the beginning. They are only aware that something is pressing for expression. This expression of their desiderata may even be masked by feelings of discomfort (in the absence of a critical self-awareness). In this case, the designer must help bring to the surface a clearer articulation of a client's desiderata as a positive, proactive impulse.

This is not always easy to do, as there are often feelings of anxiety concerning the future, and fears of unknown contexts or situations in life. People, in general, prefer what is known or predictable. For instance, a great deal of effort and resources is expended by organizations (public and private) to predict the future (i.e., "futuring") while being fully aware that most major unintended changes in history have come as total surprises (e.g., the 9/11 attacks on the United States and the economic collapse in the first decade of the twenty-first century), taking even experts by surprise (Taleb 2010). The future is shown repeatedly to be unpredictable. It is only determined by chance and necessity or formed by intention through design. Designed futures are brought into existence through the triggering affect of desiderata.

A designer, therefore, "makes meaning" for a client by empathetically drawing out his or her preformed desires. This designer does not ask the client what fully formed outcome is to be designed, but instead—through open communication—tries to discern the underlying intentions of that client's vaguely-cloaked desiderata—intentions that, most often, the client does not yet recognize fully. To be in service means to build on these gossamer findings of direction and purpose, and to concretely conceptualize them in such a way that they surpass the client's own understandings and imagination, while fully representing his or her authentic self-interests.

Design outcomes do not have to be virtuous to be considered authentic consequences of design activity; although one hopes this is, most often, the case. Some individuals may desire only to maximize their material wealth, personal power, or prestige, while others are truly interested in designing a more meaningful life for themselves. One business may endeavor only to increase profit and assure market dominance and longevity. Another may desire to contribute something of lasting social value. Some governments may attempt to respond democratically to diverse ways of life, almost as readily as other governments attempt to impose paternalistic control. A good design approach does not assure that "good" designs emerge as a consequence. Designers and stakeholders—not design approaches—ultimately are responsible for creating altruistic and sustainable designs.

Our intent, in *The Design Way*, is not to generate more panaceas by creating one-size-fits-all templates, formulaic algorithms, or prescriptive principles by which to guide design processes. Rather, we submit that a client's desiderata can best be encountered through an approach that is inclusive of both theoretical and practical knowledge; one that is reflective and experiential, and results in a virtuous design. Through a service relationship, a design is considered successful when the expected-unexpected outcomes serve the right people, for the right purpose, at the right time in the right place.

It is important to understand that service is not servitude. Instead, service treats the *other* as an equal. This does not mean being similar, as in categories of social science, or equivalent, as in egalitarianism, but equal as in equitable partnerships. Service is also distinct from helping, which, by its very nature, creates a unilateral relationship. In a helping relationship, all power and resources reside with the helper, leaving the person receiving help in a position of indebtedness: "Serving is different from helping. Helping is based on inequality; it is not a relationship between equals. . . . Service is a relationship between equals. . . . Helping incurs debt. When you help someone, they owe you one. But serving, like healing, is mutual. There is no debt" (Remen 1996).

In our Western culture, helping relationships are one of the more popular—and self-reinforcing—types of contracts available. Nonprofits, governmental agencies, and NGOs (non-governmental organizations) spend millions of dollars on behalf of the helpless, sick, unlucky, or tragedy-struck. In many instances, this may be necessary, when there are no good alternatives within easy reach and there seems to be more than sufficient justification for an urgent, unilaterally triaged intervention into the lives of others triggered by moral outrage or simple humanitarian concern.

As a consequence, philanthropy and related approaches of "doing good" have often walked a well-worn path that leads to the formation of habitually unequal relationships. These quick-fix helping relationships tend to prevent service relationships from forming when possible, and where appropriate. Those who have the power and resources to define norms often treat people who are culturally, socially, or economically different as simply needy or helpless. This is also true of individuals who find themselves victims of unhappy circumstances formed by well-intentioned but misguided fixes that have resulted in unintended consequences. Although these individuals' circumstances are the result of forces outside of their personal sphere of influence, they are treated as the loci for a helping or fixing intervention.

Well-meaning benefactors spend a great deal of their money and influence in these pseudo-contract relationships. As a result, there is a symbiotic relationship between the recipients and the providers. Often the providers, quite unconsciously perhaps, use the helpless and powerless to build a deeper sense of purpose and meaning in their own lives. In other cases, the helpless are there to be taken care of in order that the provider's status—often in reference to power or success—can be legitimized, or justified, in social contexts.

The donors need a clear and urgent call to arms in order to mask the more difficult and challenging job of dealing with the human condition in all of its complexity and potential. This includes dealing with any other human as an equal in diversity. Everyone feels rewarded, at some level, in a helping relationship defined by urgency. Important values, such as caring and love, can form the basis for the best of these relationships. However, this is usually at the expense of other important human values, including those that support dignity, equity, creativity, and individuality.

Interestingly, even though service is a defining characteristic of design, some design professions are not necessarily framed within this tradition. Architecture, for instance, can be approached as an applied science or an applied art and not forfeit its character as architecture. As we noted earlier, architecture is often referred to as a midpoint between art and science—a compromise or mean between two extremes. Other fields, such as product design and information systems design, are thought of as a mix of "hard" science and fine art. As proponents for a design culture, we would suggest that, rather than classifying these professions as somewhere between the traditions of science and art, they should instead be treated as professions within a culture of design.

Whether or not architecture, industrial design, interaction design, or any other design profession is to be approached from a design tradition is an entirely open choice. However, the consequences of this choice are significant to the praxis of the professions. This can best be exemplified by taking a look at the educational philosophies that have supported each of these professions historically. Education in art is radically different from science education. The values and structure upon which each educational process is built vary significantly. Science pedagogy differs from art pedagogy in that the purpose of education in science is to learn how to determine the true nature of the material world through augmented and controlled input from sensory data. The outcome is objective and factual knowledge that is confirmed because others can replicate it. In contrast, art education is about learning to give self-expression to emotions and feelings without the intervention of formal, replicable intellectual constructs. The outcome in this case is subjective and personalized knowledge.

For design to be accepted as its own intellectual tradition, designers must foster their own unique approach to education, as science or art have done so successfully—one that places priority on the *idea of service*. The purpose of design pedagogy is, therefore, to learn how to gain both objective and subjective understanding on behalf of another's interests rather than in one's self-interest only. It also includes the reintegration of reflective thought and practical action in a way that unifies the knowledge of "why" with the knowledge of "how."

If a generative service relationship is one of the higher goals in design, then how a designer communicates with his or her client takes on immense importance. Design communication is about listening. It is about helping people to express what they believe will help them live fuller lives. In order to do this, design communication may at times include the use of rhetoric and persuasion, as is also true of science and art. But these forms of argumentation are not a part of its essential nature. Also, a good designer does not spend time convincing clients of needs or desires they have not authored. So, "selling," in a traditional marketing sense, is not fundamental to the design process. Instead, it is the client's own intentionality—in the form of their desiderata—that should trigger and aim the process.

When a service relationship is established correctly, it brings everyone involved along at the same pace. Design communication, therefore, does not depend on selling outcomes as much as it does communicating progress. Design is, at its root, a form of democracy: not the arithmetic democracy of majority rule or the representative democracy of elected political bodies, but the democracy of self-determination through interrelationships of service. Design is the kind of democracy that can embrace the growing diversity and complexity of human interests in today's world. Design provides the possibility that each and every person's individual good can be considered, within the framework of the common good.

Therefore, service, in terms of design, demands a heightened and refined ability to "listen"—to hear what is pressing for expression as much as what is being outwardly expressed. To do this, we must utilize *notitia* (Hillman 1992). Hillman defines notitia as the "capacity to form true notions of things from attentive noticing." Notitia is an act of attention that is complete and uncompromising, one that senses every nuance and can bring into focus details and patterns of connection that elude more passive encounters with real-world situations. Notitia allows a relationship of true empathy to form between the server and served. Notitia is not a method, but rather a way of being that is highly focused and attentive in the extreme. It is a process of focusing in the way that eyeglasses bring things into clarity (i.e., focus) rather than a restricting or narrowing of perspective (i.e., focused). Notitia is the opposite of detachment and separation encouraged by contemplative traditions. It is an awareness that is open to all input rather than selective of predefined input as exemplified by routine.

Since the core social contract in the design process is between designers and their clients, a designer needs to be in a balanced and proportioned influencing and power relationship with the client. Unfortunately, it is not uncommon that this pivotal relationship is distorted. To illustrate this point, we will compare five generalized types of relationships, four unbalanced types, and one dynamically balanced type (see figure 2.1). Two of these unbalanced relationships, the designer artist and the designer facilitator, represent very simple relationships where one of the two roles completely dominates.

In the *designer artist* case, the designer has complete influence over the process and the client has little to none. The designer is not interested in the desires or needs of the client. Instead, he or she creates a design based on his or her own judgments concerning the requirements for a satisfactory design solution. The designer acts in the same way as an artist, where the need to express one's own self is at the core of the relationship. We often see this type of designer being glorified as a "prima donna" or celebrity designer, such as the case of the "star-chitect." Clients who desire prestige, or status, by being identified with high-profile designs, often seek

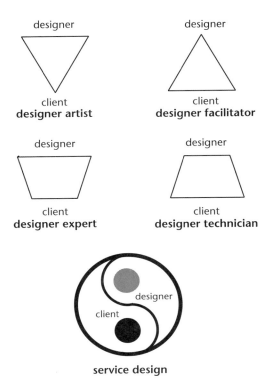

Figure 2.1
Designer/client power relationships

out this type of design relationship. The subset of this type of relationship involves consumers who are influenced to think or convinced that they need or desire a product or service developed by entrepreneurial or company expert designers.

The opposite situation occurs in a *designer facilitator* relationship, where the designer simply "obeys" any and all requests coming from the client. In this situation, it is accepted that the client knows precisely what he or she wants or needs, and knows specifically what should be done as a consequence—without any creative input from the designer. The client is, in this case, the sole creative agent in the design process. The designer becomes merely a facilitator. Although facilitation is an important part of any process, it should not be the primary role of a designer.

The remaining two forms of unbalanced relationships represent dispro-portional situations, where either the designer or the client has a majority of the influence and power. In the *designer technician* relationship, we see designers acting simply as enablers. By that we mean they don't contribute intentionally, or creatively, to any part of the design process. Instead, they answer questions, or respond to wishes from an intentional client, acting as an instrumental agent only.

In the *designer expert* relationship, we see the opposite, where the client is called to respond to initiatives taken by the designer. The designer enters the design process as a routine expert, with predetermined insights and outcomes in hand, dismissing the necessity of customized interactions with the client. As an expert, the designer determines which generalized solution, or solutions, will be adapted to the particular situation of the client.

It is difficult to find a way to visualize the full complexity of a balanced relationship between designers and the clients. To symbolize the ideal *service design* relationship, we have borrowed from the Chinese Yin-Yang model, which shows an intricate relationship where both sides are fully and authentically engaged in a dynamic design process. Both roles—designer and client—are inclusive of a part of the other. It is a dynamically balanced relation, but it is not a relation without tensions. The model implies that tension lies at the core of the interconnection. It is in the complexity of this interconnection, and in the tension between its different qualities, that imaginative and innovative design work takes place. The model also illustrates that mutual respect is vital to any effective design relationship.

Unlike the majority of group process theories, the designer-client service tradition is not an egalitarian relationship, or a hierarchical relationship. These relationships are problem focused. Instead, design is an inclusive activity, consisting of a composition of formalized roles that center on the idea of service. This integrative principle needs to guide the formation of design teams—creating a complex web of relationships with others who are, in one way or another, a part of the design process. The composition of roles for every project is unique. In any design situation, this composition has to be resolved in the earliest stages of the design process.

It is key to point out that in a service relationship, the designer is responsible to more than just the client, and must assume accountability for others who will be affected by any particular design activity. This includes stakeholders (those who are affected by an intentional change, but who are not included as part of the design process), stockholders, decision makers, producers, end users, customers, and surrogate clients (those who, when served, indirectly serve clients who are unable to represent their own interests). In addition, depending on the nature of that which is being

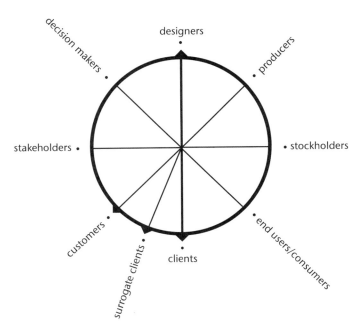

Figure 2.2
Design roles

created, the designer may need to consider future generations and the natural environment.

As we examine the service tradition in detail, it becomes quite obvious that service relationships are far more diverse and comprehensive than the singular connection that exists between clients and designers (see figure 2.2). The differing relationships and connections among design roles, as will be presented, are not exclusive of each other. The interrelationships or interconnections among any particular set of roles, in any specific situation, can be compound ones, consisting of several different types. In some cases, it may be appropriate to treat a set of relationships as one-dimensional, but this should always be a matter of intentional choice.

Which of these roles are relevant and essential to a particular design situation should be determined in the contracting process. Identifying which roles will be necessary to satisfy the design goal is the responsibility of the designer(s), in collaboration with those being served. We would suggest that a designer evaluate each interrelationship or interconnection carefully, as the essential nature of many roles may not be immediately apparent to everyone involved. We should note, these service relationships and connections are uniquely determined by the quality of each particular interaction and defined as *design protocols*.

The composition of the different types of protocols, for any given design activity, needs to be intentionally considered. It must be, in effect, designed. The resulting composition(s) can be shown graphically (see figure 2.3). Although graphic representations like these fail to show the full complexity and richness of the corresponding design protocols, they do make it quite clear that, in every design situation, the possible number of compositions is quite large.

This being the case—and given the fact that there are no hard-and-fast rules determining what compositions are most beneficial for any particular design situation—each configuration must spring from a designer's intentional design. It is also useful for that designer to experiment with different compositions, trying to imagine how these various combinations might influence the design process, and ultimately, the outcome. Finally, in the process of configuring these interactions, the designer must stay in close communication with the client, remembering that the service alliance between the designer and client is at the core of the process.

As stated earlier, it is not easy to identify all possible roles and interactions. It may not always be that formal or semiformal roles—such as stakeholders, stockholders, decision makers, producers or makers, end users, and customers—are the most useful ways to determine the interactions between or among roles for a particular design situation. If that is the case, there are other ways of representing the interactions. As a designer or client, or both, the notion of who "I" am, in relation to others, can be characterized as the interactions among the idealized protocol roles of *thou, you, us, them, other, it, all, we*, and *self* (see figure 2.4.). There may be other role types that can be imagined and developed as well. Choosing which are most appropriate for any particular design situation is a matter of design judgment.

An interaction protocol, such as *I-you*, is very different in quality from the interaction protocol of *I-other*. Building on some of Erick Jantsch's basic work, as influenced by Martin Buber and others (Jantsch 1975), the qualities of interactions or design protocols found in *I-it*, and *I-thou*, can be further developed, giving rise to other forms of design protocols such as *I-us, we-other*, and *all-them*. In addition, other combinations and permutations of roles and protocols can be created that would be specifically appropriate for different design situations (figure 2.5).

As an example of a design protocol, in an I-us interaction the designer becomes a member of the client category and thus is serving in two roles—

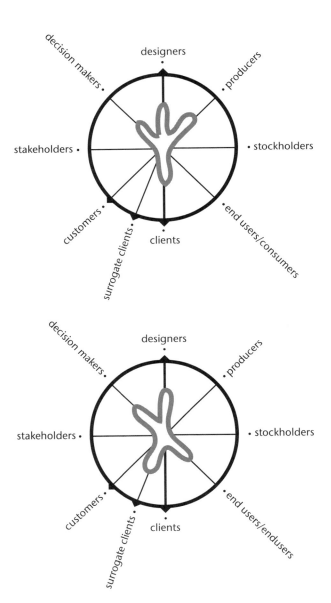

Figure 2.3
Examples of choices of role relationships

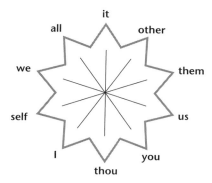

Figure 2.4
Design protocol roles

Figure 2.5
Examples of design protocol interactions

him or herself and the other. A designer in an I-it protocol interaction treats the client as an objective, impersonal entity revealed primarily through hard data. A designer in an I-thou protocol interaction relates to the client subjectively, with emotion and feeling. A designer in an I-them protocol interaction treats the client as an objective but human "other," utilizing insights gleaned from the social sciences. For these and any other set of design protocols, the interaction varies in kind and degree. Each set of interactions forms a social subsystem that must be intentionally designed with the particulars of each design situation in mind.

The way these protocols are justified and prioritized will strongly influence who takes part in the process, and under what conditions. It will affect the role of the designer and what will be expected from all other parties. Too often, intruding emergent interactions not planned for ahead of time disrupt design processes. A great deal of time and energy must be spent on redefining the composition of the team as a result, requiring that segments of the design process be repeated.

Service is a full partnership between those being served and a design team, working in a *conspiracy*—in other words, a breathing together. This notion of conspiracy transcends mere management of group process. It is similar to the concept of "flow" in the creative process, as presented by Csikszentmihalyi (1990), where normal divisions and distinctions of everyday activity blend into a seamless experience of intentionality. This symbiotic relationship is possible only if there is an exchange of empathy. Empathy, in the case of a design situation, is the ability to "be" as the other, while remaining a whole self. It is the ability to stand in someone else's place while standing on your own. These empathetic states of alignment are then given direction through the emerging understanding of desiderata—an understanding that occurs during the process of serving.

This type of design protocol forms in each particular design process a tensional, but collaborative, social system. Formal and informal agreements, or contracts, govern such design conspiracies. A design contract is a formalized relationship, where there is an equivalent exchange of value that defines the interaction. Such a contract can be between individuals who actually sit down in real time and negotiate a signed agreement known as *legal contracting*. But a design contract can also be formed between a designer and others, who are unable to represent themselves personally, such as future generations, those in ill health, or those handicapped in some way by external circumstances. These contracts need to be built on alternative, conceptual principles of agency that are made explicit. For every contract, the designer must determine the moral and legal grounds for assuming agency on behalf of a client who is unable to negotiate directly. Such an agreement is known as *value contracting*. In addition when design agency is assumed in economic, technological, or political contexts, *implied contracts* are adopted. The terms of an implied contract are not clearly disclosed to stakeholders, often leading to misunderstandings and conflict.

In any contractual relationship, one needs a clear understanding, based on agreement and consent, of the intention of the contract whether implied or actual. There are many types of contract intentions that are often categorically different from one another. For example, we can recognize different types of implied contracts, based on intentionality. These intentions include those that are based on scientific reasoning, on helping the helpless, on art-oriented aesthetic enlightenment, and on serving economic interests.

The service contract is the primary type of contract in design, although aspects of the other types may be appropriate, in different proportions, depending on the situation. These contracts are often implicit and do not necessarily represent a legal document. However, they do define a fiduciary relationship where there is ideally an equal exchange of value for agency. These contracts can exist between designers and clients who are unable to represent themselves and their desires in person, but who are represented by surrogates acting indirectly or directly in their stead.

It is important to note that even when there is a desire for intentional change, often one of the nonservice contracts are selected by default. For instance, if a specific action is needed for a certain situation, a science approach—which consists of describing, explaining, predicting, and controlling events—may be employed. This is not the kind of approach that supports making design judgments and bringing something new into the world. Science provides descriptions and explanations, but it does not provide sufficient basis for overall judgments of intention and action, especially in situations where knowledge and information are not complete or comprehensive—which is always the case in design—or given instrumental value. In a case like this, intentional change is agreed upon by a *coercion of facts* (Rittel 1988/2010).

The intentionally driven interactions that are built in a service contract—where one is serving, empathizing, and "conspiring"—form the binding forces of an effective design team. This team boasts a composition of diverse roles that are distinctly different but always equitable in character. Because of this, those in the role of "client" experience change motivated out of their own desiderata, rather than someone else's limited understanding of what is best for them. The client, in this case, is a full member of the design team. There is no assumption of inequity in the client's capacity to contribute.

So, to summarize, a designer needs to be able to form intentional service contracts with constituents—in other words, members of a whole. Design contracting therefore is not so much about agreements and exchanges between people as *among* people. The designer must keep in mind how dramatically contracts can vary, and should be sure that his or her client is also clear on the expectations that spring from a particular contract. This way, the two are aligned and integrative going into the process.

In addition, a designer needs to remember the complexity of interactions that a service contract entails, and in response must engage intentionally in a process of designing the team's compositional makeup. And, finally, a designer must be willing to let empathy lead the way. This assures that an appropriate design situation will emerge where contracts are formed, relationships and connections built, and design goals identified by focusing on desires and open communication.

3   Systemics

Designers need to be able to see relations and to identify and protect the essential connections found in real life—they need to be systemic thinkers. They must be able to create essential relationships and critical connections in their designs and between their designs and the larger systems in which they are embedded—in other words, designers must be systemic in everything they do and make. If they aren't, their way of working is fundamentally unsustainable. It doesn't matter if designers use "green" materials and process, if they use the latest environment-friendly technology, or if they follow the latest "recipe" from the most recent charismatic consultant—if they do not pay full attention to essential relationships and critical connections, they will not contribute to sustainability in the long run.

Social and natural ecosystems may be able to accommodate, adapt, and adopt designs thrown into them from outside, but in so doing each individual design perturbation becomes a crapshoot: will the design turn out to be a good thing or a critical mistake? Getting better at designing in an unsystemic way does not mean creating better designs. As Russell Ackoff said, "The righter you do the wrong thing, the wronger you get" (Ackoff and Pourdehnad 2001). Design systemics is the compound of integrative, inclusive, and connected thinking aimed at taking right action—doing the right thing even if not perfectly.

Every design is either an element of a system or a system itself and is part of ensuing causal entanglements. No design exists in a vacuum. Designers and their design activity do not live within a vacuum either. Designers, clients, and other stakeholders form a social system that is embedded in an entanglement of systemic relationships and connections. Acknowledging that complexity is the natural order of things is something too many people try to avoid and have even been trained to avoid in their educational backgrounds. Occam's razor—"the simplest explanation is the preferred explanation"—is exemplary of the more popular and simplistic *KISS* admonition—"Keep it simple, stupid."

Designing is by definition an interdependent activity that involves multiple inputs from the multidimensional realms of the real world. That is why design inquiry is systemic in nature. The systems approach and systems thinking, including systems science, are integrative *ontological* (relating to the nature of real things) and *epistemological* (relating to designs of inquiry) approaches within an encompassing schema of systemic philosophy. Some philosophers hold that the systems approach is one of the oldest forms of philosophic inquiry to be found and may be a founding schema for philosophy in general. Any philosophy is an archetypal schema that forms a unifying narrative of the human condition.

Systems philosophy and design philosophy are inseparably intertwined at the intersection of inquiry for action. The love (philo) of wisdom (sophia)—philosophy—in the tradition of design is expressed as the love of wise action or practical wisdom—*phronesis*. Every action has consequences in a world where all things are interconnected systemically to other things. To be wise therefore requires that thinking and acting be unified through the reconstitution of sophia—dissolving the separation between thinking and acting. Systemic design unifies thinking holistically with acting courageously, creatively, and responsibly.

Systemics is the fundamental basis for what can be seen as design logic and reasoning. Systemics focuses our full attention on the connections and relations between people, subjects, objects, and ideas—rather than just the things themselves. There are a variety of formalized fields of study and professional stances or standpoints that fall under the general heading of systemics (see figure 3.1). However, because of the extensive focus on analytic and reductive thinking in people's educational backgrounds and subsequent work experience, they too often focus on elements or categories

- systems thinking
- systems approach
- systems design
- systems theory
- systems dynamics
- systems assessment
- systems analysis
- cybernetics
- systems management

Figure 3.1
Systemic stances and standpoints

- entanglement   causal relationships
  complexity
- network   emergent behavior
  nodes/intersections/links
- functional assembly   synergy
  operation
- subsystem   function
  means
- system   purpose
  ends/outcomes
- metasystem   intention
  direction
- whole system   essential qualities
  adequate/requisite/vital
- emergent whole system emergent qualities
  transformation
- deep system   desiderata, wisdom
  hypostasis

Figure 3.2
Systemic categories

of elements rather than on the connections or relationships between or among events and things.

The concept of systemics is inclusive of a number of types of systems that help us to simplify and think about complexity in systems (see figure 3.2) without losing critical connections. These categories should be seen as ideal types, that is, as analytical definitions and not necessarily types of systems to be found in reality.

One of the most common categories in systemics is—as one would surmise—system. System descriptions and explanations of the natural world are some of the most common schemas in science (Ziman 2000). The term "system" has crept into the vocabularies of professionals and academics as well as into technology, business, and government. So let's look more closely at the meaning of the term. "System" denotes both a subjective means of inquiry and the objective focus of inquiry. The Greek origin of the noun "system" is *sustema*, meaning a composite whole. When "system" is used as a modifier of action, its derivative is the compound term *sunistanai*, which means "to bring together" (sun—"together" + histanai—"to cause to stand"). Thus the motivation for a systemic design inquiry is the desire to know how things are intentionally caused to stand together in unity as a design.

The term "system" has many definitions promulgated by a pantheon of contemporary systems scholars. It has been used as a description of both an "embodied way of thinking"—in other words, an *epistemology*—and the thing that is being thought about—an *ontology*. Systemic thinking is an approach to thinking and learning about the human condition. It also refers to the description and explanation of things that affect the human condition. The latter of these two definitions includes systems science—the understanding of systems as "real things," either concrete or abstract, using the scientific method approach. The former, a systemic inquiry approach, focuses on a way of thinking that enables different fields of focused inquiry to be related to each other.

Systemic thinking (see figure 3.3) is constituted of both systems science and the systems approach. It is a new and, at the same time, ancient way to undertake meaning making. Meaning making is essentially the creation of relationships of understanding, specifically between that which is experienced and the one who is experiencing. These relationships form the matrix of a belief system, which is inclusive of real, true, and ideal understandings of the world that inform actions, reflections, and imagination in specific situations.

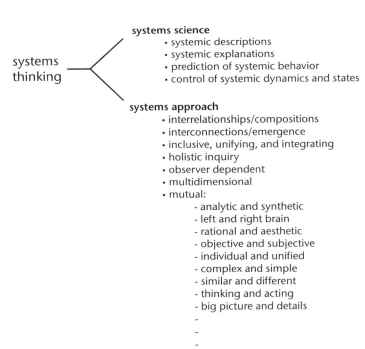

Figure 3.3
Systems thinking

Systemic thinking is both a way of observing the world and a way of being in the world, depending on whether your intention is to describe and explain it, or to take action in it. Systemic thinking represents the way people have naturally interacted with the world, as it is natural for people to bring their whole selves into the daily process of making sense out of life. The whole person is not a distillation of characteristics and attributes. This is important for the designer to remember. Distillations are inherently unnatural—whereas, compound world approaches and worldviews function in an inherently more natural way.

Systemic thinking is a distinctive form of inquiry that does not fit naturally into the traditional specifications reserved for any of the individual scientific disciplines. What a systems approach does, instead, is offer an alternative to the forced compromise between narrow specialization and broad, shallow generalization. Systems thinking focuses on relationships between domains of knowledge, and on the patterns of relationship that emerge as a consequence. These patterns provide a map for the development of hybrid forms of knowledge, and for their application in theoretically, and pragmatically, relevant ways. These patterns are given meaning through interpretation. This is similar to the scientific tradition, where raw data are also interpreted and then given meaning.

The domains of systems, systems approaches, and systems thinking do not have a predefined field of interest or content area. Like science, art, and other traditions of inquiry, they form a lens through which observation, imagination, comprehension, understanding, and action are focused integratively. In this sense, they reflect the same qualities found in the tradition of design. The processes and outcomes of systemic thinking are mirrored in design thinking.

Envisioning a systemic situation's essential nature, as imagined or observed, in order to be able to communicate it to others, is a complex and demanding task. Models, diagrams, and other forms of cognitive art are invaluable and essential (Tufte 1990) for envisioning information about systems. Our dominant mode of communicating—words—falls short when used without the corroboration of other means of representing complex, dynamic entities. Describing, explaining, and imagining systems necessitate the ability to visualize them, using representations of form, structure, and process.

Systems of all types, including designs of systems of inquiry, can be represented using the concept of systemic *compounds*. A compound is a complex set of interrelated elements, which are combined in unique blends. Coherent and consonant attributes of any particular systemic composition or composite compound can be revealed indirectly through the means of abstract, conceptual images in the form of rich schemas. These cognitive models are representative and not literal and thus more comprehensible than attempts to represent the real complexity of a situation.

All systemic phenomena are constituted of compounds and forms, which exhibit unique emergent qualities and behaviors. Systemic compounds represent the substance, but not the form, of a design, in the way that water is the substance of a hydrogen-oxygen compound, while waves or snowflakes are forms. Systemic patterns and compositions differ from compounds in that they represent form and not substance.

Systems thinking and the systems approach can be characterized as arising from a mix of different traditional approaches to inquiry and learning, which are combined in certain proportions within the constraints of the given contexts. Systemic thinking as a part of design inquiry is a *world approach* because it is action oriented. This is in contrast to scientific systems inquiry that is focused on description and explanation, and forms *worldviews*. An approach is action oriented, while a view is noninterventionist. A world approach, like design, depends on the reliability of effective worldviews but is biased toward taking action as well. Design, as a world approach, emerges as a compound of ontological and epistemological design categories. In systemics the predominant ontological interest is in types of systems and related concepts such as subsystems and metasystems.

Any description of a system requires a lens or a defined set of framing categories through which the system is examined. These framing categories can be abstract theoretical categories or based on everyday concrete aspects. An example of an epistemological design category is illustrated by the categorical set inclusive of the real, the true, and the ideal cognitive frameworks in chapter 1, "The Ultimate Particular." The particular frameworks or categories used determine what attributes and qualities of a situation or event will be revealed to the observer. Another example, with greater granularity, would be the categorical set inclusive of economics, politics, and social frameworks. When more than one framing category is used from this set to "see" a situation, the resulting images may not only be different but also in conflict or mutually exclusive to one another.

Let's focus on a real-world example of these principles. For example, look at lending policies for home purchases. A particular decision based on these policies may be considered "just good business practice" in an economic frame of reference. At the same time, it may be considered to be unfair in a social frame of reference, or may be treated with total indif-

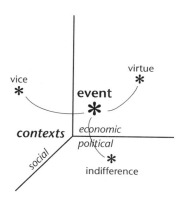

Figure 3.4
Same event—different context

ference by a legal or political framework, because it was not against the law, or was not required by law. As you can see, a real-world event, projected into three different frames of reference, can reveal dramatically different understandings, values, and meaning. Yet, at the same time, the incident remains a coherent singular event in the world. The event does not represent any specific value in itself. The value judgments about the event are made with a different set of framing categories. A specific event may be perceived negatively in one context, positively in another, and at the same time be seen as neutral in a third (see figure 3.4).

The tensions created by an awareness of two or more paradoxical images or descriptions of a system can be mediated through a systemic approach. We find an example of just such mediation in Aristotle's concept of the *mean*, the mean being a mediated judgment, where a new understanding emerges from the reconciliation of differences between things, as in the case of the type of judgment that mediates between mercy and justice resulting in compassion. From a design perspective it is vital that a systemic reconciliation occur rather than merely defaulting to compromise, trade-offs, or other forms of conflict resolution. So, how can that be done?

The first step is to dissolve the contextual frameworks that give rise to the conflicting images in the first place by *stepping back* to look into the larger system within which the diverse contexts have been formed and intentions defined. From the perspective of the larger system a more unifying frame can be constructed that transcends the limitations of the original system's purpose and from which an entirely new understanding of the event can emerge at a different level of comprehension because the focus has shifted from outcomes to intentions. This is an example of a systemic strategy for dealing with complexity as an alternative to methods of oversimplification.

The ability to use a systemic design approach is not dependent on the mastery of a set of theories, methods, and facts. It is a *stance* that can be assumed by a change in *mindset* just as we switch between being evaluative and being creative by making a change in our mindsets. We perceive observations, experiences, and reflections differently depending on our stance or mindset. If our mindset is analytic then synthesis concepts will not make sense. If our mindset is reductionist then systemic ideas never make sense. Our mindsets determine the stance or *standpoint* we take toward understanding and acting in the world, and give us access to the schemas that have been developed as aids to this stance or to the process of creating more such aids. In the case of a systemic design stance there are multiple schemas—including the scientific schemas called *theories*—to be shared by designers as well as ways of creating schemas for systemic designing.

There are a number of cognitive influences on the formation of schemas that determine what we see and how we see things in a complex world (see figure 3.5). Not dealt with here is the understanding that individuals

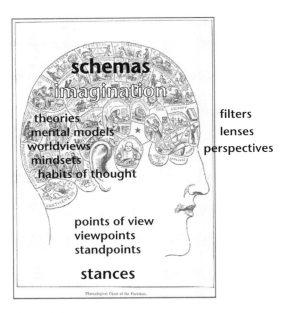

Figure 3.5
Cognitive frameworks

are of "many minds." Our minds work at the subconscious as well as the conscious levels. The integration of the multiple cognitive frameworks occur at all levels of consciousness so the challenge is to inform our unconscious minds while we further develop our conscious minds. What we see—and how we see ourselves and the rest of the world—depends on what we are inclined to see and where we are positioned in relation to what we observe.

Stance is a seminal concept in systemic design. Intention—aim, direction, bearing—is bound up in with stance, which is a matter of paying full attention in a particular way—in other words, service, imagination, and action—in a particular direction—meaning, intention or aim. There is a clear distinction among cognitive strategies such as *Weltanschauung*, mental models, standpoints, and stance. But the question of what stance is remains difficult to explain fully. Stance is a compound of ideas and attitudes such as propensity, inclination, proclivity, disposition, and attraction. It points to first intentions and next steps, setting a designer along a specific path of inquiry for action.

A mindset, however, is a set of assumptions held by individuals or groups of people, so dominant that individuals and groups continually use it to guide behaviors, choices, and responses. The concept of mindset is closely related to that of *mental models*, which are systemic cognitive representations of reality that people use to guide their interactions with the world. A mindset can also be seen as a form of worldview or Weltanschauung.

The term "Weltanschauung" (German), is composed of Welt, "world," and Anschauung, "view" or "outlook." Weltanschauung, as a designer's worldview understood from Horst Rittel's approach (Rittel 1988/2010), is a cognitive framework, a type of schema or mental model that determines what and how things will be focused, filtered, and understood. Weltanschauung is a comprehensive worldview that is the cognitive orientation of an individual or social system encompassing a fundamental set of narratives about how things work in the world including values, emotions, and ethics. It refers to a framework of schemas, theories and belief systems through which an individual interprets the world and interacts with it.

Showing the constituent elements of a system as isolated separate parts is an inadequate means for representing systems. Equally unsatisfactory is the description of the whole from a singular *point of view*—that is, a positional relationship to the system. The difficulty of seeing the whole of a situation is a challenge that has been recognized for thousands of years. The famous tale of the blind wise men and the elephant demonstrates the limits of the positional or point-of-view perspective. Each blind scholar describes the elephant based on the part of the elephant he is in touch with at the moment. Thus the elephant becomes a rope from the perspective of the one hanging on to the tail. Alternatively the elephant is a fan for the scholar holding an ear, a snake for the one hanging onto the trunk, a tree for the one leaning against a leg, and a wall for the one pushing against the side of the elephant. It is obvious to the rest of us who can see the whole animal that the scholars' descriptions are partial and lead to the wrong conclusions. Of course, the mystery is who is able to see the whole system and see that the scholars are only in touch with a part? Obviously, from a "sighted" person's perspective, none of the descriptions are accurate, nor would a summation of their descriptions render a factual representation of "elephantness."

Systemic insights into complex realities are revealed partially or obscurely through images, which are distorted by intervening factors or elements that filter or dim direct cognitive access. *Filters* such as culture, habit, and expertise are unavoidable, requiring allowances to be made. On the one hand, filters limit what can be seen, heard, and felt (see figure 3.6). Biases, bigotry, and prejudices are all-too-common filters that block what people can access. On the other hand filters help determine what is foreground and what is background, what is important and what is less so.

0) absent: tuned out
                — "self"-displacement

1) ego: judgmentalism
                — listening to "self"

2) affirming: familiar
                — reconfirming to "self"

3) critical: factual/real
                — disconfirming to "self"

4) empathic: graphologue/dialogue/conversation
                — with "other" about "other"

5) generative: insight
                new understanding/
                new meaning/
                added value/
                parti

Figure 3.6
Listening filters

Lenses are different from filters in that they make things clearer. Such lenses are not the kind that focuses things down to a point, such as a magnifying glass that can start fires by concentrating sunlight. Our cognitive lenses are more like the lenses in our glasses that make things clear rather than narrow. Of course, lenses are also tuned to certain frequencies, which select and pass information within restricted bandwidths.

Harold Linstone developed a model of *multiple perspectives*—in other words, points of view and standpoints—that he and others have used to make assessments of technologies, events, and significant disasters (Linstone 1984). When combined, the different perspectives provide a richer, more holistic picture of existing complexities. These three perspectives—technical (T), organizational (O), and personal (P)—have been used and expanded on by others in a variety of situations. Linstone's multiple perspectives model describes truth-oriented epistemological schema:

The T perspective: Problems are simplified by abstraction, idealization, and isolation from the real world. The implicit assumptions and characteristics include reductionism, reliance on scientific logic and rationality, problem-solution focus, quantification, use of data and models, optimization, and objectivity of the analyst. . . . But, as the recent work in complexity science has underscored, it has serious limitations in dealing with complex, nonlinear, adaptive systems. Unfortunately, most real-world sociotechnical systems are of this kind.

The 0 perspective: The organizational perspective focuses on process rather than product, on action rather than problem-solving. The critical question is "does something need to be done?" and "who needs to do it?" rather than "what is the optimal solution"?

The P perspective: This views the world through the eyes of the individual. While cause and effect is a fundamental paradigm of the T perspective, challenge and response animates P. Each individual actor in a decision process has a unique set of patterns that inform his or her intuition. (Linstone 1984)

It is profitable to expand these multiple perspectives to be more inclusive in the case of design (see figure 3.7). For example, with regard to design, political, economic, ethical, and spiritual perspectives would be important additions to Linstone's list. The ethical (E) perspective, for example, asks such ethical questions as who ought to be served by the designer's actions and what ought to be the scales of measurement used to evaluate the quality of the design? Who should make the decisions and who should the designers be? What resources ought to be used and what boundaries drawn around the project?

Using a different approach, the attempt to integrate parts of some phenomena into a unified whole from a disciplinary *viewpoint* requires interdisciplinary or multidisciplinary cooperation. But one of the limita-

T   technical
O   organizational
P   personal
P   political
E   economic
E   ethical
S   spiritual

Figure 3.7
Expanded multiple perspectives

tions to this approach based on stitching parts together is that, just as a dissected frog would not come back to life if its parts were stitched back together, a holistic understanding of some aspect of the real world does not reveal itself through an aggregation of pieces and parts of disciplinary descriptions (see figure 3.8).

Complex phenomena like real systems are impossible to "see" from one *station point* or *standpoint*. A station point is based on the position one has in relationship to the object of interest. A standpoint is one's outlook or attitude based on circumstances and beliefs. So one would have a specific standpoint from a unique station point.

Just as a building cannot be seen by standing at the front door but can only be fully appreciated by moving around it, up and over it, below and through it—in other words, by moving between different *station points*. A complex phenomena, or situation, may reveal contradictory images of itself depending on from where it is observed. Complex ideas and beliefs are often perceived as paradoxes, when images from two different points of view of the same complex thing are viewed simultaneously (see Schön and Rein 1994 for a similar conceptualization). When light is observed as both wave and particle, there is a desire to resolve the paradox into one or the other reality. In the social realm, where paradoxes cannot be resolved by the dominance of one over the other, differences are resolved by strategies such as compromise, or trade-off. However, attempts to resolve irresolvable differences between images are not the answer, because the images are not based on commensurable perspectives. Light appears as a wave from one position of observation and as a particle from another position.

Although complex images from systemic observations are difficult to formally model as schemas, they can be imaged. For example, the concept of a paradigm creates coherent frames of reference by defining the epistemological rules of the game for any particular system of inquiry, thus

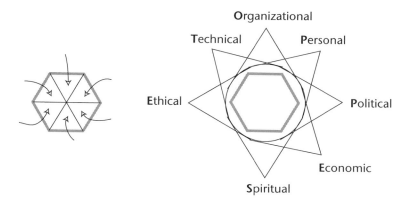

seeing the divisions

- **disciplinary**
- **interdisciplinary**
- **multidisciplinary**

challenge:
- **relationship of parts**
- **synthesis of parts**

seeing the whole

- **multiple perspectives**

challenge:
- **integration of perspectives**
- **recognition of emergence**

Figure 3.8
Seeing the parts and the whole

assuring consistent forms of knowledge are produced. The outcomes of a systemic *world approach* can be made visible through a compound of multiple projected images illuminated from different station points, by a coherent perspective.

We can sometimes only see a dim projection of the complex real thing itself from any one viewpoint (see figure 3.9). It may only be possible to imagine a design, in situ, through the dim shapes of the cast outlines and contours of a complex parti, similar to Plato's shadows of idealized forms on a cave wall, where chained prisoners could only see the shadows cast by the true forms. Plato's shadows are an example of a single viewpoint projected from a single station point onto a single cognitive surface. Such an approach is the most restrictive because it offers only a two-dimensional image of a complex, multidimensional reality.

The reflected, or projected, images are formed by the internal rules of relations for each *frame of reference* in the same way that individual paradigms dictate the theories that are congruent within their terms. Being able

Figure 3.9
Photo by Max Braun; Max Braun photostream, Flickr, 2009

to create distinct complex images and then conceptually model them in relationship to each other, as a whole, is the function—and ultimately the value—of systemics in the design tradition.

A systemic design is more than the sum of its parts or perspectives—in other words, an emergent whole—because of two important types of protocols—*ordering systems* and *organizing systems* (see figure 3.10). Ordering systems result in *compositional emergence* and organizing systems result in *created emergence*. Ordering systems are concerned with *relations* and organizing systems are focused on *connections*. Relationships define how things contrast and compare with one another while connections determine how causal power or influence is transferred between things. Descriptions focus on relations while explanations focus on connections.

Wetness, a quality associated with water, is an emergent quality resulting from the combined connections of atoms of hydrogen and oxygen. Wetness disappears as an attribute when a water molecule is reduced to its constituent atoms of gases as connections are broken. Life, as an emergent quality of biologic systems, disappears when the living plant or animal is dissected—that is, essential connections are severed—into elemental com-

ordering system
  • relationships
  • categories
  • ideal types
  • taxonomies
  • orders
  • hierarchies
  • composition

organizing system
  • connections
  • structure
  • process
  • form
  • synergy
  • emergence

Figure 3.10
Ordering systems and organizing systems

ponents. Abstract entities, such as community or family, similarly lose their emergent qualities when divided into individual components for analysis. The point of a work of art disappears altogether when categories of materials and methods are studied individually through decomposition. In contrast, gases, biologic life, communities, and families, grouped by kind according to specific types of relationships, create categories of understanding that can be lost without the application of patterns of relations.

It is relations that create unifying compositions and connections that create emergent qualities—both seminal attributes of designed and natural systems. Relations describe why artificial systems are structured the way they are. Connections explain why systems take the forms that they do, and why both natural and artificial systems behave in the ways they do. Explanations demonstrate why connections—both internally and externally—in particular, systemic situations, are necessary in order to fulfill purposes defined by larger intentions.

An example of the distinction between relations and connections in designed systems can be seen in an ancient Greek computer more than two thousand years old. The Antikythera Mechanism is a series of machined brass gears connected in combinations of gear assemblies to other combinations of gears connected to dials with inscribed letters, images, and numbers (see figure 3.11). This astonishing, functional assembly creates information that denotes the solar, lunar, and planetary (five known

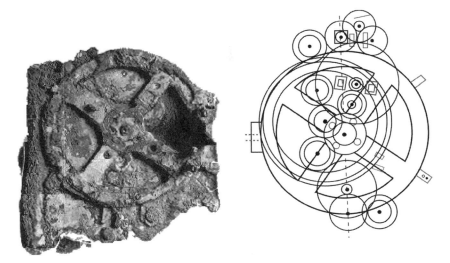

Figure 3.11
Model of Antikythera Mechanism

planets at the time) interrelationships at any point in time—their astro-
logic groupings and celestial movements. The information includes the
predicted dates of lunar eclipses and the dates of the coming Olympic
Games, the most important public event in Greek life. The connected brass
gears do not *cause* any of these astronomical or public events to occur but
their coordinated connections create information for individuals to use.
The gears are an example of an organizing system while the relationships
of the planets in constellations are an example of an ordering system. The
connected positions of the gear assembly dials and the relationships
between the earth and the sun, moon, and planets are tied together by a
human observer into a coherent information system, one integrating
both cause-effect mechanical connections and external astronomical
relationships.

Another way of illustrating the importance of a systems approach in
design is to contrast that which is essentially analog in character with that
which is digital or analytic (see figure 3.12), not only to contrast the concepts but also to show the necessary relationship between them in design.
The analog and the digital are requisite companion approaches in designing. By analog we mean a form, process, or experience that is perceived as
undifferentiated and continuous, as opposed to the discontinuity imposed
by a digital or analytic perspective. For example, the human condition,
both in a natural and historical context, is analog when life is experienced

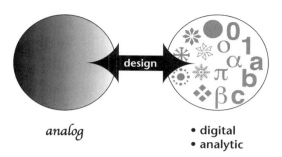

analog

- **digital**
- **analytic**

Figure 3.12
Analog to digital and back

as a flow. "Meaning making" in human experience is dependent on being contained within this analog context. Things make sense only when connected and interrelated. If things occur without connection in a discontinuous way, there is no inherent meaning present. Meaning is only attributed to that which is understood through relationships in context. This is what a systems perspective does for design. Design is a process of meaning making because it is engaged in creation from a systems perspective, holistically and compositionally.

It is only in the most recent, infinitesimal fraction of the human lifeline, when technologic cultures have pushed to the fore, that the analog experience of life has not been dominant. In some great cultures like that of China, the analog was able to remain dominant (Jullien 2004) even during the great analytic or digital transformation of the last century, though in recent years, China has slowly embraced a more digital perspective. How can a society not change, when the success of the analytic and digital in the material development of the West is so undeniable? But we would argue that the negative consequences of not reintegrating these scientific approaches in an analog life experience are becoming more and more apparent. One example of this is hydroelectric dams, which are designed and built to handle one specific aspect of reality but also interrupt the migration routes of salmon. Both fish and humans have to go to great lengths to get around (both figuratively and literally) the disruptive effects of these dams. Such examples show how an analytic and digital perspective of reality typically only depicts some aspect of the complexity and richness of the analog world, while people live in a world that is analog and where aspects can not be experienced or treated separately.

Despite a recent coining of the phrase "the digital age" to mean our current and immediate past history, the Western world has actually been digital for the last 750 years (Crosby 1997). Time, space, and energy have all been divided into packets, or abstract forms of information, which prove to be very stable over time. These packets provide information only when they are in a correct relationship with each other. Regardless of the amount of information these packets can provide, it is important to realize *the relationships themselves provide meaning*. Thus, the division of the day into hours, minutes, and seconds meters the passage of time without saying what kind of a day it was. A mapping grid demarcates traffic patterns and real estate, but does not delineate the human qualities of neighborhoods, communities, or hometowns. Electrical impulses may be digitized forms of energy, which can convert into digital modes of communication, but they cannot translate the message they are sending.

Much of modern life is experienced as a fractured and stressful whirlwind. The lack of integration between analytically designed systems and our own analog life experience can be seen as the primary reason for the current levels of angst and yearning in individuals—there seems to be a growing longing for a more integrated, meaningful, and holistic life experience. The challenge for designers is to take advantage of the benefits of the analytic in their design approaches, while at the same time integrating these elements into an overall compositional approach, which draws from the analog.

Every new design introduced into the world becomes an analog contribution to the human experience, rather than superficially attached, meaningless "stuff" or, worse, "junk." Design can be served by the analytic and digital, but every design process must finish out as an analog composition, in order to fit back into the human experience. The architect Louis Kahn said: "A great building must begin with the unmeasurable, must go through measurable means when it is being designed and in the end must be unmeasurable" (Kahn 2003).

One excellent example of this is the way in which the traditional Balinese culture integrates artistic representation, agricultural processes, and spiritual ritual into an undifferentiated, holistic, lived experience. For example, a newly designed rice plant introduced into the agricultural sector would quickly be integrated into the totality of the analog Balinese life experience, because the Balinese do not partition their lives into distinct categories such as religion, work, art, and community. They try to maintain seamless lives in contrast to many Westernized cultures.

The end products, or artifacts, of design will invariably be social systems or subsystems of social systems or parts of social systems. The designs will become networked into complex causal entanglements. This is true whatever the actual outcome of the design process—for example, a product, building, service, process, or abstract concept. This is because all things are related systemically and nothing exists in isolation. Whether an idea or a coffeemaker, it will be fully embedded in a complex system of relationships. Not only are the artifacts systems related, but also the agents of change—the designers and the design teams—are social systems as well. Design roles and relationships are systemic. Design processes are both systemic (integrative and interconnected) and systematic (methodical, sequential, and episodic). This is why it is essential for designers to understand theoretically the nature of systems and for them to use systems thinking as the basis for design reason.

Design is now understood more deeply and applied more broadly by people in domains well outside of the normative confines of the professional design fields that create our material culture. Design is coming to be appreciated as disciplined and realistic in addition to creative and innovative. A design approach can be used in complex, unstructured, messy situations cutting across traditional disciplinary boundaries and domains of expertise because of the development and maturation, over the past several decades, of foundational and fundamental concepts in systemics.

Nature is not merely a collection of organic and inorganic elements or compounds, possessing attendant qualities and attributes, which exist in isolation. Nor is humanity merely a collection of individuals in isolated proximity to one another. Everything in the real world is connected to everything else with varying levels of criticality and intensity of connections. These connections produce qualities and attributes at multiple levels of resolution and emergence. Complexity, a distinctive attribute arising as a consequence of the dynamic interactivity of connections, is the rule in the real world, while simplification, or reductionist thinking, such as ignoring the interrelationships of critical connections and concomitant emergent qualities, is a dangerous distraction. Analytic, reductionist thinking (separating into parts for the purpose of study) can create knowledge that is powerful and productive in a positive way only when brought back into a context of inquiry that takes into account the existence of complex relationships of connections and the phenomenon of emergence.

Elemental states, perceived as independent from an analytic perspective, are actually quite interdependent in significant ways; ways that generally guarantee their own continued existence. Everything exists in an environment and within a context. Everyone depends on other things for something, whether it is food, protection, or other basic needs. Such assemblies of functional relationships lead to the emergence of phenomena that transcend the attributes and qualities of the things themselves. Ecosystems are one example of this. An ecosystem, as a community of living things in close interaction and interdependence with one another, displays qualities that are experienced only in aggregation, as in the case of wetlands, a biologic community. This type of ecosystem filters and purifies the water that flows through it as a result of the complex interaction of the plants and animals that inhabit it. Another example of emergence is a house, a functional assembly of construction materials, until it is experienced holistically as a home—not merely a building. Since life itself is an emergent quality, an attribute of functional organic assemblies, it is literally life threatening, when dealing with living systems, for connections to be ignored or broken through the intervention of reductive thinking or action.

Another critical shortfall of the reductionist approach concerns the separation of function from purpose and intention in conceptual analysis. Reductionist approaches in thinking and intervention separate and isolate function from teleological ends while ignoring altogether intentional aims. But what we argue here is that the understanding and improvement or optimization of functional members and elements of a system in isolation from the intention, purpose, or ends of a system is not possible. The relationships between functional activity and teleological considerations are as important as the connections between system elements. An approach that accounts for critical consideration of relationships of connections and emergence is necessary to overcome this and other limitations of reductionist thinking.

When we view nature and human activity as interconnected and interrelating, we are taking a systemic approach, the opposite of the reductionist approach described previously. As designers, we believe that we need to view the world from this systems perspective. Systemics is the logic of design. Such an approach requires that close attention be paid to fundamental connections and relations, which result in the phenomenon of emergence. If an individual's intention is to create something new in the world, not to merely describe and explain things, or predict and control things, it is essential to take a systemic approach.

However, a comprehensive design process ultimately entails creation of the analog and the emergent as well, in order for the resulting design to weave seamlessly back into the human experience. Such a comprehensive design process will ultimately yield an understanding of what we want the analog whole to be like. But, in order to reach this vision, we need an

assessment			change and design	
systems apposition	systems analysis/ synthesis	systems critique	systems restoration	systems redesign design
that-which-is		that-which-ought-to-be that-which-should-be	that-which-needs-to-be	that-which-is-desired-to-be
• describe • explain		• critique	• repair	• reform • transform • form

Figure 3.13
Assessment, change, and design

understanding of the analog experience of reality. And, for this, we need to make *systems assessments*.

Designers are thrown into a complex milieu when invited into a design situation. In order to engage in a process of making desirable changes within this milieu in a confident and well-balanced way it is necessary to describe and explain the situation from the perspective of a change agent. This involves undertaking an assessment process that is appositional, analytic, synthetic, and critical, which evolves into a change and design process (see figure 3.13). The outcome of a systemic assessment lays the ground for the subsequent design process of reformation, transformation, or formation activity.

The assessment processes and the change and design process are complex and interconnected. Even simplified schemas of the processes and their connections can appear overly complex yet worthy of some time and attention in order to begin to grasp the systemic characteristics of the process as a whole (see figure 3.14). Figure 3.14 highlights the assessment and critique side of a binary process model of *inquiry* and *action*. Facets of the assessment process are introduced in this chapter with the design process covered in greater detail in chapter 15. Assessment and design are interconnected processes that unfold in time with mutual influence that are not necessarily sequential.

Making an assessment of a situation for design purposes involves producing descriptions and explanations of the situation using a variety of cognitive frames. In addition, making an assessment involves taking

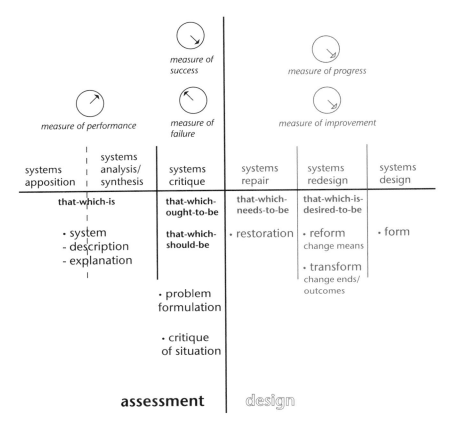

Figure 3.14
Systemic assessment

measurements of the situation in order to evaluate how well the system is performing—in other words, its efficiency—and how successful or unsuccessful the system has been in fulfilling its purpose—its effectiveness. From these evaluations a critique can be made and a determination reached on whether the situation is problematic or primarily a datum for design.

Systems assessment can be characterized as a process of "looking" in different directions from different perspectives (see figure 3.15) Systems "fit" into their environments and contexts. This fit is called apposition. Not only do they fit in place but they also fit in time. Systems have a past; they are representative of their provenance. They also have a future however brief or extended. Systems often have peer systems with which

analysis
    "looking into"
        • disassembly

synthesis
    "looking at"
        • assembly
        • form

    "looking out"
        • environment
        • encompassing systems
        • integrative synthesis

apposition
    "looking around"
        • context
        • milieu

    "looking back"
        • provenance
        • research

    "looking ahead"
        • design
        • predict

Figure 3.15
Assessment as "looking"

they interact cooperatively, competitively, or conflictually. There are larger systems that they fit into as well. Any assessment requires a process of "looking around" to see how things fit; is the system ill fitted or well fitted?

"Looking into" a system requires analysis. An analytic inventory of the parts of a system is like the inventory of all of the unassembled or disassembled parts of an automobile. The essential character of the automobile is not revealed until it is fully assembled and functional. For example, the analytic inventory of all the parts that make up an automobile does not reveal the character of the car itself, its comfort, performance, and efficiency. When the parts are assembled into a car, the car does not give any insight into the nature of the transportation system—the context and environment—which it must fit into as a functional assembly. When someone talks about being a car designer they may or may not mean taking responsibility for addressing all of these criteria.

"Looking out" of a system entails synthesis. This is the assembly of constituent elements into a functional whole, relating its functioning to the performance specifications formulated by the larger system in which it is embedded.

Synthetic thinking has become particularly effective in the ongoing development of the systemic design tradition because of the availability of more fully developed systems scholarship and research. The contributions of analytic thinking's to design reasoning are effective, certainly, but there is a caution. The challenge in design is to not allow analysis to become the dominant or exclusive thinking process.

From a synthesis approach, ingredients are not the cake. Neither are the cooking utensils, the cook's techniques, and the processes used for mixing batter and baking and frosting the cake. These are all necessary elements but do not reveal the emergent form of cakeness until all the ingredients are blended, baked, and decorated in sequence. In the same manner, in academic programs the individual courses do not comprise an education. Neither does the sequencing of classes reveal the character of the education received by the student. Curriculum is not equivalent to pedagogy or androgogy. All these elements and more are required for the emergence of an educated person to occur. This is the essence of design *becoming* and design *being*.

As we have seen, a system can be defined in many ways. A system is located both within a context and an environment, and has a different relationship with each. A system is described as being embedded in a metasystem (i.e., nested within a larger system). A system is also defined as being in relationship with peer systems, some of which may compete or cooperate with the system. A system can be profiled in reference to its boundary and whether that boundary is open or closed to energy, resources, influence, or information from the system's environment. A system is further explained through the identification of its constituent elements, units, subsystems, or other parts. Another descriptor is of the processes that animate the system's dynamics. Most important, a system is explained through the patterns and qualities of the relationships of its components. A system is further characterized by the emergent properties and behaviors, which these patterns and combinations evoke.

System ideal types are grouped by strategies of determining similarities and overarching methods of differentiation. As an example, Ludwig von Bertalanffy wrote:

In dealing with complexes of "elements," three different kinds of distinction may be made—i.e.,

(1) according to their *number*;

(2) according to their *species*;

(3) according to the *relations* of elements.

(Bertalanffy 1968)

Even though it is unrealistic to be able to know all of the different definitions and characterizations of systems, it is important for designers to have a clear understanding of how they choose to define systems, systemic concepts, and systemic thinking. No designer can practice good design by avoiding systemics. Systemic thinkers discern varieties of systems using sets of *ideal types* (Weber 1904/2007) and *categories*.

An ideal type is formed by the one-sided accentuation of one or more points of view" according to which "concrete individual phenomena . . . are arranged into a unified analytical construct" (*Gedankenbild*); in its purely fictional nature, it is a methodological "utopia [that] cannot be found empirically anywhere in reality (Weber 1904/2007).

For example, Russell Ackoff and Fred Emery (Ackoff and Emery 1972) discerned systems as mechanical, organic, or social types. Kenneth Boulding (1956) discerned system types as forming a hierarchy starting with mechanical frameworks through social systems to transcendental systems. There are additional categories of systems—too numerous to include here—that have been developed by other systems scholars that provide useful insights into the nature of systems and systems approaches. The literature is full of descriptions and explanations of immense numbers of types of systems, all drawn from the perspectives of a wide variety of individual systems practitioners and researchers.

There is extensive philosophic, and to a lesser degree, metaphysical literature on system types. Specific systemic processes have been the focus of scholarly interest, including those involved in communication and control (cybernetics), processes of making or production (poiesis), and adaptive or evolutionary behavior. Chaos theory, fractal geometry, and complexity theory are all contemporary concepts that serve as mathematically sophisticated means for explaining and describing systemic behavior. These and other systems-related concepts have been developed in great depth in recent years. Unfortunately, when evaluating these concepts, it is not transparent as to what basic beliefs about systems theory have been brought to bear, either from an ontological perspective or an epistemological viewpoint.

Systemic practitioners over the years have formulated untold numbers of sets of ontological systemic types and epistemic systemic categories. If, by happenstance, you were to be introduced to the field of systemic thinking via only one set of ideal types or categories, you might easily adopt a restrictive perspective on the field as a whole. A designer is always wise to look to the a priori selection of types or categories used in the construction of a systemic characterization of a situation or in the construction of a schema and the concomitant subset of systemic theories.

Although there is some comfort in not being confronted, at the beginning of one's introduction to systemics, with all the complexities and subtleties of systemic thinking as a whole, it is essential for designers to appreciate the fullest possible inventory of descriptors. The specific types or categories of systems in ordinary usage vary according to specific domains of interest. Of course, the challenge for a designer is to begin to make sense of long lists of ideal system types in order to become more effective at choosing which kind of systemic types best fits with any particular design project's other categories. This requires using systemic thinking as an approach to understanding the nature of design itself, as was mentioned earlier.

A particular categorical set does not delineate an exclusive group of ideal types, but only determines the conditions for inclusion of a type within the set. Another way of stating this is that a categorical set identifies the common ground from which each particular systemic type is differentiated. It is a matter of judgment as to which set of types or categories will be used to support the systemic designer in his or her work.

The illustrations of systems and systems concepts in this chapter present ways to approach design through the means of systemic design aids that might be found in a designer's personal "how to" manual. We should note that the examples are not meant to be used as true descriptors of systemic designs and processes, accurately explaining systems structure and behavior. Instead, they are pragmatic ways to communicate certain complex ideas and are merely schemas or tools meant to assist in the ultimate design of more specific, custom-tailored designs from a systems perspective. They are examples of how a designer can form his or her design palette using a systems approach.

From a systemic perspective, distinguishing a systemic category or type is guided by the strategy used to define what is common about the set and what distinguishes groupings from one another within the set. The categorization of systems is not restricted to a singular classification logic. Such a strategy is dependant on the epistemological frame of reference used in the process of making distinctions. For instance, a set of ideal types of systems can be defined from a scientific approach, or it may be defined using humanistic, artistic, technologic, spiritual, or other distinctive tradi-

Client
• purpose of system
• measure of performance of system

Decision maker
• boundary between environment and system
• components of system

Planner
• implementation of designs
• guarantor-of-design system

Systems philosopher
• significance of systems approach
• enemies of the systems approach

Figure 3.16
Churchman's categories for planning and design

tions of inquiry. This implies that a particular system, and its type or category, can be defined or described using epistemological approaches that draw from a variety of traditions or designs of inquiry. Now, what does this mean to the designer? It means that there are no given categorical sets, types of systems, or categories of systems, or even categories of elements making up a system. It means that determining such things is all a matter of judgment.

The particular sets of elements within each type of system are also a matter of approach and judgment. The work of one well-known systems philosopher, C. West Churchman, provides a good example. Churchman chose to describe teleological social systems from an approach in which people are the dominant elements in his social systems category (see figure 3.16). He identified four categories of essential roles people play in the activities of teleological or purposeful systems, including planning—in other words, design activities. He further developed these categories to include descriptions of role responsibilities and accountabilities (Churchman 1979).

From this set of categories, Churchman developed a series of questions to investigate any situation that was too complex and unstructured for analytic problem-solving approaches. His questions constitute two sets. The first set of questions asks for an objective determination of the situation. The second set asks for a deontic or ethical determination—that which "ought to be"—of what should be taken into account including issues of fairness, equity, and social justice. This is a mix of two traditions of inquiry—one objective and the other value based. The process of answering these questions provides a good first foothold in a complex, real-world situation. It allows the next steps to unfold with care. Those next steps include determining the make-up of the particular system in a way that will best serve that system's inhabitants' unique situation. This process is similar to that of the artist, who must choose the palette of paints from which to create a painting.

Such a systems approach not only integrates both objective and subjective thought processes, but also weaves in multiple traditions of inquiry including: design, scientific, philosophic, artistic, humanistic, metaphysical, religious, professional, spiritual, pragmatic, and technological traditions. All forms of system inquiries are brought into focus by a particular frame of reference. This frame of reference is based on a set of categories and typologies. How a designer formalizes the types and categories of the systems he or she is working with is up to them. It is a design judgment, and therefore a matter of choice.

Some systems designers create "totalizing" systems they believe should be adopted by everyone. When people don't, frustration tends to build in the system designer. In the worst case, this frustration leads to attempts by the designer to coerce acceptance from clients and stakeholders. This is an unfortunate form of a design approach. For purposes of justification, this approach is an application of systems science even though it is marketed as systems design. This is neither good design nor good systems science. In other instances systems design is merely assembling parts into a functional assembly. There is more to systems designing—to intentionally cause a desired thing to come into existence—than method and technique.

Designing takes place in complex settings, is a complex process itself, and results in complex augmentations to the real world. So how is it possible to work with all this complexity without defaulting to simplistic approaches with all the inherent dangers of that choice? We have experienced the consequences of one-dimensional designs in the past. How do we bring epistemological and ontological insights together with the design fundamentals of relationships and connections? How do we utilize the general and universal truths of scientific inquiry in particular projects that result in ultimate particular artifacts? There are many ways to make things more simply accessible by design without falling into becoming simplistic (Nelson 2007; Stolterman 2008).

One example of working with complexity is the schema of a *design palette* that demonstrates one way of designing systemically. Relations and

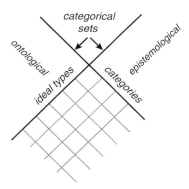

Figure 3.17
Design palette

connections are key concepts integrating design and systemics in the design process. Emergent compositions and qualities are the result of relations and connections in design process and in designed artifacts. Relations allow us to recognize or create patterns, categories, and types using ordering systems. Connections allow us to see or create critical links that define the structure and behavior of systemic phenomena.

In order to explain what a design palette means we can use the metaphor of an artist's palette. The artist chooses an inventory of colors to array on his or her paint palette—an inventory of the elements that will be used in the creation of a painting. As the artist proceeds, he or she makes choices concerning the framing of the composition and the tools that will be used to produce the painting and the principles of composition. By bringing the different colors into relationship with one another, an emergent image appears that transcends the particulars of the colors, strokes, and texture of the elements.

Design palettes serve the same purpose as an artist's palette in the chain of events of the design process. The design palette is formed by interrelating general or universal ontological and epistemological categories in matrix fashion. The examples of design palettes that follow are two-dimensional but they can be multidimensional as long as there is at least one ontological dimension and one epistemological dimension present in every case (see figure 3.17). The designers and stakeholders choose the sets of categories to take into consideration and choose which particular category or grouping of categories will be used to supply the inventory of elements for the *palette of particulars*.

As the designers begin to refine their alternative categorical sets and develop individual categories and ideal types of individual systems, they form the matrix of a design palette from which design judgments will then be made. Throughout the design process, a designer has to make judgments and decisions about how to approach the project at hand. And, as noted, the designers and stakeholders accomplish this by selecting the categories and ideal types for a design matrix. Can any of them guarantee that the choices made are the absolute correct ones for the design project in question? No.

There is no way to predetermine the consequences of such choices in the ultimate particular situation. The choices always are made based on the particular design intention. Most important, designers and stakeholders must realize that all of these choices are inevitably made. They cannot be avoided and therefore will be made whether or not the designers, clients, and other stakeholders are aware they are making them. A conscious approach is most definitely preferable. This requires the designer to acquire at least a working knowledge of different ideal types and categories from which to choose, as well as to devote considerable time to reflecting on the specifics of the present design situation and what is considered to be a desirable outcome.

Potential design palettes—in other words, design matrixes formed from divergent ontological types and epistemological categories—are numerous; as stated previously, the choice of which is best in a particular design situation is a matter of the designer's judgment. A palette matrix combining different contexts and approaches (see figure 3.18) can be used to create multiple particular palettes. For example, a religion-based context can be a compound of both ideal and real approaches to inquiry, thus mixing spiritual and practical concerns in a manner that fits more easily into the contemporary life styles found in the technically developed West. Another example would be a political context that is a compound of both ideal and true approaches to inquiry, resulting in a science-based utopian approach to policy design. A legal contextual category can be matrix related into a compound of true and real approaches to inquiry (legal systems based on precedents) or a compound of true and ideal approaches to inquiry (legal systems based on codes).

Once specific types or categories are chosen, they are brought into conjunction with one another. This becomes part of the development of a particular palette for an ultimate particular design (see figure 3.19). Particularized categories of contexts and modes of inquiry create concomitant cognitive frameworks that assist in explaining or describing the parameters

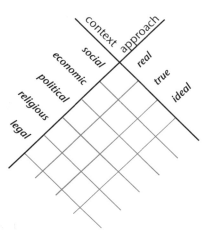

Figure 3.18
Two-dimensional design palette

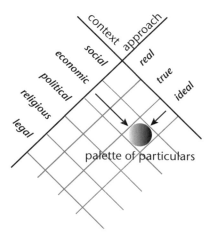

Figure 3.19
Palette of particulars

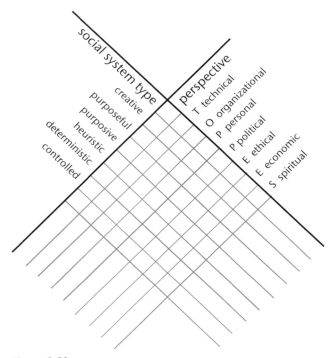

Figure 3.20
Two-category design palette

of a particular project. These frameworks can also help in the design conceptualization of a new designed addition to the particular situation. The capacity to create design palettes comprised of ideal types in relationship to different categories of inquiry is essential for managing complex design projects.

The different types of systems listed on the left side of the matrix in figure 3.20 collectively represent only one possible set of types and are not meant to be a comprehensive list of the correct things to include, which is also the case for the categories listed on the right side of the matrix. Other systems types can be presented through alternative sets while maintaining the same categories of inquiry as listed on the right side of the matrix. A common mistake in systems design is to assume that there are universally optimal archetypes—that one size can fit all, so to speak. In reality, this is never the case.

Any particular categorical set of systemic types and categories formulates a design palette matrix, from which designers and others can work

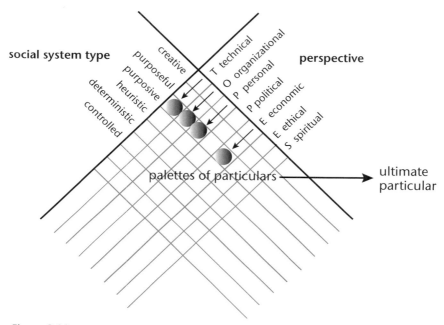

Figure 3.21
Multiple palettes of particulars

using the methods and tools of their personalized design approaches. The example of the formulation of multiple palettes of particulars (see figure 3.21) shows how the choices for filling in the design palette lead to concrete differences in the unfolding development of particulars in a design situation, which will inevitably lead to different ultimate particular outcomes of the design process.

It is easy to imagine in a real-world situation that there would be complexities requiring the formation of a compound design palette where more than one type or category needs to be included (see figure 3.22).

It is also easy to see how the two different design palette choices shown in figures 3.23 and 3.24 will lead to very different understandings and interventions in the same design situation. When a designer approaches the situation at hand, with these two divergent conceptual frames, different things will be made visible and considered important in each case.

As we examine the nature of design and designing, it becomes increasingly clear why systemic thinking is the organizing element in design reasoning. Systems, as objectified things (whether concrete or abstract),

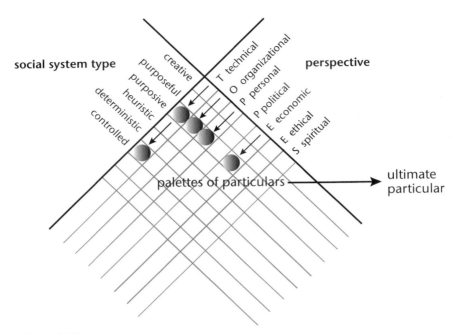

Figure 3.22
Compound palette

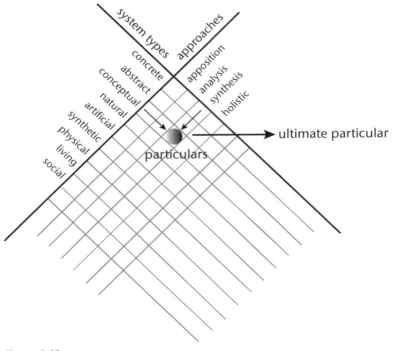

Figure 3.23
Simple palette of particulars

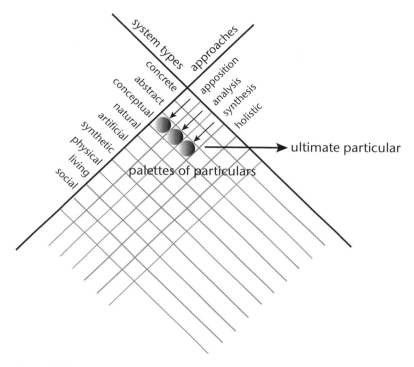

Figure 3.24
Complex palette of particulars

provide us the necessary context and focus for design activity. Also, design palettes are essentially formed using a systemic approach to choice and judgment. As every design is part of an environmental system, formed by a systemic context that carries systemic consequences with its implementation, the best design is one that is a whole-systems design. Systemic thinking is a necessary and essential approach in design. Indeed, design inquiry and action is systemics in action.

4 The Whole

What do we mean when we say that a design constitutes a whole? What does it mean to design holistically? The term "whole" and derivative forms—like "holism" and "holistic"—are used in diverse ways. The term "whole" unfortunately is often taken to mean the entirety of existence, the complete or comprehensive collection of things, whether abstract or concrete—an all-inclusive perspective. The term "whole" is also understood—from the spiritual concept of oneness—that all things are merely glimpsed reflections of a unitary reality. A permutation of this is the understanding that all things are connected or interconnected systemically. From a design perspective, the concept of *emergence* as the consequence of *composition* and *assembly* is illustrative of what is meant by whole or holistic. Emergence is the instantiation of wholeness.

One of the foundations of design is its holistic character. A good design never exists in isolation. It is always part of a larger whole and is itself whole. In design, when we say that something is a whole we mean that it is a complex ensemble of relations, connections, and an underlying unifying force or principle—that which causes things to stand together—that when taken together results in emergent qualities (see figure 4.1).

Let us take a look at the elements constitutive of compositions and assemblies. A *compound* is a blend of elements—abstract or concrete. It is the stuff of which things are made, not the form or shape of things. For instance, the compound known as water is made up of hydrogen and oxygen and exhibits the emergent quality of wetness. The variety of forms water can take is quite large and can be seen in such diverse things as the spray of an ocean's surf or a crystalline snowflake. A compound can also be a composite of sounds that form a musical scale, which can be formed into an almost infinite number of melodies.

Meaning, as form, is revealed to us through the ordering and organizing of elements into systemic relationships and connections that have been

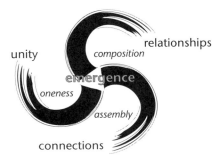

unity relationships

connections

Figure 4.1
Dimensions of emergent whole

created intentionally, in response to purpose, in fulfillment of an end. With this we mean that those unifying forces that cause things to stand together, in unity, provide comprehensible emergent qualities of presence, significance, and value, thus forming meaning for individuals who are part of the whole or served by the whole. Presence is the emergent essence of the whole. This essence is brought into reality, conceptually or perceptually, through different levels of apprehension, including appearance, character, and soul. Significance is when the emergent whole pushes to the foreground of awareness and value can be placed on it. The value of the whole can be determined by examining if it augments or merely attaches itself to human nature.

When a designer employs a holistic approach he or she must be careful not to disaggregate, compartmentalize, polarize, or ignore attributes of undifferentiated life experiences. Traditional distinctions that work against integration, such as mind and body, science and art, reason and imagination, are examples of nonholistic approaches representative of popular intellectual habits of mind. It's hard to break the analytic habit of dividing things into distinct parts, with distinct, categorical differences. For example, in the process of developing and presenting ideas that are foundational to the design of this book, we were continually challenged to remain inclusive, relational, and contextual. It is difficult to hold things together in unity and not to be drawn too deeply into a focus that lands primarily on distinctions and divisive separations. It was the principle of holism that constantly reminded us what we needed to attend to if we were to stay congruent with our initial intention to present design as a third culture and a tradition of inquiry that was unique in itself.

Although it's true that "the whole is greater than the sum of its parts," we must also acknowledge that the whole is of those parts. This idea has important consequences. Namely, you cannot design a whole without taking into consideration the selection of parts or elements for inclusion on the design palette. You cannot conceptually (or concretely) impose a whole onto parts. It is not possible to design a whole, and impose that emergent quality onto parts that cannot belong in the whole a priori. The whole takes its emerging essence from the nature of its parts. There is an inseparable relationship between the parts and the whole. We also need to remember that any whole is always part of something more comprehensive—another whole. This means that a whole—made up of parts interacting systemically, functioning to serve a particular end—invariably is the means for an even greater end.

It is not uncommon for the concept of "vision" to be used as representative of a desired and future whole. But this can lead to confusion in relationship to design. A vision is not the manifestation of a whole, that is, it is not an outcome of the process of composition. A whole can never be fully described before it is fully formed, even with the parts at hand. It is not possible to impose a predetermined vision of wholeness onto parts, in order to obtain a specific whole as an outcome. To create wholes, it is necessary to compose and assemble them from particular elements—elements that are then destined to lose their individual identity to a transcendent identity. Early definitions of holism were concerned with this relationship of parts and wholes. For example, from the 1927 edition of *Encyclopaedia Britannica*: "Holism shows these opposites as reconciled and harmonized in the whole. It shows whole and parts as aspects of each other."

There is no agreed-upon standard understanding of holism, as shown by the variety of definitions employed in contemporary philosophies and theories of holism or holistic approaches. Some common concepts share the trait of "claimed comprehensiveness" as mentioned earlier. The term "whole" is used in this case to imply an inclusive understanding of the relationship of everything to everything. This definition arises from a systems science approach to the concept, where "wholes" are defined as the study of comprehensive systems. The underlying assumption here is that you need to know everything about a phenomenon in order to understand it. It also implies that everything is connected to everything, with no natural boundaries. This comprehensiveness requires that everything with a relationship to the phenomenon of interest be included in its analysis. Such a view can easily lead to different forms of analysis paralysis. Luckily, holism can be viewed from a variety of other angles.

One such alternative perspective defines the whole as a comprehensive understanding of the world in metaphysical terms, such as spirituality and mysticism. In this case, the belief is that there is a whole from which everything emerges. Sometimes, this is expanded to include the concept that each and every thing in the world is a holograph of the metaphysical whole, reflecting the whole at every resolution of detail. Like the scientific approach to holism, this understanding treats the concept of complete knowledge as the ideal.

These scientific and metaphysical approaches to holism are manifested to varying degrees in various contemporary schools of thought, including deep ecology, Gaia theory, the theory of implicate order, and the New Age sciences. These movements advocate a belief in the holistic character of reality, and advocate that this belief should become the first, and sometimes only, ordering principle for change. These definitions of holism are stimulating and important antidotes to the overpowering dominance of reductive analysis, but they are not fertile ground from which to develop design principles. From a design perspective, the whole is not something merely to adapt to or emulate.

Another definition of holism comes from the perspective of a systems approach, where the concept of emergence is a seminal attribute. As indicated earlier, a commonly stated belief in systems thinking is that "the whole is greater than the sum of its parts." This means that there are emergent qualities of a whole that can only be revealed as transcendent properties, different from those properties displayed by the individual and separate parts of the whole. These emergent qualities are the result of the relations and connections binding the elements together in unity. This perspective of whole introduces a concept that provides an important insight leading to a deeper understanding of design as a process of intentionally relating and connecting elements in order to evoke emergent qualities, in addition to the functional synergies that result from compositional assemblies.

What do we consider to be an emergent quality? In design terms, we are talking about a deterministic outcome that is the necessary consequence of the relationships, connections, interactions, and collective behavior of the constituent elements of an integrated system. For example, this could be something as simple as the aggregate action of a flock of birds or school of fish that is seen as a distinct and unified behavior pattern (i.e., "flocking" and "schooling"). It can also be something as complex as someone's personality that is apprehended as a unified expression of an individual's character. Or, it can simply be the essence of a work of art.

Emergence can be either a predictable or an unpredictable outcome of holistic constructs. The concept of an unpredictable, emergent quality

natural whole

- inclusive
- required
- being
- viable

designed whole

- adequate
- essential
- emergent
- vital

Figure 4.2
Whole as functional composition

highlights the role of chance in natural wholes—while the predictable highlights the role of necessity. Emergence can also be the outcome of intentionality in designed wholes. Emergence embodies not only an aggregation of the collective elements of a system, but also the qualities of the underlying structure of the system. In this light, emergent qualities can be understood as general qualities, brought into existence by the way a whole is bound together by substance and order through relationships and connections.

One way of defining wholes, and one that is a foundation of design, is the characterization of the whole as a composition and an assembly. This definition applies to both natural and designed wholes (see figure 4.2). Natural creations are defined by the emergent qualities of contingent (i.e., depends on circumstances), or universal (i.e., without condition or exception) wholes. In contrast, designed creations are ultimate particular wholes, thus unique and singular. This type of whole is evoked through intentional acts of composition and assembly, undertaken for specific purposes, at a particular time and place.

Natural wholes can be defined as having attributes such as being comprehensive, necessary, emergent, and viable, plus they have a presence in the world and an influence on it. The properties of designed wholes are equivalent, but different in kind, in contrast to natural wholes. For example, in the case of a designed whole, the attribute of being adequate replaces the attribute of being inclusive.

A natural system is comprehensive from the perspective of what can be said that is true about it. Its comprehensiveness, however, can never be fully disclosed because of its complexity. A designed system is adequate because it is only as complex and comprehensive as it needs to be in order to fulfill its intended purpose. Relatively speaking, its complexity is comprehensible because it is the product of human intention. In similar fashion, designed whole attributes—such as essential, emergent, and vital (for social systems)—stand as counterparts to the relevant attributes of natural wholes. These attributes of designed wholes become guides for the intentional composition and assembly of wholes. These guiding qualities are relevant, both in relation to the process of compositional assembly and to the designed outcome.

Often, we are more familiar with the designed whole attributes of health expressed in terms of aesthetics and ethics than we are with the first three listed—adequate, essential, and emergent. Unfortunately, in contemporary processes of designing, the holistic attributes of the adequate, essential, and emergent too often are substituted with criteria that lack the same depth of meaning. The adequate generally is substituted by the attribute of more, the essential by faster, and the emergent by the quick fix, or short-term gain.

The most elusive and unfamiliar concept in design—from a holistic perspective—may be the idea of the *adequate*. This concept can be difficult to understand, given the unquestioned assumption that any plan for action must be grounded in comprehensive analysis. It is an article of faith, left over from the days when being comprehensive was believed to be not only possible but also necessary. In the Age of Enlightenment, the abiding faith of the Encyclopedists was that all that was worth knowing could be known. Their faith also held that this knowledge could be brought to bear on any situation, providing a clear, accurate description and explanation of the situation at hand, and thereby illuminating right decisions. This hypostasis has become the benchmark upon which professional decision making rests to this day.

For designers, there are two problems with this belief. The first problem is that design choices are certainly based on reason, but they are not made by reason. That is, design draws on rational thinking (e.g., the systems science, disciplinary thinking, and the scientific method), but it is not merely a rationalized, logical process. It is a process that includes imagination, intuition, feeling, and emotion as well. The second problem is that the explosion of information in the past century has made it impossible to be comprehensive about anything. Those who continue to cling to the belief that comprehensibility can be achieved will invariably experience analysis paralysis.

Design is often assumed to lie comfortably in the shade of the "comprehensive decision making" umbrella, because it is frequently understood to be primarily about making something concrete, or planning for something specific, or simply making something aesthetically pleasing. Although these are common outcomes in traditional physical design, there is actually much more to design than what these ends would imply. One of modern design's key distinctions is that design choices are made through design judgments, leading to the creation of something that did not exist before. And, it is an inescapable realization that these crucial design judgments always are made within a context of the *adequate* rather than the comprehensive.

Every design process unfolds within a unique situation: a complex and dynamic reality. A designer always acts in response to that reality. We do not have unlimited freedom, resources, information, or time to fully understand that reality. We can never achieve absolute comprehension of any situation nor can we achieve perfection in design even if that were possible. Rather, we embrace the adequate. By adequate, we do not mean the mediocre or compromise. This is not about dampening or limiting a designer's ambition and passion. Instead, we use the term "adequate" as simply a way of framing the real nature of design, which is to work within limited time and resources to do the best that is possible.

Design is not the pursuit of a perfect concept. It is not the creation of an ultimate vision, in a perfectible world, where everything, including sufficient information, authority, and resources, is in the hands of the designer. On the contrary, design can only be fully actualized by all the circumstances and specifics that make a design situation uniquely particular. As championed by Follett (1930) we are not trumpeting compromise among ideals, or surrender to the imperfections, shortcomings, and incompleteness of each unique situation's appreciation. Instead, we are saying that we need to explore the splendor of the possible, to create something not yet existing based on the fragile and incomplete understandings of the realities of each unique situation that encompasses the desires of real people who are mysteries even to themselves. A holistic understanding of real situations, and the integration of limits to understanding real situations fully, leads to a design approach deemed to be adequate and therefore realistic. As Follett noted, "Integration might be considered a qualitative adjustment, compromise a quantitative one. In the former there is a change in the ideas and their action tendencies; in the latter there is mere barter of opposed "rights of way" (Follett 1930).

It is important to appreciate the danger of creating a design motivated by a quest for the absolute ideal design solution. This often leads to the creation of something that cannot be supported, maintained, afforded, or controlled by the proposed beneficiaries of the design. Attempts to create perfectly glorious designs can bring ruin, or the threat of ruin, because they are not formed by the intention of designing the adequate, but by the unrealized quest for the comprehensive and utopian. Therefore, establishing a firm grasp of the adequate may be the most difficult and important judgment made in a design process. This judgment will, in turn, have impact on all other design judgments in the unfolding process.

The adequate can also be understood as an emergent quality evoked through judgments of mediation (see chapter 8) that bring together things of very different or diverse natures to form an integrated and integrative whole. A designer's judgment is used to mediate among such differences using principles like proportion, measure, balance, and complementarity. Mediation in this case means the ability to judge the mean in the Aristotelian sense rather than a determination of an arithmetic average, utilitarian trade-off, or political compromise. The quality of mediated difference is exemplified by examining the challenge of creating a holistic composition out of the distinctive differences between justice and compassion, tradition and innovation, creativity and control, or stability and change. These are all examples of concepts that are valuable in themselves, but that become even more so when combined in a composition of mediated wholeness. Other examples can be as simple as the obvious functional difference between fire and metal that, when mediated with skill and good judgment, results in a great work of art or a functional tool. Instrumental judgments that combine material differences of this type do not result in reconciliation, resolution, or trade-off, but in an *adequate* creation. They also do not result in an idealized, or perfect, design. Compositional assemblies are never the result of a recipe or rule. Rather, they are an outcome of judgments. The essential value of each difference is enhanced and enriched, by being brought into a particular, relational connection that adequately facilitates the desired outcome of an emergent design.

Finally, a definition of the adequate, seen from the perspective of the whole, states that the elements of a whole are formed with respect to the aim and purpose of the whole, meaning that components, relationships, and connections may be suboptimized in order to optimize the performance or behavior of the whole. Components need to be adequate, certainly, but they cannot be optimized according to some standard external to the whole. They need to be formed, ordered, and organized, taking into account the emergent nature of the interactions and interconnections of all the elements of the whole.

Getting back to our initial list of designed whole attributes, we now consider that which is *essential* in design. By essential we mean discernment, and the inclusion of anything that is judged to be an intentional necessity for the design, in order to fulfill authentic human needs and desires. This would include all desiderata at both the particular and collective level. Often, there is a sense that something important is missing in a design, something that not only frustrates its function, but blocks its service capacity as well. In such a case, the thing that is missing is an essential attribute.

Another attribute of designed wholes is related to *significance*, which is connected to meaning making. Designed wholes are created by intention, to evoke emergent forms and behaviors that embody the essence of human potential more fully. Some of what we assume to be a natural element of our humanity is in actuality the consequence of a design originally. For example, human "rights" are the outcome of historical social system designs, which gave significance and meaning to such entitlements.

The attributes of the designed whole can be used for two purposes. They can guide intentional compositions of designed wholes, or they can act as a foundation for a critique of designed wholes. A designer needs to have the skill of discernment, a sensibility for proportions, which is essential to compositional mediation, and competence in judgment making to actively compose wholes with these attributes.

One way to acquire these skills is to examine and critique existing designs. By critiquing different types of designs, from the perspective of wholes, a designer can begin to acquire a sense of designs that work as wholes and those that do not. It is also possible to expand this critique using different frames of inquiry (see figure 4.3).

With these critical attributes in mind, it is possible to make an evaluation of all sorts of wholes. Such an exercise might help a designer to better understand what distinguishes a designed whole from other types of designs. These attributes are not exclusive to one another or to other sets of attributes—a wise designer would not dispense with the attributes of the ideal, or the true in favor of the real. In fact, he or she has to act within all three types of inquiry, never forgetting that the outcome of a holistic design process is a designed whole. In order to assure that a design process is robust and adequate, it is essential that it is a compound of the real, true, and ideal.

Some attributes, such as efficiency, are easier to evaluate than others, as they have a tradition, in our technical culture, of being measured and critiqued. The most difficult attributes to evaluate are those associated with the real because they are unique and particular. These attributes have a quality that, by necessity, brings the designer into a mode of service that

inquiry	critique
real	• adequate • sufficient • essential
true	• efficient • rational • reasonable
ideal	• aesthetic • ethical • desirable

Figure 4.3
Critique of functional wholes

demands a higher level of empathy and communication, with all those to be benefited by the design. Also, the attributes are relational and incommensurable, and therefore cannot be measured by some general standard.

Compositions and assemblies result in emergent qualities that are the expressions of holism. The notion of the whole applies not only to large comprehensive designs, which by their size or impact make them natural to consider as wholes, but also to small designed artifacts and processes. Thinking in terms of emergent wholes is important for every design no matter the scale or consequence. In fact, the degree to which each design may be experienced as a whole is determined by the judgments of the designers and not by scale or quantity. The notion of the whole is a foundational property of design that is realized through the careful and creative ordering and organizing of elements through intentional relations and connections.

III FUNDAMENTALS

The design approach requires us to acquire a certain number of fundamental competencies. These skills make up the palette that sustains and nourishes design inquiry and action. Although you will be able to intellectually understand these skills, these *fundamentals*, you will never be able to learn them abstractly. Fundamentals for a design approach are an open-and-shut case of "learning by doing." They require continuous practice. In effect, they are acquired in the same manner one learns fundamentals for sports, art, or music. Mastery of these fundamentals is not an end to be reached, but an exciting, ongoing process. Accomplishment is measured in terms of excellence and quality.

The fundamentals of design thinking include desiderata, interpretation and measurement, imagination and communication, judgment, composing and connecting, and craft and material.

5 Desiderata

Intentional change in our world can be initiated in basically two ways. People can take action to move away from situations they do not like, or they can take action to move toward what they believe to be more desirable situations. People are often forced to be reactive because a change suddenly occurs in their lives due to external causes. Sometimes they are aware of unpleasant or undesirable things that have occurred in the past and they take action to prevent or prepare against such changes if they were to recur. The need for change can arise for a number of reasons, with one of the most challenging emerging from the felt need to change a situation from the way it is to one that is more desirable.

Too often, the good intentions that arise from the recognition of a need for change lead to paralysis. This means that agents of change are often paralyzed by the complexity of the challenge they are facing. This is because the strategies for change, to which most of us commonly default, lead to dead ends, rather than next-best steps. Some of these dead ends include analysis paralysis, wicked problem paralysis, value paralysis, and holistic paralysis. These forms of paralysis are primarily consequences of attempts to be comprehensive. Analysis paralysis occurs when too much divergent information is generated, without any effective means for convergence. The paralyzing effect of confronting wicked problems, rather than tame problems, comes from bumping up against the limits of rationality itself (Rittel 1972). Value paralysis occurs when any and every value system is taken into account because they are considered equally relevant without any means of transcending the differences and diversity. The paralysis of holism occurs when there are no automatic means for bounding or limiting comprehensive expansion.

This unfortunate situation exists because all of these strategies have a common foundation in "problem solving." Their focus is on only that-which-is (description and explanation), versus that-which-ought-to-be (ethics and morality), and without consideration for that-which-is-desired (desiderata). Now, we can, and do, cause actions that lead to change in the world. Some of these actions are based on that-which-is because we believe in a true, logically structured reality; one based on natural laws. We hold fast to a reality that can be understood through science and changed by technology. Most people think of the world as a given, already completed design, and they behave as if they were put on earth to react and adapt to this design. Even in postmodern thinking, which postulates the temporary stature of human-defined natural laws and the relativity of anything in the category of truth—particularly social truth—it is commonly believed that change is based on stabilized, universal principles of cause and effect.

However, there is a missing insight in this view of reality: *description and explanation—science—do not prescribe action, nor do prediction and control—technology—justify action.* Around the world, billions of dollars are spent on studies and projects based on science and technology. This is done in the belief that rubbing the two together will generate the spark of prescriptive action. Unfortunately, this never happens, because the spark must flare from a different source.

It is also important to note that we can, and do, cause changes based on that-which-ought-to-be because this, too, is believed to be a kind of truth. It is truth that is logically formed and based on ethical laws, religious precepts, and moral codes. Yet our actions in this case always seem to stem from a reactive mode. The trigger for this cause of action is anything from an uneasy sense of ethical transgression to moral outrage. The outcome is as diverse as good works and holy wars.

We also create changes based on what we want, including that-which-can-be, as demonstrated by our emphasis on technologic innovations. We can create everything from biological clones to smaller, faster, more complex electronic devices. Because we have the ability to create them, we then become convinced we should want them, and that they are needed. Yet even though what we want is most often driven by our immediate short-term needs and interests, there is sometimes a deeper, more profound sense of want, which is expressed in the aesthetic terms of values. This deep sense of wanting occurs even without a belief in natural order.

These three approaches to intentional change have the following correspondence. What we *want* can be seen as our aesthetics. What we believe *ought to be* relates to our ethics. That which *is* or *needs to be* corresponds to reason. In any particular situation, however, there is never just one approach present. Depending on what we perceive as the basis for intentional action, there will be different proportions and balance among the three: aesthetics, ethics, and reason. In real-world contexts, everything is blended.

In this book, we use the concept of *desiderata* (i.e., desires) as an *inclusive whole*. That is, we view desiderata as a concept that includes all three of the approaches: aesthetics, ethics, and reason. But within this concept, the aggregated effect of these three approaches transcends their summation, forming an emergent quality that is characteristic of compositional assemblies, or wholes. Desiderata are about what we intend the world to be and it is the integrative outcome of all three approaches in concert. Desiderata as a concept is the escape route from the strategies for change, which box us into paralysis, blind action, or slavish mimicry (see figure 5.1). Desiderata form the imperative voice of design.

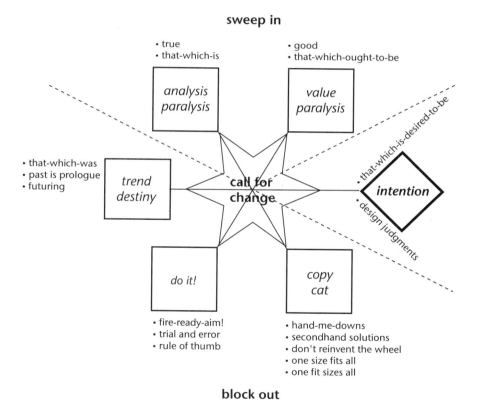

Figure 5.1
Change strategies

When there is a call for change in society, people generally use one of two typical strategies to take action: the "sweep-in" approach and the "block-out" approach. Sweep-in approaches are characterized by an ambition to rush in and discover the right solution to the problem by applying a comprehensive examination of the needs in question. This type of approach often leads to analysis paralysis or value paralysis as a consequence.

People become paralyzed because they are confronted with too much information—while at the same time they feel they have a need for even more information. Comprehensive, rational analysis creates more questions than are answered. Rather than converging on an optimal design solution, the process diverges endlessly into greater and greater numbers of details.

Conversely, block-out approaches try to use simple, often ready-made strategies to make decisions, without investing the time and energy on in-depth examinations. Every particular design situation is complex and unique. Design solutions that have been created for other complex, unique situations do not necessarily match the particular situation at hand. In addition, generalized solutions that fit all or most situations are coarse and grossly formed. They do not have the complexity and refinement of detail sufficient to match the richness of a unique design situation. This does not mean that designs must be complicated, or expensive, or excessive in any other way as a consequence. The best design for a situation may be elegantly simple and economical, while at the same time being the most appropriate response to the unique requirements of the design situation. For example, when a universalized global or generalized national policy is applied to particular populations of people, in particular places, at particular times, it is often disastrous because it is ill fitted to the situation at hand. To illustrate, an educational policy may work for one school, or set of similarly structured schools, while being ineffective, or worse, ruinous, to a diversity of schools in the same administrative jurisdiction.

Clearly, neither of these options, block out or sweep in, is ideal when dealing with a call for change. A more relevant and rewarding path leads one to engage in an intentional approach, based on a careful consideration of desiderata guided by design judgment (see figure 5.1). So, how does one start down this road?

How do we use a design approach to assess and respond to a call for change? To begin with, a *needs assessment* may be necessary but is insufficient alone. Too often, this is the initial, inadequate step in approaches to intentional change. More appropriate for a design approach is a *desid-*

erata assessment. Determining needs is a responsible activity for any agent of change to engage in on behalf of those who are in need of change. However, for those wanting to be served, it is essential to assess what is felt to be desirable. This is particularly true when the change involves the creation, or modification, of new social structures, such as business organizations, governmental agencies, or social institutions.

It is important to note that assessing need is very different from creating need. The latter is a common approach to change, but decidedly more suspect—especially when focused on the creation of new technologies, commodities, and services. Taken too far, this approach can lead to over-consumption, addictions, and self-destructive behavior, as demonstrated by the tobacco industry. Recently, the way technology has been used has also been considered addictive and self-destructive. For example, the artifacts of advanced technology, especially computer technology, including computer games and the World Wide Web, have been criticized for the negative effect they may be having on human beings concomitant with the benefits they promise.

The aggressive and manipulative character of advertising and marketing, when focused on creating need, has been successful in shaping markets for products and technologies that people did not contract for out of desire, but which they have been successfully coerced into adapting. Similarly, the tradition of science has also been used as a justification for creating need. The motto of the 1933 Chicago World's Fair, as Donald Norman (1993) reminds us, was: "Science Finds, Industry Applies, Man [sic] Conforms." Scientific breakthroughs and the resultant applied technologies are treated as predestined realities for humans. A typical response to questions of what the future may look like is: "The technology is there, it will happen!" It is considered to be a matter of "trend destiny."

A created need is an imposed desire. It is a faux desire, which originates outside the individual's own generative nature. It is preformed and impressed upon a person in their role as consumer or end user, through persuasion or manipulation. Still, when moderated, the creation of need can, and does, act as the engine for an effective free market system, with all its benefits and successes. It is also important to remember that the creative work of artists and innovators elicits new expectations or needs, as people encounter and are influenced by the new and unexpected creations of individual expression.

At this juncture, we want to emphasize that with any of the preceding approaches, there are problems with focusing too heavily on *need* as the key human motivation for change or innovation. Need implies that the desired situation is clearly understood, and that the real state of affairs, which is also clearly understood, is an undesired one. The difference between the desired state and the actual state is framed as the problem. It is also assumed that there is no difficulty in determining the needs that must be satisfied in order to realize the desired state. It is assumed that the process of satisfying needs can be efficiently accomplished through a rational and pragmatic problem-solving approach.

However, focusing strictly on our needs has allowed the fields of our desires to go fallow. Our understanding of motivation, triggered by what we believe to be desirable—in other words, *desiderata assessment*—as opposed to what we need, remains remarkably undeveloped. Human intention, when motivated by desiderata rather than need, reshapes the entire process for intentional change. To be intentional from a deep understanding of that-which-is-desired, rather than from a difference between that-which-is and that-which-needs-to-be, reverses the assumption about what can be known from the beginning. A needs-based change, animated through a problem-solving approach, assumes that the right outcome is known from the start.

In this frame of reference, when people speak of a "vision" as a goal to reach, it is often as a preformed image, whereas a desire-based change process leads to a desired outcome but does not start with that outcome already neatly in place. Needs-based design is founded on the erroneous assumption that a need or problem is easily discerned. The reality of course is that needs are not clearly understood at all. What do people really need beyond the needs of basic survival? People in the developing regions of the world live with much less than people in developed economies feel they "need."

People desire to flourish and not just survive. They may not need music or art to survive, but they certainly desire them both. A need is a baseline condition that must be mitigated in order to support and stabilize a given situation. The hungry need to be fed and the cold need to be sheltered— but people desire to be more than "needy" creatures. Desire is the destabilizing trigger for transformational change, which facilitates the emergence of new possibilities and realizations of human "being."

In today's world, the newspapers are filled with reports of action that came from a reactive need for change. Regardless of whether it stems from business, political, or personal affairs, change emerges out of negative reactive responses to events, or situations in the world. The justification for action arises out of what is broken, what we fear, what makes us angry, what hurts us, what we hate, or what is humiliating us. Politicians in democracies around the world demonstrate leadership by identifying what, of the many things that threaten us, ought to be dealt with, in which order, and in what way. Voters participate by identifying all their own reactive issues—scared into action against threats both real and imagined.

These reactive responses lock us into an understanding of the world through the filter of problem solving. Ackoff (1978) has pointed out that getting away from what we don't want does not guarantee that we will get what we do want. On one level we inherently understand this. We know that if we back away from danger, we might back into an even more dangerous situation. Still, everyday conversations are filled with the language of problems, problem recognition, and problem solution. But as we've intimated earlier, rather than allow our various problems to run our lives, we would be wise to approach the world from a design perspective and look to our desiderata for direction in our approach to intentional change.

As stated earlier, the term "desiderata" refers to those things that are believed to be desirable. Desiderata can be expressed through distinct domains: the body's desire, the mind's desire, the heart's desire, and the soul's desire. A desideratum is something that is roused out of a desire, a hope, a wish, a passion, an aspiration, an ambition, a quest, a call to, a hunger for, or a will toward. In our culture, desires are often treated as low-level needs—things that we wish for but could live without. But desiderata are not a response to the problem of an unfulfilled human need. The negative impulse toward action, which arises out of such a felt need, is completely different from the positive impulse born out of the desire to create situations, systems of organization, or concrete artifacts that enhance our life experiences. Rather than treating the source of these aspirations as needs, we believe it is helpful to refer to them as design intentions.

Desire can be understood as the "force" that provides us with intrinsic guidance and energy. Desires constitute that which we long for. As humans, we use our desires as a way to understand how we can fulfill our lives and how we can become more human. But desires are not all good. To reveal our desires, we have to name them, reflect upon them and examine them. When we examine our desires, we often find the bag fairly well mixed, with both the good and the bad. It is necessary in this process to accept both types of desires. Over time, we learn to discipline the negative desires and live out the positive ones. To differentiate positive desires from negative ones is one of our lifelong tasks as human beings. Rosaleen Trainor (2001) has called this process "befriending our desires." She explains that when we become aware of and comfortable with our desires, they begin to have an accepted place in our lives and can function as a form of guidance. They help us form and name our intentions.

Let's take a look at an example of how a desideratum can function as a guide in designing. The "desire" for love is universal, but it is experienced differently, depending on the particular design of inquiry for action that we choose. In the framework of the "real," love takes on the form of eros—love of the physical world. In the "true," love is manifested as agape—an abstracted form of social love. And, in the "ideal," love is elevated to philo—an unconditional love of an ultimate possible.

This example of love, as a particular type of desideratum, seen through the lenses of three different forms of inquiry, demonstrates the symbiotic relationship between desiderata and intention. In a philosopher's sense, intentionality is much more than just intending to do something. For example, it can mean any way that the mind has of referring to objects and states of affairs in the world (Searle 1983). As Searle points out, intentionality is two-pronged, consisting of belief and desire. We would add that intentionality is an expression of the aim, direction, or bearing of human affairs animated by will and volition. It is at this level of resolution, within this very big idea of intentionality, that the concept of design intention, as an expression of desiderata, is developed.

One of the key concepts concerning intention arose in the philosophic discourse of the Middle Ages. At that time, the idea of *aim*, as in aiming an arrow, became central to the unfolding meaning of intention. That is, that intention is not the target, not the outcome, nor the purpose, nor an end state, but is principally the process of choosing or giving direction to effort. This distinction is an important one for design, because it is this judgment of intention that ultimately determines what direction or bearing the strategy of inquiry for action will take in any particular situation.

The form of action decided on affects the concomitant modes of inquiry associated with it. These systems of intention are often referred to as cultures of inquiry and affiliated action, and are defined in terms of academic categories, such as design, science, art, the humanities, spirituality, and technology (Snow 1959). Although each culture can be inclusive of the others, there is a distinct "aim" for each which is directed away from the others. Some of the intellectual activities, born from these cultures, include creativity, innovation, research, management, and problem solving. As in social cultures, different combinations of intellectual traditions live within different cultures of intention. For example, science at its best is inclusive of both creativity and objectivity. The humanities are inclusive of research, rational problem solving, and individual innovation. Design, when fully

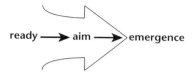

Figure 5.2
Intention as aim

formulated, is inclusive of creativity and innovation, practical art, applied research, and project management, to name an exemplary few.

The intentional approaches associated with design also happen to be fundamental to the development and application of good leadership. This is no accident. Leaders require many approaches and skills to wisely serve their charges. One of the most important, yet most undeveloped, is design. Two terms often define good leadership; these terms are "character" and "vision." The need for vision dominates almost any discussion of leadership today. Leaders are expected to have a vision, around which followers can rally and toward which they can surge. Vision becomes something that is given, a solution to a problem. Strategic planning, and similar methods for the management of change, have grown out of the belief that vision, and visionary leadership, are a priori factors in any intentional change process.

Intention is best understood, not as a vision, but as the aiming and subsequent emergence of a desired outcome (see figure 5.2). Desiderata help to aim and name one's intentions. Unlike the vision approach, the outcome is not in place when the design process begins. The outcome only emerges based on the situation and desiderata's prescriptive intention. This process is very different from many common approaches, where action is seen as a consequence of defined goals or outcomes. Now, in any intentional process, we know that we can easily produce goals and objectives that would be closer to our desires than the present. But intention is not only about where to get to, it is also about which direction to go to get there—how to aim so as to move closer in proximity to our desired ends.

Within the Zen tradition, a deep understanding of intention, as a process of aiming, has been developed. In the classic book *Zen in the Art of Archery*, Herrigel (1953) shows how the notion of aiming can be developed by careful, attentive preparation and by letting go of our everyday assumptions on how to reach our goals by aiming "at" them. The process of aiming—intention—can be expanded upon by elaborating on the conceptual context, within which intentionality takes place. In the case of

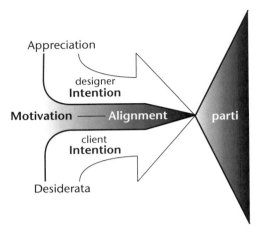

Figure 5.3
Design aim and outcome

design intention, vision is the outcome of a process triggered by desiderata that is framed and contained by appreciative judgment—distinguishing foreground from background (see chapter 8, "Judgment"). It is animated by motivation and intensified through the alignment of design behaviors among participants (see figure 5.3). The design breakthrough insights that are revealed emerge as an intense but undifferentiated *seed of wisdom* known as a parti (the idea of parti is further developed in the chapter 9,)

Through the design team's energy and focus, the parti is developed into an analogous image from which vision is then formed. Therefore, vision is the outcome of creative, design-based leadership rather than the starting point. Simultaneously, this developmental process also reveals an understanding of purpose for this particular case and ultimately expands to include the general, as a representation of an unfolding telos—in other words, purpose. Just as vision is an outcome of an intentional design approach, so too emerges an ultimate understanding of purpose. Neither vision nor telos begin as input but emerge and are revealed as output.

This also differs from the more traditional design process, which first develops concepts and then implementation plans. Post-implementation evaluation and redesign follow production and innovation of the intended design. In all of this we notice that the parti was preordained—presenting itself bright-eyed and bushy-tailed—at the very beginning of the process. Under the traditional approach, all improvement occurs during the final redesign process, through a concrete reinterpretation of the parti. The majority of design efforts by current professional designers actually fall within this realm of redesign. The designers do not, as a rule, begin with the trigger of desiderata, but instead begin with a revisit to the accessible images generated from the original parti. However, if progress, rather than just improvement, is desired, the process must be initiated with the client's expression of desiderata.

This is the quintessential expression of leadership in the framework of design. Leaders are required to be many things, but their most essential character is that they are designers. Leadership is not defined by a particular role, or a blend of character traits, or a position in a hierarchy, but as the consequence of participation in an authentic engagement with the process of evoking vision from an initial expression of desiderata. At this point, we should note that desiderata are not the only initiating points triggering the design process. They need to be matched by an appreciative judgment of what is to be considered as real, in any particular situation. Appreciative judgment, as Vickers defines it, is not a comprehensive description or explanation of what is real (Vickers 1995). Instead, it is a judgment of what is to be treated as the essential background, or foreground, of the design situation.

As an example, when a decision is made to draw a perimeter around what or who is to be included in any particular project, it is done by making an appreciative judgment—based on appreciating what is important to consider and what is not; whose interests need to be taken into account and whose do not; and what level of complexity must be maintained as a substitute for never-ending comprehensiveness. It is within this context, and against this environment, that the design process unfolds. An appreciative judgment creates the frame for design inquiry and action, as well as the container—thus providing the limits that are so necessary in any creative work (May 1975).

Motivation is also key to any design leadership process. In design, ideally motivation should be intrinsic, but can be augmented by extrinsic influences as well (Pink 2009). We'll more fully discuss intrinsic motivations in a moment, but let's take a quick look at some extrinsic motivators. For designers and others, they include such traditional rewards as money, acclaim, and influence. Business literature abounds with methods for motivating people to be creative and innovative, including both negative and positive feedback reinforcements. These extrinsic forms of motivation, however, do not seem to be of critical and lasting influence.

That is clearly not the case with intrinsic motivations, which spring from a vital source, the client's desiderata. For the designer, motivation flowers from an empathy for a client's desiderata. But there are other motivations as well. Often designers speak of responding to a call that cannot be ignored, as if they are compelled by a necessity born into them to engage in designing (Hillman 1992). There is also the pull of what appears to be both a psychological and biochemical reward for engaging in a creative act that results in a breakthrough insight. This process of coming to emergent knowledge, through a design means, is both biologically and spiritually reinforced.

Beneath these intrinsic motivators resides a compelling quest for wholeness, as defined in the traditions of the perennial philosophy—the "immemorial and universal belief in a divine Reality" (Huxley 1944). Designers and clients seem to understand that by engaging in design, they are expressing a god-like capacity to engage in the co-creation of the experienced world, and in doing so, make clear what it means to be human. They are expressing a deeply embedded script, which plays out the human potential to become more than we are in the present. This is the myth of Hephaistos, being played out every day, in every corner of the world.

Alignment can be seen as a synthesis of both group process and team dynamics (see figure 5.3). Group process is necessary, but insufficient in support of collaborative design work. Group process is a bit like maintaining the operating systems of an airplane. It is absolutely necessary that all motors and control systems are kept in prime condition. This state of being well maintained and well tuned, however, does not get the plane off the ground, into the air, and onward to its destination. Flight requires the airplane to be animated by a flight team composed of pilots and service personnel with flight plans and a clear purpose for the flight. This alignment of function and intention is necessary for the design process as well. The condition of alignment integrates the intentional behavior of all the individual participants.

This is quite a task, given that design teams—as purposeful social systems—are made up of distinctly different human beings, each with his or her own unique understandings and desires. An example is the designer-client team that is inclusive of everyone with a stake in any particular design process and outcome. In effect, they are a multiminded social system (Gharajedaghi 1999). The ability to create an alignment of these independently powerful and capable minds brings focus to, and magnifies the potential within, the design process.

There are many ways in which a successful alignment can be described. A popular metaphor for this alignment is jazz improvisation. Each musician plays impromptu, yet contributes to the musical unity of a collective effort. Other musical metaphors, as well as metaphors based on team sports, point to the same felt experience of unity in diversity. Participation in alignment has been characterized as the experience of flow that is an experiential state of cognition without the normal distinctions and distractions of measured time and space—an analog state of being. This concept also has application to individualized activity, as an unself-conscious experience of empathy, timelessness, and unity (Csikszentmihalyi 1990).

The capacities that become important to the designer, when desiderata are the focus and starting point of design, are those abilities that allow a designer to compose, imagine, and make good professional judgments. Engaging with desiderata as that-which-is-not-yet demands creativity and innovation. It requires attention, imagination, and communication in order to manifest a world not yet seen. This is true no matter the size of the design project; even the smallest design is subject to that process.

Desiderata, as the initiator of design action and designed change, are the intentional links between human capacity and human achievement. They are the enabling sources of guidance for intentional human evolvement. Design is the change of evolution into an intentionally directed process rather than a consequence of necessity, luck, or accident. Reactive triggers to change—such as fear, hate, hurt, humiliation, anger, distress, and need—drain energy and hope from human potential. Desiderata create energy, and hope, fueling the generative capacity of humans individually and collectively. Desiderata reflect the innate human understanding that the world is not complete as it is. Desiderata make design possible and necessary.

6 Interpretation and Measurement

Every design situation is unique and complex, constituting an ultimate particular, which is unique and singular in and of itself, without commensurable qualities. To create and introduce new designs into the real world, designers must adequately know the world that already exists, at a level that makes meaningful design possible.

In our modern society, we have at our disposal a large number of approaches to inquiry that have been developed solely for the purpose of creating such understandings. For some, the only way to reach a true understanding of reality is through the strict application of the scientific method. Others believe that there are intuitive approaches based on trusting their innermost feelings, intuitions, and instincts. Still others believe that an understanding of reality can only be reached through the help of a higher power, making reality accessible through spiritual experiences. Each of these approaches offers us a way to interpret the world we live in.

The "real" nature of the world is revealed when it is explored as thoroughly as possible in breadth and depth, in order to understand its basic constitution. However, the real does not always divulge itself to us in a form that is necessarily meaningful or easily understood. We can quickly be overwhelmed by the immense complexity of the real. Information comes to us through direct sensory experiences that are filtered or focused by our perceptual lenses and ordered by our conceptual scaffolding. Or we collect information we have gathered from a variety of secondary sources looked at through a variety of cognitive frameworks. The challenge is to make sense out of all the diversity of data and information.

Surveys, scoping, statistical analysis, observation, and direct measurement help us to discover more about reality objectively. These approaches make diverse facets of reality accessible through measurement and categorization. Typically, the idea of objectivity leads us to consider only variables that are unproblematic. So, we focus on life situations that present reality in forms that we can easily interpret, which we hope makes it possible to understand and control them. More subjective approaches, with the capacity to see with greater acuity into the richness of reality, include qualitative methods of observation and discernment. These types of investigations do not use standard scales of measurement, but rely on qualitative interpretations of more ambiguous information.

All of these approaches are common tools in the scientific tradition. But even with the most objective and rational approach, there is still a need for interpretation, and this can present a problem. Within the realm of science, for instance, we find different lines of reasoning for how to go about interpreting data. Some researchers argue that we must use methods that reveal the true core of reality, without being colored by our innate subjectiveness; while others argue that any true understanding of reality can only be achieved by relying on our own subjective ability to adequately interpret reality. Our desire is to break down this polarity in the case of design. We are interested in putting forward a holistic approach to assessing the real world in design situations. To do this, we must further investigate the act of interpretation.

Interpretation is a subjective process. Interpretation, as a part of the design process, serves the same purpose as evidence and proof do in science. Interpretation is part of our endeavor to grasp the conditions and contexts that exist in a design situation, which will set the stage for conceptualizing new designs. We need to apprehend the situation we are going to change. Design, though, is not only creating change that results in difference in the existing situation. It is also creating a new emergent whole, by adding something new to something already in existence. Every design must fit between the existing and the not-yet-existing. It is a compositional assembly. In a holistic design approach, everything is embedded in a milieu, an environment, and a context framed in time and place. For designers, the context consists of those things that have been selected to stay unchanged in the face of designed change even though they could be changed. This is in contrast to the environment, which constitutes those external things that must be taken into account, but which cannot be changed by design. Designers need to be able to observe, describe, and understand the context and the environment of the design situation as adequately as possible.

There are many ways of approaching the world in order to discern the preconditions for a design. Most of these approaches have quite narrow capabilities. This means they can only reveal a few limited aspects or properties of reality. In attempting to interpret the full complexity and richness of reality, we are wise to use a variety of these limited methods. For example, if the design task is to create a new organizational structure, it is common to begin by trying to define the present structure in both formal and informal terms. We might choose to conduct interviews and surveys with employees to see how they would describe what is good and what is problematic about the existing structure. We might study competitors, the marketplace, financial trends, technological developments, and so on. There is no end to the breadth and depth of research with which we can be occupied. There is no limit to how much data, information, and knowledge we can generate.

No matter how selective and limiting, these traditional approaches are essential to the process of understanding a design situation. The tradition of science has always been aimed at revealing the truth about things—an objective understanding of how things are. Given this, science has well-developed tools and methods for the purpose of observing existing conditions and then describing and explaining them as carefully and accurately as possible. In design, these methods and tools are invaluable as they help us to form a basic, factual understanding of the world.

But there is a difference between how facts serve truth and how interpretation serves meaning. As designers, we are not only interested in facts that reveal what is true about a situation; we are even more interested in creating something that is going to become real. Since a designer is not obligated to replicate something that is merely true, it is not necessary for him or her to apply only methods used exclusively for the discovery of truths. Rather, a designer is obliged to use whatever approaches provide the best possible understanding of reality from a design perspective. This does not mean that anything goes, in an undisciplined way, or that one method of interpretation is as good as any other method. It simply implies that the means of validation and acceptance of pieces of information have different criteria in design than they do in science.

Design is intentional; therefore, design interpretations are also intentional. It is intention that predisposes or directs us toward certain data and values. This means that interpretation cannot be done without an understanding of a direction. Another way of saying this is that the act of interpretation allows us to observe and understand the world through the lens of our design desiderata. It is a means to discover if the real world holds a valence for our designs and if there is good fit between our chosen design and a specific situation.

In design, interpretation is not about determining a solution by closely and objectively analyzing reality in order to be informed of what action to take (as in the German word *Sachzwang*—a coercion by facts). Interpretation in design is not a search for the objective, true, and precise design imperatives, hidden somewhere in the richness of reality waiting to be observed. Instead, design interpretation is an act of judgment. A scientific assessment is an accounting of objective factors, while a design interpretation is an *appreciative judgment*—a picking and choosing of what is to be considered and in what way. For example, appreciative judgment is the type of judgment that determines what will be considered as foreground and what as background, what is important and what is unimportant, what is valuable and what is of little value. Whenever a part or aspect of reality is considered important enough to be assessed, a judgment has been made. In design, interpreting reality cannot be done without imposing judgment, which is guided by intention.

This does not mean that an understanding of reality based on scientific methods is useless or misguided. Rather, we would like to bring scientific decision making and judgment together in a way that is guided by intention and is holistic in its approach. But this is a difficult task, since it requires a move toward meaning making rather than meaning finding. Thus, it is not an approach focused on deductive or inductive scientific reasoning, but on making connections and seeing relations among a diversity of candidates pressing for attention. The making of meaning is not an activity of scientific inquiry; however, as a designer, it is vital to your process. You participate in the creation of a real world. To do that, you need the world to make sense to you. To design is not to create things that make the world more reflective of the true. It is rather to create a world that has more meaning, that makes more sense.

Aristotle saw attempts to make meaning out of the world's complexity as a dilemma. Nussbaum tells us how Aristotle argued that we have to accept a third type of choice and action, other than the quantitative approach and the guess (Nussbaum 1990). For Aristotle, the third way is based on *qualitative judgment*. Nussbaum argues that there is no reason we should be defensive about the scientific community's steadfast assertion that objective measuring is the only way to proceed if we want to be rational. For Aristotle, it was not possible to reach a true understanding of the complexity of a situation by means of objective reasoning only. It is his practical wisdom in the form of qualitative judgment that sensitizes us to the critical, consequential, and vital aspects of a concrete situation. This is an *overall judgment*, where we sweep in the contributions of each distinctive approach to design inquiry, without the restriction of a rigidly logical, coherent framework. Aristotle argues against the idea that all aspects of a

purpose	outcome
explorative interpretation	finding meaning
generative interpretation	creating possibilities of meaning
compositional interpretation	making meaning

Figure 6.1
Design interpretation and meaning

situation are comparable as equivalents. He makes a defense for making specific judgments, prior to the more universal ones, along with a defense for feelings and fantasies or imagination—as important aspects of a true *rational judgment* or choice (Nussbaum 1990).

Aristotle's philosophical musings mesh well with our belief that a complex design situation needs to be approached holistically. We can assess and measure a situation, but any overall understanding can only be reached through design interpretations, which are, in turn, achieved by means of qualitative judgments. As designers, we create meaning in a situation as a whole, including the systemic or emergent qualities that arise from the interactive relationships and connections of the elements composing that whole.

When we enter into design interpretation, we distinguish between different acts of interpretation with different purposes and outcomes (see figure 6.1). As we've said before, in any design situation, it is important to find out as much as possible about the existing conditions we are thrown into as designers. But the amount of information that can be gleaned from a situation is, in fact, infinite. We can never know all there is to know and it is possible go on gathering facts forever. As designers, we have to accept this reality and not expect to be completely comprehensive; instead, we must endeavor to construct meaning out of the complexity and chaos that constitute the real world. This is an act of exploration of possibility. Because the capacity for information gathering is infinite, exploring empowers the designer to depend, not just on acquired skills, but on synchronicity as well as on intention. The availability of an infinite amount of information means that a fully rational analysis of all information is not possible. Therefore, to explore any real-world situation, we are required to stay focused on intention and desiderata, while remaining open to the possibilities that reveal themselves in fortuitous ways, since meaning is never "out there" to be "found"—external to the inquirer.

A different type of interpretative process occurs when the intention is to create possibilities of meaning. To conduct generative interpretations is to imagine possible meanings. It is a way to interpret the present, in relation to the not-yet-existing. Reality, interpreted this way, makes it possible to imagine an infinite number of new realities. This process is creative, generative, and always done in relation to the meaning produced in the explorative interpretation. The purpose of generative interpretation is to experiment with different interpretations of reality, in order to create possible futures that are in line with our intentions and desiderata. This is an imaginative process disciplined by intention and desire, while being grounded in real-world considerations. Divergent thinking and brainstorming are just a couple of examples of common ways in which designers generate possibilities.

As we introduce a third form of interpretation, it is useful at this juncture to examine the nature of interpretation from a different angle. Instead of thinking of interpretation as a way to find the difference between that-which-is and that-which-is-envisioned, it is often productive to think about interpretation in relation to a context and environment. In every design situation, there are things that are impossible to change (environment), or things that we do not want to change (context), or both. The context forms a contrasting background to that situation's desiderata. This is not the same thing as finding the difference between two states of reality. Rather, we see desiderata as something that contrasts with context. Therefore, we begin to compose and assemble a whole out of what already is in existence (the background) with what we desire to make come into existence (the foreground). It is in this sense that design interpretation becomes compositional and creational.

The meaning of the outcome of the design process is examined through the lens of a connective and compositional interpretation. Building on the other two modes of interpretation, the designer goes through a compositional and assembly process as described in chapter 9. The found meaning and the possibilities of meaning are fused into an interpretation that embodies both a holistic and systemic character.

Design interpretation is a way to find out where we are and if we can move in the desired direction, in alignment with our intentions. To do this, we need a background or a foundation, against which our interpretations can be considered. This foundation is not common knowledge or truth—instead it is the *measurements of life*. The measurements of life

AREA OF FOCUS	STANDARDS OF LIFE	WAYS OF LIFE	QUALITIES OF LIFE
	commensurable measurement	*nominal measurement*	*incommensurable measurement*
Environment	• Level of environmental degradation. • Cost of preservation. •	• Type of environment. • Use of natural resources. •	• Pleasure or fear of environment. • Fit with environment. •
Health	• Number of sick. • Cost of health care. • Availability of services. •	• Definition of health. • Definition of illness. •	• Well-being. • Control over healing and renewing. • "Good" health. •
Housing	• Housing quantity. • Housing price. •	• Spatial allocation. • Style of construction. •	• Fit with users' character, preference and location. • Means •
Nutrition	• Quantity of food. • Level of nutrition. •	• Kinds of food. • Methods of preparation. •	• Sensual enjoyment of food. • Communion thorough food. •
Education	• Access. • Literacy rate. • Test scores. •	• Curriculum content. • Pedagogy. •	• Intellectual development. • Self-worth. •

Figure 6.2
Examples of measurements of life

involve the consideration of what makes up the worth of our lives, so that we are not simply measuring a set of variables.

Life is too rich and complex to be reduced to the sum of rigorous computational scales. Designers must use a more adaptive approach using scales appropriate for the measurements of life. These scales consist of four measuring and valuation systems: standard of life, way of life, quality of life, and spirit of life. The first three can be contrasted and compared as shown in figure 6.2.

The fourth measurement of life—spirit of life—unlike the first three is not easily put into contrasting categories of similarity. However, the spirit of life can carry the most influence in how such things as artistic endeavors, special places, cherished people, life experiences, and personal desires are given a sense of worth in someone's life. The spirit of life is much too expansive to be covered here in any adequate way—but it cannot be entirely set aside. We sincerely recommend an honest exploration of the many spiritual traditions or traditions of deep inquiry that have arisen in the course of human evolution, in addition to your own introspective journeys.

Of these four measurements of life, only standard of life relies primarily on traditional scales of measurement, which include ordinal, ratio, and interval scales. The other three engage in interpretive meaning and value. They can be applied only through the use of intentional judgment.

In design there is always room for traditional measurements in the process of interpretation, but they have limited applications and should not be considered to be adequate in any design situation. For example, in designing development policy in Indonesia, a nation that embraces hundreds of language groups and cultures, the standard of life measurement of calorie requirements for the average adult may be constant across the nation. However, the sources of those calories are a measurement of way of life, so that fish, or corn, or rice may be the preferred source for a staple food. The quality of life measures the availability and freshness of the food supply. The measuring of spirit of life relates to the relationship of food to spiritual beliefs and practices. Taken together these four measurements provide one holistic metric of Indonesian life. When only one or two measurements are used, the result is a pale and simplistic shadow of the full potential of a design's effect in life.

Interpretation and measurement are at the core of design activity. They make us realize that all our creative, intentional designs have to fit into an already existing world. They also enable us to appreciate how each new design, each addition, each change, actually changes the whole. Every designer is part of the "big" design—and every design contributes to that whole.

7   Imagination and Communication

Design is about bringing things into the world that have not existed before. It is about creating the *not-yet-existing*. One of the great design mysteries is where the image of the not-yet-existing comes from. In earlier chapters, we presented the concepts of desiderata and intention. We explored how our desiderata give direction and guidance to our intentions. Now, we find that there are processes that have to be in place for this to happen. As we discussed earlier, description and explanation do not prescribe what productive actions ought to be taken in any design situation. Scientific descriptions and explanations cannot determine what solutions are best for a particular design situation, or what creative insights should be implemented. The most careful scientist, using accurate instruments calibrated to the closest tolerances, cannot observe or quantify that which proceeds from the human imagination as an outcome of intentionality and purpose. The reasoning and logic behind an accurate explanation of an existing reality are not the same as the rationale and imagination used to determine what is desired that does not yet exist. Principles of observation and experimentation cannot transcend their own context and become an epistemological link to other cognitive frames of inquiry. Designs of design inquiry always have their own unique rational structures and coherent forms of logic that allow for the disciplined integration of diverse epistemologies or ways of knowing.

One of the processes most people think of when design is mentioned is *creativity*, which is related to the production of novelty, but to design is to be *creative* as well—in other words, to bring things into existence. This means that design causes things to stand together in unity—abstract and concrete—through conceptualizing, schematizing, forming, assembling, and other formative activities of relating and connecting. Bringing something new into the world involves much more than just creativity—it encompasses the production of originality and novelty. It is a more complex and involved process of preparation and realization. Two major ingredients of that process are *imagination* and *communication*.

In order to create something, one must have the ability to imagine what the something is and how it can be made real. Imagination is demanded in all fields and all phases of design, no matter what the situational demands on the designer are. Even a very restricted design situation, one that is similar to many previous cases the designer has encountered, requires a certain amount of imagination to create the right composition for that specific situation. This means that every ultimate particular design is envisioned through imaginative thinking. It can never be merely copied from a template or example. Every situation should be imagined anew and only then can the determination be made whether to replicate an existing exemplar or to create something entirely new.

Imagination is also inherent in the process of interpretation. To make an interpretation—a form of judgment—of what specific aspects of reality are important in a design situation, given all the possible choices, is a vitally necessary activity. Architecture, organizational design, curriculum design, urban planning, information systems design, industrial design, and social systems design all require designers that are able through interpretation to conceptualize and give form to their ideas in a way that makes them communicable and comprehensible to everybody involved in the design process.

The ability to give form to an idea—meaning, to create a schema—can be described using a concept borrowed from Kant as the *formative faculty* of the designer (Makkreel 1990). In his thinking on the formative faculty, Kant had been strongly influenced by his contemporary colleagues, but he broadened the original scope of the concept to include a whole range of imaginative skills. Kant showed the importance of recognizing formative skills focused on at least two different categories of objects: given objects and not-given objects—that is, existing things and not-yet-existing things.

In design, there is a need for formative skills in both of these categories. Unfortunately, they are not always regarded as equally important. Often, the formative skill required for the description and explanation of given objects is accorded greater emphasis because it is based on observation or other "objective" sense data. These are the empirical inputs required to make a "true" representation, or image, of something already existing. This preference and emphasis on the given, over the not-given, leads to situations in which many designers and stakeholders are not sufficiently skilled in the art of apprehending or making not-given objects (abstract design ideas) visible, communicable, and understandable. The formative faculty of imagining not-given objects has to be recognized as a necessary and equally important ability in all design activity and projects (Stolterman 1999).

The nature of formative powers, or imagination, has always been an intrinsic part of many philosophical debates, even if it has rarely been acknowledged as a major question for philosophers. Subsequently the act of imagining has not been emphasized in traditional disciplines. This is predictable, when you consider that science has, as its major purpose, the creation of true knowledge about reality—the given. There has not been a similar kind of focus on how to change reality through the process of imagining and creating new additions to reality.

Kant also made another distinction between formative powers based on temporal relations. He talked about direct image formation in the present, reproductive image formation of memories of the past, and anticipatory image formation of the future (Makkreel 1990). Using these distinctions, it is clear in Kant's terms that design is an act of anticipatory image formation. It is an act whereby designers and clients imagine the future, the immediate future, as a not-yet-existing but immanent reality.

It is clear that all these modes of image formation are dependent on imagination. Imagination is needed not only when we want to produce the future, but also when we are called on to describe the past or present. A situation can never be described exactly as it is. Every description of the past or present is based on a choice of the attributes of a situation that are important enough to bring forward in time or hold in time using the faculty of imagination. This kind of judgment making can only be done using well-developed imaginative skills. Based on this, we can conclude that no matter what kind of formative actions designers are engaged in, imagination is always at the core of that activity. Also, we need to note that there is no such thing as a straightforward direct depiction of something—a "direct image" formation—without the involvement of imagination and judgment.

Imagination emerges as the foundation of all types of formative activities. It is a basic cognitive process underlying other design fundamentals, such as interpretation, composition, and judgment. The ability to imagine is required in virtually every step of the design process. A designer relies on his or her imagination and formative skill to transform ideas and visions into something that's possible to share with other people—this means he or she must render not-given objects into images of what will become given objects.

Imagination is therefore something different from creativity. Creativity is the spark that ignites the emergence of novel ideas that have the potential to become normal ideas. These ideas are seminal, integrative, and cohesive. They are formed from latent, autonomous elements of experience and intuition—forged from within an individual's life experience. Creativity is often described as the creation of new and viable ideas, with the implication that this means creating new truths—as in science. Graduate students at universities are regularly required to engage in literature searches to assure that their own creative research leads to new truths, which can then be added cumulatively to the body of information containing every other seasoned truth. New truths can be the product of creative thought in this way, but this is not the limiting criterion for creative thinking.

Creative ideas are often situational and particular rather than universal. In other words, creativity is the process of bringing forth that which is new and novel in the life of the inquirer. A creative thought, act, or product is creative if it is new and novel to the creative thinker, within the context of that individual's life. It is not required to be unique among all thoughts, acts, and things, any time and anywhere, although it might be. It is also not required to be true always and everywhere to be considered a product of creative thought. It is only required to be a new and novel product of an individual's imagination in the real world of that creative individual, with the potential to become a viable addition to that world.

Imagination gives form to the creative idea as an image. It is, in effect, a type of skill that can be developed and improved through training. But being able to imagine how a new design might look, feel, act, and behave in a given situation is only one side of the coin. A designer must also be able to communicate that image. One of the most common and persistent beliefs among the general public is that designing is primarily about drawing pictures rather than revealing images and that these drawings are designs. Patterns of decoration are defined as design—as are plans and schematics. Many dictionary definitions reinforce this perception because the list of possible meanings of the term design begins with these basic understandings. Visual representations as such are important elements in design communication, but they are far from being sufficient. Among the list of dictionary definitions there are usually one or two that refer to design as a form of intention. It is this definition that is most closely related to the meaning of design that is explored in this book.

The communication of intention involves more than the creation of visual representations of finished design concepts. Design communication is essential throughout the whole design process and is heavily dependent on the creation and communion of images. Images are fundamental to human communication whether with others or ourselves. We all have experience with the phantasmagoric flow of images in our dreams that Sigmund Freud considered communication between the id and ego. Many of us are also aware of the universal images, or archetypal images as Carl Jung called them, which all humans seem to some extent to share. Images are primal and a rich means for human understanding that go beyond simple graphics or text. And although words may evoke images, they are not a substitute for them.

Therefore, design communication is not merely graphics, text, or language dependent—design communication is image based as well. For example, the popular creative technique of "brainstorming" is a group verbalization process used extensively by product designers, organizational consultants, community activists, and others working with teams of people. The verbalization approach has limited effectiveness when used in isolation, because true creativity is image rich as well as image dependent. However, when a collaborative, language-dominant technique is used as part of an inclusive design process—to assist in the generation and communication of images—it has much greater potential as a truly creative tool.

Design images are diverse in appearance and substance. They can be found anywhere along a continuum from complete and total psychic abstraction to literal representation. In the idealized design process, images are created deep within the psyche of the individual, transmuted and communicated to the mind's eye. This newly formed image is further transmuted and displayed in the realm of sense data. This process is reversed or repeated many times within the confines of an individual's mind. This is as true for the client's images of desiderata as for the designer's breakthrough creative insights. This internal communication process is eventually linked to others: design team members, decision makers, stakeholders, producers, and others involved in the design process. This external process is most often a developmental process involving communicating images that are being translated into less abstract, more concrete versions of themselves, with iterative feedback loops along the way.

Design communication between designers and clients is somewhat unique in that this involves a process striving to re-recreate the internal image development process—in reverse—in the "other." A translation of an external sense-data image into an internal image in the mind's eye is then translated into an image in and of the psyche. When the "other" is the designer, the outcome is empathy. When the "other" is the client, the outcome is service. Engaging in design communication at this level is to engage in a design conspiracy—a form of systemic intimacy that is synergistic of, but not suffocating to, individual gifts of imagination.

There are many ways to communicate design images. In this chapter, we make the case for a particular method of design communication that fits the intention and character of design and serves the variety of people involved in the process, including both clients and designers. It honors the complexity of thought processes that are dependent on both solitude and collaboration and also enhances individual strengths and group synergy. It is a process that allows a design team to expect the unexpected outcome, in alignment with the client's desiderata.

This is an *allopoietic* design communication process, different in kind or degree from other types of communication in both form and purpose. Design is a process of making something on behalf of the other—in other words, *allopoiesis*—similar but not identical in meaning to the German term *kunst*—creating something outside of self. Therefore, a design communication system must be one that can support *poiesis*—the Greek term for the process of making—with the expectation that it is not merely making as an instrumental process. It is the act of creating something intentionally on behalf of another's desires and purpose—it is design. A related process of making, one that can be characterized as being on autopilot, is called *autopoiesis* or "self-making." Allopoiesis, conversely, is a term meaning "other-making"—the making of something outside of one's self, with and on behalf of the other (see chapter 2).

This type of ideal process involves imagining and creating that-which-does-not-yet-exist, but which we desire to be in existence, in the service of humanity in general and specific people in particular. It is about the significance of human intention and purpose in the creation of the real world. This is quite different from a typical Western technological approach, which prescribes that something ought to be created, simply because it can be done. This assumed prescriptive reasoning is lifted from an economic frame of reference where money—as the measure of value and return on investment—stands in for deeper aspirations and intentions. Humans have an immense capacity to cause things for many reasons—ignoble or noble—to come into existence, which then becomes the reality of our experienced world.

The ability to communicate and consummate images of that-which-is-not-yet is essential in this process of imagination. Communicating the not-given is different from the process used to communicate inductive or deductive reasoning, which is the communication that is used for description and explanation. Communicating that-which-is-not-yet is a nonlinear, complex, and highly dynamic emergent process that grows out of the systemic relationships among individuals engaged in the design process. Each individual plays a different role and brings different skills, perspectives, and authority to the intentional process of engaging in inquiry and communication for the purpose of taking actions, which cause new forms to come into existence where none existed before.

These systemic relationships encourage the communication of desire, purpose, and imagination. This includes the communication of images, which are diverse and unique in nature and the communication of individual perspectives on trust and common intent, of common and uncommon understanding, and shared beliefs necessary for collective action.

In order to facilitate the use of imagination to create rich images in the service of human intention and in support of design judgment, we need a special type of communication, one that works both intrapersonally and interpersonally. For successful design communication, the use of written or spoken prose is necessary—but not sufficient. Visual communication, using approaches spanning from cognitive art (Tufte 1983, 1990) to virtual reality modeling, is also important, but still insufficient. All of our senses contribute to the work of the imagination—creating images—but the imagination labors in the realm of non-sense as well. Therefore, design communication is dependent on both sense and non-sense as carriers of the design messages. It is a form of communication that is both phenomenal and noumenal. It is dependent on sense data, and at the same time, independent of it. Reason and logic inform it, yet it is equally independent of the laws governing formal logic and reason.

Communication modalities, such as formal *dialogue* or *visual literacy*, are essential to the process of making design images concrete realities. Yet as powerful as these methods are, they are not sufficient when it comes to successfully conveying the emergent images and insights of a design imagination. Formal dialogue—the Greek term *dia-logos* refers to creating meaning through words—is very effective as a collaborative communication method (Isaacs 1999). It is a process for gaining common understanding and common meaning among individuals in a group. This method is quite useful whenever members of a design team or group need to reach a common understanding of the past, the present, or a future situation. But these dialogues are not designed to reach into imagination's depths and extract new ideas.

Visual literacy and cognitive art utilize denotative signs and connotative symbols, graphics, schematics, sketches, and other types of concrete images

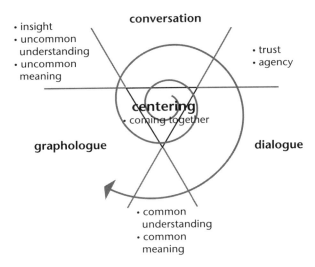

Figure 7.1
Design communication phases

to convey simple or complex ideas by taking advantage of the eye's extensive cognitive capacity (Tufte 1983, 1990). In addition, music and other nonvisual types of communication appeal to other natural senses, helping to form shared understandings in diverse and divergent ways. But shared understanding is just a part of the requisite communication needs of design.

Design communication needs to convey comprehension, meaning, and the promised value of that-which-is-not-yet. This can be done through the utilization of *diathenic graphologue* or simply *graphologue*, which means to let a thing be seen through its "image." One way of understanding the complexity and richness of diathenic graphologue—the communication of the not-given—is within the context of what we call an allopoietic design communication process (see figure 7.1).

This design communication process unfolds through four iterative stages followed by an implementation phase (see figure 7.2). The first stage in the sequence—a coming together—is a centering and engagement of all stakeholders and is followed by iterations of the next three: conversation, dialogue, and graphologue. After an adequate conceptual design has been developed and agreed upon, we enter the last phase, which is the implementation phase of making or production. In the case of design, implementation takes form of an *innovation*—the transformation of the creative concept into a concrete particular addition to real life. Of course, in reality,

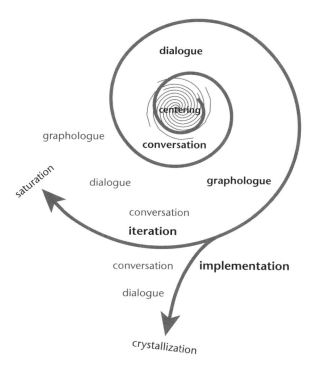

Figure 7.2
Design communication phases and stages

projects are probably not this clearly delineated by step and phase. Yet the process remains true in spirit and intent to the archetypal process animating allopoietic design communication.

Although the arrow of time flows through these stages in sequence, the sequence is not necessarily linear—it is sequentially emergent. This means that the subsequent stages are dependent on the outcomes of the preceding stages. The initial step reflects the obvious need for initiation of "contracting" with the "other," the potential design clients. The contracting can be a face-to-face connection, or it can be an empathic connection with clients who can never be in a face-to-face situation—for example, future generations—or who cannot represent their own interests to the fullest extent—for example, children. It can, to a lesser extent, be a customer whose needs are represented by governmental or corporate providers acting as *surrogate* clients.

The first stage of design communication, centering, begins with the triggering of the design imagination within each individual designer (see

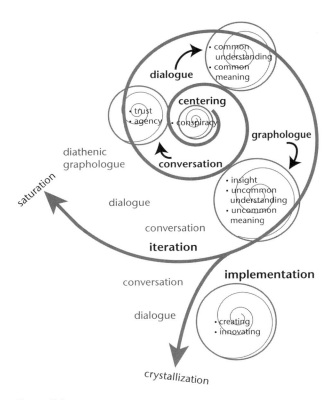

Figure 7.3
Communication outcomes

figure 7.3). The explicitly and implicitly communicated needs and desires of the clients initiate this response. The ability to listen to the other is at its best when the exchange is heard as if it's a *conspiracy*—in other words, a breathing together—initiating the second stage, conversation—a turning together. To have a conversation is to pay full attention to the other, to find relations and connections that can serve as starting points for contracts and even fuller relationships. This is a very sensitive process, in which the possibilities for emerging contracts and relationships must be carefully developed. The ability to go slow, to be patient, to pay attention from a first contact to a full conversation, are the building blocks to a good designer/client relationship.

The conversation stage is followed by the third stage, dialogue. With dialogue, there is a move toward shared understandings and expressions, motivated by the desire and intentions driving the specific situation. This phase of the process is essentially the creation of a common understanding among those within the process. It is not a process of identifying a truth that has been carried in from the outside by an expert participant. It is not a give-and-take process of coming to compromise, where pieces and parts are either accepted or rejected, as part of the common ground. It is simply reaching a common understanding, given the particular context of people, time, place, and resources. A dialogue can be designed in many different ways. It is important that the way the dialogue is set up resonates with the people involved and the specifics of the situation. To reach a common understanding does not mean that everybody has to have the same understanding of the situation—it only means that everybody is clear about one another's understanding.

Once common understanding is reached, it is time to move toward uncommon understanding, a transcendent state of insight into new possibilities. The not-yet-existing cannot come from an understanding of the present situation primarily—it has to come from the imagination of the possible as well. This fourth stage focuses on graphologue. The process transports newly formed seminal images of *that-which-is-desired* from the birthplace of their creation, from within a single individual's imagination, connecting them with feelings and emotions along the way, where they're imprinted with details from the color and texture of the histories of the clients and the character of the designers. They make their way into the shared conscious world of the senses—to be more fully formed and synthesized in collaboration with other designers' formative imaginations. These seminal images trigger new, emergent, or divergent images in other's imaginations that can become triggers for even more images.

These matured images are then encoded with communicative artifacts. Graphologue-affiliated approaches, such as cognitive art, are intended to evoke the experiences legislated by the images. This allows clients and others to feel, imagine, or be moved by the sublime quality of the ordering and organizing principles of these images—images that embody the clients' expressed and unexpressed expectations. They allow critiques by designers, clients, and other stakeholders to be expressed fully and authentically.

Acceptance often comes in the form of surprise at the recognition of met expectations, embodied by images that have emerged from the creative imagination of an individual designer, further refined and transformed by others. Neither client nor designer could have imagined these images on their own, or held these images a priori to the design experience. These candidate images arise from an individual intimately bound to others in the systemic relationship of service. The uncommon idea becomes the common ground for intentional change. This occurs when the creative insight of an individual is transformed into a commonly shared experience among designers, clients, decision makers, stakeholders, surrogate clients, and essential others.

At some point in this communication process, a judgment is made that an image is sufficiently rich and mature for the next stage of iteration or the final phase of implementation. Design communication can become cyclic at this point, moving from the process of gaining uncommon understanding, to transforming this into a common understanding, and then back again into an uncommon understanding and back yet again. This cyclic process can occur as many times as there is time and need and until a satisfactorily adequate image of a desired outcome has been reached. This image can be seen as an emergent insight coalescing from a supersaturated mix of ideas and images created from iterations in the design communication process. The image continues to be further crystallized and concretized through the implementation and innovation phase. At this point the adequate, common understanding of a new design transitions into a concretized addition to the real world. The artifact then takes on its own life history, contributing both intended and unintended outcomes to the lives within its sphere of influence.

A designer's formative powers are needed both in the process of coming up with the unexpected idea and in giving form to that idea so that it can be communicated. Imagination and creativity are so closely related in design that one is almost worth nothing without the other. Yet creativity and imagination alone are not of any value without the ability to communicate. Good designs must be given form and communicated.

In summary, imagination is not only needed as a way to create the unexpected, but is also invaluable in the process of interpreting the present—the client's needs and desires, as well as future demands and possibilities. Imagination is the reflective skill designers use to evoke and assess an overwhelming number of ideas that are possible in every design situation. Through imagination, we can visualize future possibilities and explore the consequences of bringing any particular one into existence.

8 Judgment

Judgment making is essential to design. It does not replicate decision making but it is as necessary. The ability to make solid design judgments is often what distinguishes a stellar designer from a mediocre one. By judgment, we mean that which is at the heart of design wisdom—inquiry resulting in wise action—in all of its manifestations. Judgment is the means, and wise action—wisdom—is the outcome. In fact, design wisdom can be defined as good judgment, which enables right action aimed at appropriate change.

Judgment is not a form of decision making as commonly understood. It is not dependent on rules of logic found within rational systems of inquiry. Judgment is not founded on strict rules of reasoning. It is more likely to be dependent on the accumulation of the experience of consequences from choices made in complex situations. However, judgment is not irrational, because it follows its own form of intuitive logic. Learning to make judgments is not a matter of learning to follow the steps of a technique, or to follow directions dictated by a method or algorithm, or to impose the a priori constraints of a theory. Wittgenstein stated: "What one acquires here is not a technique; one learns correct judgments. There are also rules, but they do not form a system, and only experienced people can apply them right. Unlike calculating-rules" (Wittgenstein 1963).

Judgment is, by definition, an elusive animal. It is the expression of the work of the subconscious mind, and as distinct from rational decision making as it is from intuition. Judgment has practical, pragmatic value and academic legitimacy, without having to be codified and generalized, as science demands on behalf of its cousin, reason. We believe the capacity to judge can be learned and then applied in design circumstances, without destroying its essence and value. This is unlike the case of intuition, where too much intellectual attention is often feared by artists who feel that reason, at its best, is the opposite of intuition, and at its worst, a mortal enemy. The ability to make good judgments is as essential in design as it is in business, law, medicine, politics, art, or any other profession. For a skill that is necessary to so many endeavors, it is surprising that judgment is so little understood and so seldom a part of one's formal education.

There have been a few significant exceptions to the lack of attention paid to the formal development of the concept of judgment (with the exception of training regimes). For example, Immanuel Kant, the German philosopher living in the eighteenth century, placed judgment as one of three cognitive faculties of human beings. For Kant, meaningful propositions were not just the consequence of empirical fact or analytic logic. They were also the consequence of *normative judgment*. In addition to his categories of judgments of fact, he developed philosophic concepts of judgments of ethics and aesthetics as well. His concept of *aesthetic judgments* (Kant 1790/1987) does not focus on the same outcomes as the concept of *design judgment* developed in this chapter, but there is a common foundation nevertheless.

John Dewey (1910) stated that there is an intimate connection between judgment and inference. The intention of inference is to terminate in an *adequate judgment* (which is equally a good judgment) through the interpretation of facts. John Henry Newman, a nineteenth-century Christian apologist, proposed that judgment was made possible by the intervention of the "Illative Sense", which informed reasoning, leading to correct judgment (Dunne 1993). Joseph Dunne develops another well-grounded argumentation for judgment, by elucidating the distinction between the two Aristotelian forms of knowledge, *techné* (a Greek term for productive, technical knowledge) and *phronesis* (a Greek term for practical, personal knowledge). From this, Dunne argues for an understanding of *practical wisdom* that makes it possible to take the complexity of reality into account through judgment making (Dunne 1999).

Contemporary examples of judgment-focused scholarship include the seminal contributions of C. West Churchman (1961). Churchman defines judgment as a *well-substantiated belief*, a belief held collectively by a group, in contrast to a belief held by an individual. As mentioned earlier (see chapter 5), Sir Geoffrey Vickers (1995) is known for his development of the concept of *appreciative judgment* in public policy design. Appreciative judgment is the capacity to understand, or appreciate, a situation through the discernment of what is to be considered as background and what is to be considered as foreground, in the formulation of a project context. Horst Rittel, another example of someone who has formally developed the concept of judgment making, focused his attention on the fields of design and planning (Rittel and Webber 1974). Rittel went so far as to state that every logical chain of thought is ended only by an *off-hand judgment* (one of several types of judgment he considered) and not by reasoned decision making. Recently, focus has been put on decision making in high-stake situations that are ill defined and time constrained—a form of judgment referred to as *naturalistic decision making* (Zsambok and Klein 1997). Judgment as an educated guess about what is true about a situation or context has been defined in research as *intuitive judgment* (Kahneman 2002). A popular science concept of judgment as adaptive, unconscious mental processes that come to quick decisions based on simplified information abstracted from complex situations has been introduced as a means for choosing actions based on hunches or *snap judgments* (Gladwell 2005).

A lack of regard for judgment as the legitimate alternative to formal decision making at critical junctures in design situations is not only revealed by its absence in curricula and professional discourse, but by the negative connotations one hears in everyday conversations regarding judgment. These conversations are full of comments that are indicative of the distrust of judgment: "Don't judge me." "Don't be judgmental." "That's only your judgment." "Withhold judgment."

Judgment can best be understood when it's considered within the context of knowledge, knowing, and the knower. To put it simply, judgment is knowing based on knowledge that is *inseparable from the knower*. By this we mean that judgment is based on a type of knowledge that is generated in the particularity or uniqueness of a situation; knowledge that is inseparable from the knower and is only revealed through the actions—cognitive or physical actions—of the knower. This is in contrast to decisions that are made, based on the type of knowledge that is of value primarily because it is separable from the knower.

Judgment knowledge cannot be stored in libraries or in databases. Colleagues in controlled experiments can't replicate it. It can neither be memorized nor accumulated in any quantity so as to build a field of routine expertise. Judgment knowledge has instrumental value only for a particular situation and loses its direct and immediate relevance in the next setting except as experience. Therefore, it becomes clear that separable knowledge deals in that which is universal, or generalizable—while the inseparable knowing of judgment deals with particulars and ultimate particulars. This implies that designers can learn to make better judgments, but cannot learn—a priori—the specific kind of knowledge necessary for particular judgments at the moment they occur—namely, adaptive and design expertise.

Skills and competencies can be practiced and mastered, in support of future judgment making, but should not be confused as knowledge for a particular judgment itself. Scientific knowledge, the ultimate separable knowledge, plays a necessary supporting role, through decision making on behalf of good judgment making. However, it is very different in character from the knowing that's embedded in judgment.

Knowledge that is separable from the knower is an end point in a continuum that transitions from data, to information, to knowledge. There is no similar continuum in relation to judgment-produced knowledge. There is, however, a direct connection to wisdom. Sagacious action has been considered as evidence of wisdom and the source of such action is always "good" judgment.

We will use these general definitions to examine judgment—particularly *design judgment*. We argue that a better understanding of the concept of design judgment and its different specific manifestations is needed if we want to improve our design ability. Although design judgment cannot be separated from the designer, designers can reflect on the nature of their own judgment making and begin to improve on their ability to make good judgments as an essential key to gaining access to *design wisdom*.

Unfortunately, judgment is often framed as an inappropriate alternative means of decision making. It is also deemed to be an inappropriate foundation for action or belief. Judgment is put into the same category as mere opinion or conviction, which, since the time of Socrates, has not been considered a legitimate form of knowledge in the Western tradition. Thus, it is not considered to be a fit candidate for access to design wisdom, the necessary precondition for right action. It is paradoxical that when others want some demonstration of our personal accountability we often receive the advice to "trust your own judgment."

Judgment is also touted as the enemy of creativity. Students of creativity are constantly admonished to suppress their judgment—actually their *judgmentalism* (which is mistakenly conflated with judgment)—to hold it in abeyance and allow the free flow of their ideas to emerge. Creativity and innovation are often proffered as the polar opposites of judgment. In reality though, well-managed judgment is a necessary component in the synthesis of creativity and innovation. Without exercising judgment, creativity is diffuse and innovation rootless.

Where judgment is acceptable is in day-to-day settings in the arenas of life that traditionally require judgment calls to be made. Judges are required in beauty or sports competitions, in order to decide who is the most "beautiful," or to make decisions on what is fair play, what is worth a game penalty, or whether a specific behavior is good sportsmanship. Judgment takes on its most serious role in the realm of law. In this case, judges are expected to make considered judgments based on their own experience, as well as their understanding of the qualitative and quantitative truth of a particular situation, in relationship to an idealized code of law or an aggregation of the consequences of past legal judgments.

And, lest we forget, there is another form of judgment that has concerned humanity for millennia, often called "the final judgment." In this situation, a Supreme Being sits in judgment of an individual's life, in anticipation of the inevitable end of worldly existence and the beginning of eternity. The anxiety and fear of this form of final judgment filters into attitudes about more corporeal forms of judgment that carry the threat of some form of punishment from an authority figure. Police, judges, bosses, parents, teachers, and others with positional authority are surprised by the negative reaction against their potential for authoritative judgments. The antagonistic reaction to this kind of ultimate authority and power, over the measure of an individual's worth, often results in the rejection of the idea of judgment altogether.

Our distrustful attitude toward judgment is quite fascinating when you stop to consider that people are engaging in judgment all the time. It is as common as breathing. In fact, nothing would ever get done, without the small judgments being made by people every minute of their lives.

This is because real life is complex, dynamic, and uncertain. Truth is difficult enough to know even with the best science, but reality, the domain of human experience, can be overwhelmingly complex and beyond comprehension. Careful, accurate descriptions, concomitant with clear explanations, are necessary but not sufficient in the quest for enough understanding to allow wise judgments to be made.

Therefore, without the opportunity to authentically engage in judgment, there often emerges a situation, commonly cited as "analysis paralysis," and its frequent companion, "value paralysis," which are also addressed earlier in this book. These two types of paralysis result from the popular assumption that decisions need to be based on a comprehensive understanding of the specific situation at hand. Further, there is an assumption that this comprehensive understanding, imbued with rational logic, will eventually lead to the "correct" choice of actions to be taken in particular situations. It is also assumed that this approach renders results not influenced by any personal preferences; in other words, that it is an objective and unbiased process.

Aiming to be comprehensive, such approaches in fact often lead to problematic oversimplifications. This is because in order to be comprehensive it is necessary to deal successfully with an unimaginable amount of sense data and objective information. And in order to deal realistically with the complexity and complication of large amounts of information within a reasonable amount of time, it is therefore necessary to find ways to simplify. This means ignoring or leaving things out that cannot easily be characterized or quantified. It also means using generalized abstractions to stand in for the multiplicity of particular constellations of sense data. In the process of simplification and generalization, nuances and subtleties are lost in the particulars. Even characteristics that are obviously apparent are lost because they are not easily understood and conveniently accessible through descriptive or explanative frames of reference. There are obvious dangers in the inability to deal with the full richness and complexity of reality, including, for example, dehumanizing individuals in favor of abstracted profiles or stand-in avatars.

The value of judgment is that it allows individuals to overcome their paralysis and engage in the challenging complexities of life in a way that, when done well, can bring function, beauty, and dignity to human existence.

Formal, rational, decision-making processes often are held up as the standards to be used by businesses, governments, institutions, foundations, and individuals, when engaging with complex, dynamic issues. The irony in this is that decision making, based on rational analysis alone, actually creates more options and divergence than it does convergence (in the form of focused outcomes) because of the never-ending need to be more comprehensive. In contrast, judgment is a convergent process. It brings diversity and divergence into focus; that is, it gives form and comprehension to aspects of messy and complex real-world situations. Best of all, it is "on time" or "in time," which means that it takes place within the constraints of a reasonable time frame based on a time line of realistic expectations and limitations. This is the discipline of judgment: making good judgments in a timely way without the delays associated with never-ending studies.

We believe that judgment is a basic human activity. But what exactly is this phenomenon? Is there just one kind of judgment? We don't believe so. Reality presents itself to us in extremely large quantities of sense data and bits of information at each moment in time. In addition, the imagination and other faculties of the subconscious mind deal with an immense diversity and an unimaginably large profusion of types of information as well. This has forced us to develop different types of judgment, each appropriate to the magnitude and diversity entailed. In any situation, in any field—where there is a need to create choices and take action—we rely on a number of categories of judgments. These include intellectual judgments, practical judgments, ethical judgments, systemic judgments, professional judgments, and design judgments.

These various sets of judgments relate to specific aspects of our experience of reality. People use these judgments to deal with the problems, questions, and challenges they face. Keep in mind that we never find any of these judgment types in their pure form; there is always overlap between and among them. Because we are interested in how judgment making affects us as designers, we take this opportunity to focus more intently on the category of design judgment.

Design judgment holds many things in common with the other categories of judgment, but the outcome is distinct because it deals with volition and desiderata. Design volition—using one's own will to pursue desired ends—forms the distinctive character of design judgment. Design judgment facilitates the ability to create that-which-is-not-yet. It is a form of judgment making that is related to the type of processes that bring new things into existence, making them a reality as emergent compositional wholes or the constituent elements thereof. When design judgments are executed well, they create beauty and evoke the sublime on the one hand and commodity on the other.

Design judgments are essentially nonmetric decisions or understandings. That is, they do not rely on a science of measurement to determine an objective or subjective outcome in their deliberation. Design judgment making is the ability to gain subconscious insights that have been abstracted from experiences and reflections, informed by situations that are complex, indeterminate, indefinable, and paradoxical. This results in the emergence of meaning and value, through the creation of relationships and connections that cause the appearance of unities, forms, patterns, and compositions, out of apparent chaos. Judgment is, in effect, a process of taking in the whole, in order to formulate a new whole. The outcome of judgment is not predictable based on rational anticipation. Nevertheless, the outcome of good judgment complies with the criteria and constraints supporting the driving intention and expectations of any particular purposeful process. The operational outcome of any judgment is dependent on the nature of the intention. *Intellectual judgment* may lead to an understanding of a general principle, and *creative judgment* leads to new concepts, while design judgment leads to a concrete particular understanding and concomitant action, within a specific contextual setting.

In our examination of design judgment, we have found it encompasses several different "ideal types" of judgment. For instance, as designers we face situations where we have to make an overall judgment on the quality of a specific material used in a design. At other moments, we have to judge how the chosen parts of a design fit together as a whole—as a composition and functional assembly. These two situations are not only different in their focus, they also reveal how different the act of making a judgment can be, and how our skills and knowledge underlying a judgment may differ.

We do not claim that the types of judgment presented as follows are an exhaustive or comprehensive list. We want to be careful to emphasize that our focus is on design judgment making only—this is not a discursive, generalized theory of judgment making. Also, this not an attempt to define the design judgment category as resident in the realm of the true. Instead, design judgment is a concept that dwells in the realm of the real. Our aim is to create an image of design judgment making that is practical enough to help designers and nondesigners to better understand how designing works, and to improve their capabilities and skills as designers.

Reflecting on design judgment, we can initially distinguish between the categories of *client judgment* and *designer judgment*. We also divide design judgments into domains of conscious or unconscious acts. The term "client" as used here does not simply mean the one who has signed a contract. "Client" is used to broadly mean the ones who are being served by the design activity and the subsequent design itself. The term unfortunately is best known in legal or commercial contexts, but at the moment there is no good substitute term in the context of designing.

Before we explore the designer's types of judgments, let us briefly discuss the client's types of judgments—which include judgments that are made at the conscious and unconscious level, or at the boundary between the two (see figure 8.1).

A client, first of all, has to make the *judgment of approach*—an assertion of intention. For a client, it is always possible to choose—or not to choose—design as a way to approach a particular situation. The client can make the judgment that design is not the appropriate strategy and may instead choose a straightforward problem-solving approach, a scientific approach, or even an economic, political, or religious approach. Design is, in every situation, only one of many options. And, design is not necessarily the

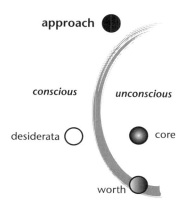

Figure 8.1
Client judgments

right option. If a client needs a process that will lead to a guaranteed and predictable outcome, design is not appropriate. This is because design is the act of evoking the yet-to-be-imagined and the not-yet-existing. This judgment of approach, if made in favor of design, marks the entry into a design project and is always properly made by the client or on the client's behalf.

Once within the design process, the client must make a *judgment of* desiderata and thus a *purpose* based on their perceived desired outcome. It is the client who has to make the overall judgment about the direction and purpose or desired end state that would result from engaging in a design process. This does not mean that the client is deciding what the particularized outcome will be. By making this judgment, the client will only be setting the direction for the design process, providing the designer, or design team, with a first approximation of the criteria and constraints for all their energy, imagination, and actions.

In the design process, the client is also responsible for making *judgments of worth*. A designer cannot make that judgment in place of a client. He or she might be able to suggest, or try to influence or educate a client to appreciate certain qualities and certain design consequences, but the final judgment of the worth and intrinsic or extrinsic values of a design to the client is in the hands of that client.

These initial client judgments will affect the designer's judgment on whether or not to choose to serve the client in the first place. The making of these seminal judgments by the client not only creates restrictions on possible actions by the designer, but also instills accountability and responsibility for the designer, especially concerning the systemic effects of his or her own judgments. Because of the mutual influence clients and designers as well as other stakeholders have on one another, there is rarely a clear demarcation between these client and designer judgments. This means that the judgments of the designers have an impact in the clients' realm of judgment, and vice versa. These initial judgments are modified and refined throughout the design process by the cross-catalytic effect of judgments being made in the different domains of responsibility and accountability.

It should be obvious at this juncture that the client does not merely provide the entry point into the design process. The client plays an ongoing role throughout, by having the continuing responsibility for the judgments already described. Design judgments are never finalized once and for all. New ideas, creative insights, changed conditions, and increased understanding and knowledge—all change the context for the judgments being made. Judgment in design is fully dynamic and dialectic, between conscious and unconscious judgments and between the clients' and designers' judgments.

Designers are expected to make a larger number of judgments than clients are, and are held accountable for the consequences of these judgments by clients and other stakeholders. These judgments are not all of the same type, going well beyond the difference between being conscious and subconscious, or the liminal zone between the two (see figure 8.2). Depending on which category of judgment the designer is engaged in, different strategies and tactics are needed, which require different commitments of time and energy.

So what can be said about the designers' judgments? *Framing judgment* is the passkey to the overall formation of the design palette. This type of judgment is at the very heart of the deliberation that determines the adequate and essential conditions for design to take place. It is used for defining and embracing the space of potential design outcomes. It also forms the limits that delineate the conceptual container—a virtual crucible—that is required to contain the intense emotional and intellectual heat of creative activity. This entry point—a portal or gateway—for a designer into a design process is marked by an altruistic and pragmatic judgment of whom to agree to serve—a judgment of who the clients, in the broadest sense, are or ought to be.

Finally, framing judgment is used for determining what is to be included within the purview of the design process—in other words, what are the "edges" of the project and what lies beyond consideration. This initial

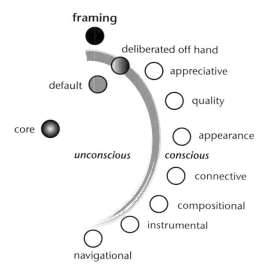

Figure 8.2
Designer judgments

framing judgment can elicit the most anxiety because it is divergent from a designer's belief in the value of being inclusive and realistically comprehensive. At this point important things may be left out and unimportant things left in; questions of what is adequate or sufficient dominate. Errors of omission are the primary concerns here, followed by concerns over errors of commission later in the process.

Enabling framing judgments are what are necessary in the early phase of any design, when the designer faces the full complexity of a real design situation. Hit by all the demands of the client, with a feeling of having too few resources or too little time, with a conviction there is not enough information readily available—anxiety can creep in.

Still, as designers, we must be able to take action. We have to start the design process by setting the stage, by framing the situation, and by moving it toward a satisfactory outcome. This means we will find ourselves intentionally deciding to ignore some aspects, in order to focus on others. In the same way that a photographer chooses what will be included in his or her photo and what will be left out, the designer must make framing judgments.

To an inexperienced designer, this may be the most difficult type of judgment to make. Before it is made, all possibilities are still open, while afterward, the design outcomes are limited. It is a judgment of great importance. Often, after a designer has become more experienced, he or she finds this is one of the most rewarding stages in the design process because it exemplifies the essence of intentionality—the direction a design adventure will take in the quest for the next evolutionary step, small or large, in human progress.

Once the enabling framing judgments are in place, with all their concomitant relationship building, agency contracting, and related activities, a design project can be initiated. Here design judgments are divided into ten different ideal types. These judgment types can be explored in great detail of course, but we will only briefly introduce them even though they deserve much more attention. Our purpose is primarily to make the case that a better overall understanding of design judgments is fundamental and essential to the development of a designer's competence in particular types of design judgment making. Just as the client is responsible and accountable for client judgments—approach, purpose, and worth—the designer is fully responsible and accountable for the ten design judgment types presented here. The ten types are as follows: default, offhand, appreciative, appearance, quality, instrumental, navigational, compositional, connective, and core.

Default judgments, made without deliberation, are a nearly automatic response to a triggering situation. In some ways, default judgments resemble instincts. The difference is that default judgments can be introduced where they did not previously exist; they can also be modified and refined, or replaced by new ones entirely, whereas instincts are genetically based—"hardwired" and unalterable. Default judgments are expressed as a "bodily knowing" enabled through kinesthetic intelligence. In the craft tradition, they are the "artless art"—an apparently effortless application of high-level skill without conscious deliberation (Platts 1997). Action is taken without recipe, formulas, or deliberation. A designer invariably encounters situations where they use default judgments. It is usually seen as a sign of experience when a designer can make good default judgments in pressing situations—a sign of good "adaptive expertise."

Default judgments are accessible through the process of deliberated *offhand judgments*. A good example of this concept is learning how to ride a bicycle. As many of us remember, this begins with full attention and deliberation, until our judgments of balance become second nature and no longer require conscious attention. Riding a bicycle then becomes a known skill that we have acquired.

Relearning to drive on the left-hand side of the road (after initially learning to drive on the right) is an example of the process of surfacing

offhand judgments—to bring them up from their habitation in the unconscious and modify them by making them open to deliberation. Every
unconscious move must be surfaced, consciously inspected, and modified.
This often happens in an environment of extreme complexity, with overwhelming sensory data barraging the driver. After some period of time,
driving decisions can once again recede into the unconscious realm of offhand judgment calls. All skills are developed in this way, whether they are
in sports, arts, or manual labor.

As defined by Vickers (1995), the *appreciative judgment* is a matter of
appreciating any particular situation from a type of gestalt perspective. By
this, we mean determining what is to be considered as background and
what requires attention as foreground. It is a process of assigning importance to some things, while not to others, without the intervention of
hierarchy. This form of judgment is key in the determination, or appreciation, of what is to be considered as context in a design situation.

An *appearance judgment* is complex and multilayered. It includes deter-
minations of style, nature, character, and experience. Determining if a
particular judgment outcome is something that contributes to the overall
whole is a stylistic consideration. This is because the choice is made as a
subjective preference for something that looks attractive, or seems preferable due to its pleasing attributes, efficacy, or membership in larger patterns of familiar phenomena. This type of informed judgment is not guided
by a literal matching of attributes on a one-to-one basis, as is the case with
scientific correspondence, which is used to create rational taxonomies—
groupings based on logical relations of similarities. Instead, an appearance
judgment is aesthetic whether focused on artifacts or experiences.

Judgments about appearance—as related to the nature of that which is
being designed—are concerned with the material substance and temporal
experience of the design as well as the fundamental character of that which
is being designed. Considerations about character concern attributes such
as form, occurrence, essence, and excellence. Character is about the appearance of difference, as a consequence of being unique or singular (Hillman
1999).

Appearance and *quality judgments* often seem related, but there is an
important difference between them. Appearance is usually associated with
taste, while quality is associated with craftsmanship and connoisseurship.
With regard to taste there is a presumption that desired attributes are recognizable in concrete particular examples. In this case, the challenge of
judgment is to determine whether there is enough of a match between
aesthetic norms and standards and the proposed design. Most designers

know what is "in style" in their specific field of design. But styles do change over time, sometimes fast and dramatically. It can take a lot of work to stay in touch with what is "in" and what is passé.

However, quality judgments do not typically have external templates to look at. These judgments are made within the boundaries of the concept itself, a unique addition to the real world, without reference to generalized examples or archetypes. Concepts like craftsmanship, connoisseurship, or artistry point to an understanding of the unique thing, in contrast to those things that are prototypical. It is a matter of the choice of materials—including temporal as well as substance—refinement in unifying materials, and precision and skill in crafting materials. The quest for excellence in the creation of things and experiences of beauty, sublimity, and practicality is often considered when a designer makes decisions regarding quality. Quality judgment also relates to the complex relationship between the designer's personal preferences, the desiderata of the client, and the richness of the design situation.

Instrumental judgments are the basis for the artless art that highly skilled craftspeople speak about, when referring to their interaction with their materials and the tools of their trade. This sensibility is what Jim Platts refers to as *competence* (Platts 1997). Instrumental judgment deals with the choice and mediation of means within the context of prescribed ends. It is the process of mediation that considers not only technique and which instruments to use, but proportion and gauge, as well. This is the form of judgment that takes technology into consideration. Any type of crafting requires instrumental judgments that meld absolutes into compounds of realistic possibilities.

Navigational judgment involves making the right choices in an environment that is complex and unpredictable—the core of adaptive expertise. The outcome of navigational judgment is based on securing the desired state of affairs for any moment, in the moment, by staying on track and proceeding in the right direction—in other words, maintaining an intentional heading. At a basic level, successful navigation is fundamental to survival. At another level, it is the ability to gain advantage in the moment. At the highest level, it is making choices that will guarantee the success of a design endeavor on behalf of clients and a larger social good. Navigational judgments are not predetermined and are, therefore, only accessible in the moment. This type of judgment is essential in every aspect of human life.

Navigational judgment is not done "by the book." It is the ability to formulate essential situational knowledge that is applicable to the conditions of the moment. It is ability gained by the experience of utilizing this competency and the experience of the consequences of doing so. Ship navigation is an archetype of this type of judgment:

> The experienced navigator will sense when to follow the rule book and when to leave it aside. The "right rule" in such matters is simply: do it the way an experienced navigator would do it. There is no safe guarantee at all, no formula, and no shortcut. And yet this absence of formula does not mean that we have laissez-faire, or that any choice one makes is all right. There are many ways of wrecking a ship in a storm, and very few ways of sailing it well. (Nussbaum 1990)

For instance, navigational judgment is important to managers and, consequently, this skill is taught in schools of management through the methodology of case studies. These studies provide the student with virtual experiences of navigational judgments, made in concrete, particular business settings. In the same way novels and storytelling provide larger, more complex examples of navigational judgment that have relevance beyond institutional boundaries. The danger of case studies is that people too often look for formulaic or algorithmic answers—in other words, panaceas—rather than for patterns of judgment making—learning that is "caught" rather than taught.

A signature type among the varieties of design judgment is *compositional judgment*, which is about bringing things together in a relational whole. This type of judgment is at the center of the creative process and includes aesthetic and ethical as well as sensual considerations. Using compositional judgment, relationships are created among a palette of elements, with an eye toward calling forth an emergent unified appearance. This whole displays the qualities, attributes, nature, and character particular to an ultimate particular. This compositional whole is formed within the guiding domains of aesthetics, ethics, and reason—in the mode of synthesis.

Intimately related to compositional judgment is *connective judgment*. Such judgments make binding connections and interconnections between and among things so that they form functional assemblies transmitting their influences, energy, and power to one another, creating synergies and emergent qualities that transcend the nature of the individual things that are being connected.

Unlike the famous example of blind scholars describing an elephant while touching different parts of the animal, the function of connective judgment in concert with compositional judgment is not merely to create a synthesis of different perspectives, but also to build a functional or teleological assembly from the behaviors of different elements. The challenging point in design is that there is no elephant a priori, just waiting to be imitated or mimicked; there is nothing given—only that which has been imagined. Connective judgments along with compositional judgments are therefore seminal to the creation of that-which-is-not-yet-in-existence.

Core judgments, the last of the ten types examined here, are buried deep within each individual, but unlike offhand judgments they are not easy to access. Core judgments make themselves known when one is being pushed by "why" questions concerning one's judgments and decisions. At some point, this process of interrogation stops, because it has reached the point where meaning and value are fixed. By fixed, we do not mean in the sense of the biology of instinct; we mean in the sense that creating, modifying, or rejecting these core judgments takes a great deal of effort in both time and intensity. We all know the uneasy feeling when we are challenged at a level that we recognize as signifying "who I am." We lose our ability to argue in a rationalistic way. We might even react like children, when we cannot justify our side of the argument but still feel deeply that we know what is right. Collingwood (1939) uses the notion of *absolute predispositions* as a label of our most intimate and personal beliefs that we cannot justify in a rational way. Core judgments are rooted in our individual absolute presuppositions.

Even if core judgments as absolute presuppositions are buried deep inside us, they seem to be accessible through at least four channels: the individual's character or "genius," and his or her life experiences, creative experiences, and experiences of the sublime (see figure 8.3).

Inborn character is the concrete particular identity that comes into the world with us, as a promise waiting for fulfillment (Hillman 1996). Core

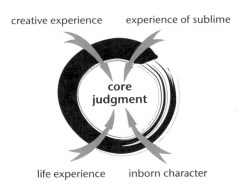

Figure 8.3
Dimensions of core judgment

judgments seem to respond to choices that either contribute to this fulfill-ment, or detract from it.

Also, core judgments are a composite of meanings and values, formed during the experience of living. These are not the products of reflection, or deliberation, but are embodied as lived experience. As life is experienced anew, the influences of old experiences are modified and new meaning and values are infused into one's core.

In addition, the experience of the creative process, which results in a deep insight of consequence (i.e., not just a matter of cleverness or cunning), contributes to the creation of new meaning and value. This new understanding becomes a part of the designer's datum for core judgments.

Finally, an experience of the sublime—an experience that moves us and transcends senses, feelings, and emotions—can also cause changes at the core. There may be other ways to influence a person's core, but these four seem to be access points to core judgment, which we can attend to most carefully.

So, in summary, both clients and designers are players in a complex relationship, which is animated by the interaction of many different types of judgment. Judgments are continually being made, and then refined, throughout any particular design process. Each set of judgments, whether designer or client related, must be made by the accountable individual or individuals within their appropriate roles. If, on the one hand, clients give over to designers' judgments of purpose or worth, or both, then the process becomes one of art, rather than design. If, on the other hand, the clients dominate judgments regarding composition and connection, or framing and containing, then it becomes a process of facilitation, rather than design.

The key point is that design is a system of social relationships and con-nections, which include a variety of roles and responsibilities (such as designers and clients), from which design activity, and outcomes, emerge. Designing is a design. Designing in each unique situation is a process of composition and functional assembly that depends on the interaction of different design roles for the desired outcome to be produced. In the same way that flour, sugar, eggs, and other ingredients combine to form the flavor of a cake, each design situation has its own particular emergent flavor of combinations of judgments.

The flavor of any cake is an emergent quality, not present in any of the ingredients when tasted in isolation. Similarly, the role of designer is not the determining element of design. For designerly activity to be expressed as an emergent quality, designers, clients, and all other design roles must be in the mix.

The plethora of judgment types forms a rich and complex map of inter-relationships and interconnection. In a design situation, however, neither the client nor the designer can use this "map" as a trip ticket. The map simply makes us realize that design is an involved process, guided by design judgments of astounding variety and type. There is no temporal aspect in the map and there is no priority to any type of judgment necessary. In real situations, these judgments are made all the time at the right time in a dialectical relationship with one another. Of course, some design processes require specific mixes of types of judgment, while others demand other proportional mixes. Yet the general map of judgment types is still valuable as a tool for reflection and for an intentional effort to improve one's design judgment-making ability. The map can even be used as an analytical tool. For example, such an analysis would be helpful in exploring one's own approach to a design task and laying out a strategy.

At this point we need to add one more type of judgment: *mediative judgment*. All of the judgments presented so far will, in one way or another, contribute to a final designed outcome. A designer needs to make judgments on how this whole should be orchestrated and brought together. Thus, he or she must balance and apportion the different types of designer judgments, through mediative judgment. In the manner that justice and mercy must be mediated in the crafting of a just society, different design judgments must be mediated into a holistic consequence. Mediation is not a process of averaging or compromise, but of instrumental intervention between absolutes, ideals, and creative ideas. Mediation between the chisel (the unbreakable) and the stone (the easily broken) results in the appearance of the desired sculptural form.

Mediation is about the retention of difference in processes of unification through composition. For example, a well-functioning design team is a formation of diverse individuals that does not compromise their integrity as unique human beings. Mediation is at the heart of the application of skill and talent, often through technology, onto inchoate material with the intention of attaining a desired end. Mediation is not a dialectic process of postulating a thesis and an antithesis from which emerges a synthesis. Nor is it a process of resolving or compromising differences. Mediation is a means of managing and integrating the power of differences using a holistic instrumental approach that is emergent rather than aggregate.

The final design outcome, the whole, is the result of all the judgments made in a design process (see figure 8.4).

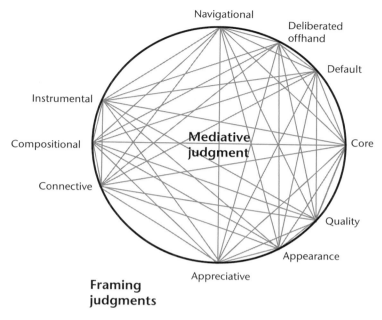

Navigational
Deliberated offhand
Default
Instrumental
Compositional
Connective
Mediative judgment
Core
Quality
Appearance
Appreciative
Framing judgments

Figure 8.4
Design judgments

The meaning of the whole, in relation to judgment and design, is one of the most crucial aspects of design, in effect, distinguishing it from other traditions of inquiry. Design judgment has a special character, since the resulting real design is something produced by imagination as an ideal—something not-yet-existing. In its various forms, design judgment relies on all our capabilities as humans. It is based on rational and conceptual thinking, as well as aesthetic and ethical considerations, and its fundamental starting block is the character of the designer.

As stated at the beginning of this chapter, we believe that design judgment is a full and equal partner in any intellectual pursuit in design, on a par with rational decision making. Competence in design judgment making is not jeopardized by an improved understanding of its nature; as opposed to the mystery of intuition, which can be threatened by too much self-conscious examination. The judgments that constitute design, as illustrated in this chapter, are based on the conviction that it is possible to understand and improve our capacity, competence, and skill in making any judgments—particularly design judgments.

Again, we should emphasize that we are not talking about making judgments about what is believed to be true. Instead, we are talking about treating design as an aesthetic and purposive form of intentional action, whereby we make an imagined ideal real, using our ability to make good, adequate judgments. Design is about making critical judgments, ranging from reflexive offhand judgments, to judgments emerging from our core being. It is about attending to the whole and all its systemic relationships. Therefore, being more reflective, in order to understand more about the activity of judgment, will not interfere with a designer's ability to make good design judgments. It can only help to improve those judgments.

This way of understanding design judgment leaves us, as designers, fully responsible for our judgments and our actions. There is no way to escape from this responsibility. Designers, in relationship with the client, have complete responsibility and accountability for their designs. This is because they have chosen, based on their design judgments, to make a particular conceptual design a concrete reality, without the protective cover of justification by truth. This leads us to the conclusion that good design is possible to achieve. The process of achieving it can be improved by learning to treat designing as an informed process of intentional judgment making and not something that simply happens or is acquired by logic and reason alone.

9 Composing and Connecting

A design is always a *compositional assembly*—in other words, made up of unifying relationships and connections between elements. To design is to be creative and innovative; but more important, to design is to cause things, including people, to stand together as a unified whole—a compositional assembly. Creating such a system of unification means bringing parts, materials, functions, structures, processes, activities, and events together in such a way that they have an emergent presence or an appearance in the world. To design a compositional assembly is to use an integration of several strategies for unification. These strategies use rules of relationships—protocols—and binding forces in the creation of compounds, functional assemblies, patterns, systems, and wholes.

Visiting a museum, where art objects are placed in large exhibit rooms, is an aesthetic experience. It is this type of an experience in two ways. The first is fairly obvious, as each art object creates an aesthetic experience in one's viewing of it. But there is also the overall experience of viewing the exhibition itself as a design—as a composition. We are attracted to each individual art object's qualities, but in addition we are influenced by the way it is related to other art pieces and by the physical space creating a unifying experience of the exhibit as a whole. In a similar way, a new car consists of many parts, each with its individual purpose, structure, materiality, and form. They all contribute to the design of the car in different ways. When we approach a new car, we might have different tastes reflected in preferences for individual elements, but we are most affected and influenced by the composition and functional assembly of the car as a whole.

Individual elements in a composition are made to reference and resonate with each other, to fit a certain style or pattern. Maybe they are related by being similar in the way they are shaped, their color or texture, or how they behave. Maybe they are made to contrast, or create tensions, as part of an overall design strategy. For example, in organizational design, this could be achieved by introducing creative change agents into a highly structured company with strong intrinsic stabilizing forces. Sometimes the elements of a composed whole may be integrated into a coherent blend. Sometimes they may be made to stand in stark contrast to one another. In either case, the elements are part of a compositional assembly—bound together by relations and connections.

Every intentionally formed design is given comprehensibility and meaning through its unique compositional assembly. That composition is the result of the intrinsic ordering system of the finished design while the functional assembly of the design is based on an organizing system. A compositional assembly is not merely patterns of parts: it is an assembled whole that displays emergent qualities that transcend the qualities of the elements in isolation or summation. In addition, the substance of this compositional assembly gives a design its sense of integrity. This substance is reflected in a variety of ways including the compositional assembly's character and appearance.

The act of ordering and organizing the elements of a compositional assembly is pragmatic and inclusive. In order to compose and assemble design elements, designers are required to acknowledge and accept restrictions governing the design challenge. This does not mean that a designer's work should be unquestioningly dictated to by real or imagined restrictions. Neither should he or she be constrained to predetermined possibilities or outcomes. Restrictions, as well as a priori conclusions, must always be carefully examined and challenged. This is true even of the stated needs and constraints presented to the designers by clients and other stakeholders in the initial contracting phase of the design process.

The processes of composing and assembling design elements should be based on a thorough understanding of what can be done, what should be done, but most of all, what is desired to be done. A compositional assembly should emerge in response to what has been found to be the client's most authentic desiderata. At the same time, the process of ordering and organizing is pragmatic, in the sense that it is an act of finding an adequate—not a perfect—solution. It is making judgments as well as reasoned decisions. To compose connections is to engage in design judgments and reasoned choices on an ongoing basis.

It is not the intent of design to reach for an absolute perfect solution, or to confirm the one true answer to a design challenge. Rather, designers must create a holistic outcome that adequately responds to the intentions of the client, in relation to the reality of the particular context. Compositional assembly is an act of creating the particular or the ultimate particular. There are no universal, a priori compositional assemblies for generalized design applications without imposition or substantial adaption. Ideally, there is only the specific particular approach in designing. As such, there is little gain in directly copying or imitating earlier designs. There is no need to survey other designs, with any other purpose than to influence or stimulate creativity and catch a sense of the mood of designing as an activity, unless it serves the purpose of historical or critical interests.

Even though there are no standard or universal solutions, studying earlier designs as case studies helps designers become aware of the specifics of each unique design situation, of the design judgments made in response to that unique design challenge, as well as of the final outcome. This immersion in the totality of past design projects develops a sensibility and appreciation in designers for the process of creating an ultimate particular design, but it does not provide pat answers for future designs—only the mood and spirit of good design.

Composing connections is an activity where judgments are made, using aesthetic principles like balance and symmetry. It is an activity that creates relationships between details and the whole and cause and effect. When Rudolf Arnheim (1995) writes that the goal in design is to create "a symmetrical, coherent and well-balanced whole," he is pointing to this important aspect. It is about making judgments on how to best integrate a particular design into a specific context and fit it into its environment. In particular, it is about how to match a design's actual potential to the client's expressed desires.

Framing, compositional, and connective judgments are creative acts. Designs express creativity not because they may consist of new innovations, like the latest high-tech materials or novel social functions. Rather, the level of creativity in a design is expressed in the way things are brought together—in how they are related and connected in ways appropriate to the ultimate particular conditions and intentions.

Understanding creative acts to be a form of compositional assembly, we can now see how many activities—not commonly considered as such—are acts of design. For example, the formation of public policy, the creation of new educational programs and curricula, the formation of intentional communities of interest, the development of entrepreneurial business plans, the design of one's own life, or the development of a new philosophy of life, are all compositional assemblies—in other words, designs. Understanding the essence of composing connections means more than having a familiarity with the inventory of relationships of relevant

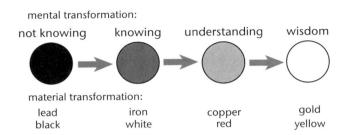

mental transformation:

not knowing   knowing   understanding   wisdom

material transformation:
    lead   iron   copper   gold
    black   white   red   yellow

Figure 9.1
The alchemy process

elements and domains of application. It means understanding design as a process—an interrelating and interconnecting process.

The archetypal design process has had many representations throughout time. This includes the archaic "four stages of the alchemy process" (see figure 9.1), which interestingly enough, is as representative of the creative design process as many of the contemporary models of creativity developed by psychologists and creativity consultants.

Besides being a fascinating early metaphor for the design process, it introduces an adjunct metaphor of the essential *design crucible*, which is an intentional construct made anew by the designer for each new design situation. The process of going from unknowing to wisdom or enlightenment—for example, from lead to gold in the alchemy metaphor—requires the presence of an effective crucible: one that can hold the "pressure" and "heat" of such a dynamic process, mentally or materially, by defining the sure limits, and therefore the space, within which the process is enabled to unfold effectively. Without such a container, it is impossible for the process to take place. This is especially true when it comes to the pragmatic conditions of real-world design. Limits and space need to be defined by the presence of a design culture, a design environment—for example, studio culture—and the particular criteria and constraints of a design project as defined by the client's desiderata.

In addition, the monomythic "hero quest," schematized by Joseph Campbell (1968), is another representation of an archetypal design process (see figure 9.2).

The mythic journey of separation from the collective conscious and entry into the individual unconscious ends with the questing individual's return to the collective conscious, in possession of a boon or insight, in service of the collective's good. This hard-won gift erupts into the real world, to be rejected or accepted, depending on the interrelationship

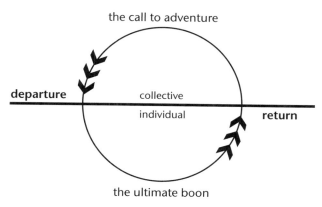

Figure 9.2
Hero quest

between the hero and the collective. It is a reconciliation process fraught with danger, flavored by fear and anticipation, much as the traditional medicine man is feared and revered simultaneously for the services he performs and the benefits he provides to the health and vitality of traditional communal life, for example.

In a more contemporary version of this design process, the sudden appearance or emersion—from the unconscious to the conscious mind—of an idea that represents the generative seed of a design solution—a parti—identifies that part of the design process that is considered the essence of creativity. The condensation of parti, the formative germ, from the swirling clouds of imagination occurs at the intersection of the subconscious uncontrolled mind and the conscious controlled mind. The parti often is experienced as a sudden flash of insight, a breakthrough thought that is sometimes referred to as the "ah-ha!" experience among creativity experts. It is an explosive appearance of a *simulacrum*—an encoded solution to a complex design challenge (see figure 9.3)

Figure 9.3
Emersion—breakthrough insight

Figure 9.4
Particular ideal to ultimate particular real

This emergence phase in the design process is marked by the precipitation of a viscous, rather than crystalline, nucleus idea. From this formative ideal—a "liquid" seed—a mature design concept grows. It is the initial germination of an idealized form. The parti can emerge in a singular moment, or in a drizzle of proximate moments with equivalent effect.

The phases in a design process that are of particular relevance to compositional assembly begin at the point of emersion and end with innovation. This involves a transitioning from the particular ideal—parti—via the particular real, culminating in the ultimate particular (see figure 9.4).

These consecutive phases of the design process consist of two very different forms of creative judgment. The initial phase is a subconscious, uncontrolled activity, resulting in the spontaneous appearance of parti. The next phase is the conscious and controlled activity of compositional assembly (see figure 9.5), resulting in a fully matured design concept ready for development and innovation.

A parti is a compelling organizing template, guiding the designer in the succeeding design process steps. The parti is the seed or germ of an ideal compositionally assembled form. It is similar to the *logos spermaticos*—the seed idea of the rhetorician's persuasive argument. In the case of design composition, the parti is the *grafos spermaticos*—the seed *image* of an ideal composition to be used to form a real, particular design solution.

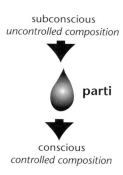

subconscious
uncontrolled composition

parti

conscious
controlled composition

Figure 9.5
Parti

The parti is seminal and essential, enabling a designer to draw together, to compose and connect, a complex set of elements into an integral whole. It is this binding ideal that the designer then is obligated to turn into something real, with an accessible presence in the world. A compelling parti guides the designer in making many types of judgments and decisions in the process of creating a whole. To be sure, a parti, or guiding image, is fluid, always "tentative, generic and vague" (Arnheim 1995). But, for the designer, this vagueness is not a drawback. Instead, it opens up a whole range of possibilities, without commitment to any one of them. Arnheim writes: "Being undefined in its specifics it admits distortions and deviations. Its pregnancy is what the designer requires in the search for a final shape."

The design process typically is misrepresented as a "problem-solving process" and a design challenge is miscast as a "problem statement." Designing does have a problem-solving aspect. However, it is quite different from the case where problem solving is treated as the primary or dominant strategic intent of design (see figure 9.6). The problem-solving activity relates to a struggle to find concrete expressions of the essence of the parti. The parti, as the conceptual whole of an ideal design solution, is impossible to apprehend or communicate fully, without being transformed into images, or schemas that become accessible as real and concrete particulars. Therefore, a design "problem" is the perceived difference between the elusive ideal solution, as represented in the parti, and the realistic, pragmatic schemes needed to represent it as closely as possible in concretized real-world terms. The ongoing development of concrete concepts is a cyclic process of "problem framing" and "problem solving" (Schön 1983).

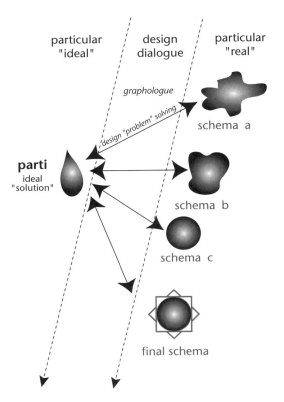

Figure 9.6
Design development

This suggests that designers problem solve using a form of dialogue or graphologue (see chapter 7), that involves the formulation of design schemas, as particular, real teleological compositions. They do this through an iterative process of schema formulation, comparison to the ideal parti, further schema development, and additional comparison to the ideal solution (see figure 9.6). This iterative process includes clients and other stakeholders, who become intimate with the essence of the parti through the emerging concrete images of the schemas. The test of a good parti is when clients recognize that their desires and needs have been met, or exceeded, by the emerging design revealed through these images.

This iterative design process is continued until a judgment is made to cut off the design graphologue and dialogue to focus on the development of one schema, which has been deemed an adequately realistic representation of the ideal solution. This design dialogue is never terminated because of measurements of perfection, efficiency, or comprehensiveness. The design dialogue is cut off because of judgments of adequacy, essentiality, and significance, for example.

Although the initial ordering and organizing process, leading to the emergence of the parti, is uncontrolled and takes place mostly at the subconscious level, it is possible to prepare and facilitate the process through intentionality. Because of this, there can be an expectation that the parti that emerges embodies all the attributes and qualities that were intentionally stirred into the supersaturated "solution" that was the catalyst for the parti—the abruptly transformed and crystallized breakthrough insight. It also assures that the parti is not a random product of novelty-generating creative behavior, focused on imaginative indulgence rather than purpose.

As we mentioned earlier, design skills, especially skills in composition and assembly, can be developed through focused reflection and analysis of earlier designs. It is also possible to develop design skills by critiquing existing designs. Each time a designer formulates a critique, he or she further develops a sense of the *why* behind each particular, of the integration of details into the whole, of how the integrity of a design is manifested through its form and appearance—how all of this holds together as a composed assembly. The sensing of *why* in each case forms an archetypal understanding of the design process and of the compositional qualities of designs.

Compositional assembly skills also include the ability to envision and evaluate a design that is not-yet-present but only imagined. These skills require a foundation based on creativity and imagination, combined with a pragmatic sense of what is real, what is controllable, and what is appropriately not controllable. Learning to hone these skills requires a different means of gaining competence. Traditional designs of design education don't work adequately in this way. Learning how to design needs to be understood as learning how to fuse—to bring together and compose connections between elements. The development of critical and analytic thinking skills, a dominant focus of education, ought to be balanced with creative and synthetic thinking skills in order to facilitate the development of compositional assembly competence. In addition, a curriculum based on systemics, the essential intellectual foundation of design, supports compositional learning by providing a logical framework focused on relations and connections in support of composition and assembly.

The concluding compositional phase, the segment of the process that is controllable and operates at the conscious level, can lead to excellent design concepts or mediocre ones, depending on the design skills, tools, character, and competencies of the designers. In any case, the final schematic form is the design that will become present in our world and will represent, for good or bad, the parti's concretized essence. Clearly, the successful expression of the parti's full essence, beauty, and splendor is dependent on the ability of the designers to translate its promise into reality.

This final schema can also be understood as the sum of the fundamental design principles realized in the concretized design form. However, a formalized design schema is not the same thing as its corresponding design principles. At this point, compositional assembly is not just about process—it is also about the actualization of design principles.

That something is a compositional whole does not guarantee it is good quality or "good" design. We can find many low-quality and bad or even evil designs in the world, including buildings, products, services, urban plans, organizations, and governmental institutions. We can see mediocrity in all the things where the relationships and connections among elements, structure, function, and form are inadequate, ugly, or morally wrong. In some cases we experience this because an intentional underlying order or organization is absent. This is typically the case when we find an artifact or system incomprehensible, with no emergent qualities or any sense of wholeness.

Although designed wholes are consciously formed through the intentional actions of designers, other types of composition can emerge as the consequence of discrete decisions and actions not aimed at the creation of designs formed from a parti, but rather, designs formed by accretion—growth and development by incremental additions. But even these accidental compositions are the consequence of agents acting, although often unconsciously, as composers of connections.

If a designer fails to transform the parti into a designed whole that forms a viable addition to the real world, then his or her design will not be recognized as a coherent system, process, or artifact, with integrity and unity. In other words, the final schema must be a viable conceptualization of the parti expressed in the real world, as an ultimate particular design.

In our discussion, we should note that there is still another translation that needs to be made: from final schema to appearance. A compositional assembly can be given presence in the world—can be made to appear as something real in the world—in whatever way the designer deems appropriate. There is no single correct appearance for any concept. In fact, there is any number of acceptable ways to give a design concept its appearance in the world. This, too, is a matter of design judgment.

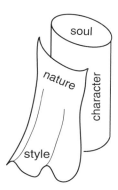

Figure 9.7
Appearance

A design's ultimate appearance can hide or reveal its true nature, its character, and its soul. The most immediate form of appearance has to do with its presenting features—the qualities that inform the senses most directly, such as material, structure, movement, and shape. Designs gain accessibility and significance by providing meaning through such mean-ing-making elements as affordance, representation, association, and information.

Style or fashion is often taken to be the essence of design, yet it often represents the most superficial level of appearance. A design can appear to be both trivial and significant at the same time. Appearance, in addition to style, is also manifested through nature, character, and soul. A critically acclaimed artifact of high fashion may, at a deeper level of appearance, reflect a character of gluttony and the soul of indifference in a design environment requiring sustainability and commitment.

Looking at a face, your own or another's, gives you a sense of age, skin tone, shape of face, and color of eyes and hair, revealing a person's style and nature. But it is the next level of appearance that comes closer to the truth of the person. That is the appearance of character, which is revealed through a more discerning means of sensing who this person is, as a unique individual. Looking into the "eyes" provides access to yet another level of appearance, that of soul, the spiritual essence of the individual.

Similar levels of appearance can be manifested in compositional assem-blies (see figure 9.7). These are levels of resolution that require attention from the designer, if his or her design is to be fully realized through the emergence of appearances and experiences at every level. The appearance and experience of a design can be treated superficially, in which case its value to people may be no more than its superficial nature. Deciding what level of appearance and experience to attend to is, once again, a design judgment.

As stated earlier, designed artifacts are most commonly recognized by their most immediately accessible level of presence, their style or fashion. Style and fashion are characteristics of presence that appear across the compositions of the one designer, or school of design, or across eras of material culture. When particular design principles are used together regularly and consistently implemented in multiple artifacts or system designs—a style is born. Some traditional design schools have used the idea of style-specific compositions as their organizing strategy for curriculum and pedagogy. On occasion these styles have become famous, for example, the Bauhaus style in material culture. To anyone familiar with the Bauhaus style, it is possible to recognize a design as that style without knowing the particular designer. However, some styles are reflections of certain cultures, or societies, and came to be without having been the consciously designed compositional trait of one individual. Most people at one time could recognize Scandinavian furniture design, or Japanese home design. This recognition occurred because the characteristics of these general styles had become so well known and widely spread. The same is true for styles of organizational design. Even social systems, for example, have recognizable styles that are based on belief systems as found in their religions and cosmologies.

When a system is merely assembled but not composed, it can still serve functionally, which will most likely be that of a cause-and-effect assembly: a simple system without any unifying form, with only local or regional organizing principles—a *tectonic* design. The Internet is an example of such a design. People have a difficult time trying to create an image of the "Web" [World Wide Web] as a whole. In similar fashion, systems like the American economy are difficult to map or comprehend, because they too are not composed—merely accreted.

If a compositional assembly is drawn together with skill and grace, it will give the resulting design a satisfying sense of wholeness and comprehensibility. If well presented, the composition gives users an overall apprehension of the design, where everything relates and each detail contributes to the whole. This helps to fulfill the design's purpose and function. The design will then have the appearance of a teleological whole—an *architectonic* design.

At this point, we should note that when one works architectonically, the relationship between details and the whole is always taken into consideration. This implies that every single detail is vitally important to the whole. Given this state of affairs, a designer can quickly wind up with a crisis of complexity, if his or her focus on details is not balanced with principles of order and organization, such as systemic thinking. A systems approach allows complexity to be taken into account without leading to paralysis. Systems thinking provides the organizing and ordering design logic needed for dealing with complexity (see chapter 3).

Once a design is complete and innovated into the world, it's not always easy to decipher the underlying elements of its compositional assembly. This critical activity demands a certain amount of skill. Sometimes, a strong impression is made by a certain design's presence, but the reasons for this impression may be difficult to deconstruct simply by viewing the whole. A composition can be subtle and elusive, requiring a highly developed skill of discernment. Every scale of measurement, including ethics and aesthetics, should be used when critiquing architectonic designs. Once evaluated, such designs will be judged to be efficient, effective, good, just, frightening, evil, beautiful, or sublime. This depends on how the client and other stakeholders, including the environment and future generations, ultimately are affected—a judgment on design judgments.

The ultimate valuation is prophesized by the designers and verified by the real world. The real value of a design is determined by its success in meeting the desires of the client and the intentions of the designers. Its intrinsic worth is further determined by the unexpected presence the design exhibits on its own, as it becomes an agent of influence and change, thus, in effect, recreating its creators.

Compositional assembly—the creation of real things—is an overwhelmingly important aspect of design. To compose connections—to shape the world—is a great responsibility, as the designer and his or her design becomes part of the ongoing creation of our reality. That is a daunting prospect, but when designers dive in fully, it is one of the most inspiring and rewarding activities imaginable.

10   Craft and Material

Design is often dominated by creativity, its most glamorous trait. While the creativity it takes to imagine new possibilities and realities clearly is important, it's easy to forget that there are other, more down-to-earth strategies associated with designing that are just as essential and influential. A new conceptual idea is not worth much if it is not made manifest in the world. All designs must be innovated—in other words, made real. Innovation is not the same as creativity, a conflation of terms that happens too often. In order to become innovations, designs must be *crafted* as concretized or *materialized* things that have appearance and can be experienced. This requires that a number of hands-on activities be brought to bear on making a creative concept real and ready for innovation. Such activities, which bring design concepts to life, all involve craftsmanship and materials selection as well as the skills and tools these entail.

This chapter explores the nature of the process of bringing a design concept into the real world. It's a delicate evolution, one in which authentic attention (*notitia*) must be paid to the maturation of a design, especially during times of vulnerability to external influences. Giving birth to a design is a matter of craft. Craft is the skill set a designer needs to use when working with the right materials, in the right proportion, with the right tool set in order to *produce* a final desired, designed outcome. An underappreciated aspect of craft is that it is involved in the conceptual phases of the design process and is not limited to just the concretizing phase of designing. There is a craft element involved in design imagination, design interpretation, design composition, as well as in the process of prototyping, modeling, and finally in the making of a real design.

Craft is where the hand and the mind come together in the process of bringing the not-yet-existing into the world. Craft is not a process defined only by causal force, but rather, by caretaking as well. Wise crafting allows for the nurturing and maturation of a design through a deliberate and skillful manipulation of the material world. All designs, in the process of becoming real, need caretakers, who enable conceptual ideas to take on material form, and to develop and mature in safety and security, thus allowing them to move toward realization of their full potential before being tested and judged by unfiltered reality. The close connective relationship between caretaking and craft means that a design, in the process of becoming real, should not be handed over to someone who is not authentically engaged in its design process.

Craft is also a process characterized by carefulness. Desirable attributes, such as quality, excellence, and aesthetics, are gained only when close, careful attention is paid to both the process and the materializing design itself. Carefulness is giving one's full attention to the work at hand in full measure of the design's worth.

The final production of a design should not be separated from its conceptual designing. When this happens, the design does not mature in consonance with the formative ideas underlying it. We will focus on two aspects of production; the *material* of design—its real substance—and the *craft* involved in the production process. Our basic assumption is that both aspects need to be founded on an understanding of carefulness—a concerned attention and caretaking—a protective trust, and an understanding of the close connection and interdependence between thinking and doing during the design process.

The fact that we distinguish between the act of creativity and more pragmatic or concrete activities does not mean they are separated in the design process. Creativity is founded on imagination and inspiration, innovation stands on ingenuity and skill. Creativity demands an open mind with the ability to cross and expand conceptual boundaries, exploring new ideational terrain. In turn, innovation requires experience, a sense of limits and a feeling for material realities.

The company that is famous for its well-designed technology products, Apple Corp., is an example of the power of well-managed product crafting leading to highly successful innovation. The company became famous for its success in taking concepts developed by others and turning them into products that set standards in the industry, becoming must-have design icons of consumer technology. The creative conceptualizations were in some cases done elsewhere but the careful crafting of material products became Apple's hallmark. Because of the well-crafted and human-connected nature of the products, innovation became a consumer-driven process as much as a company-driven process.

Innovation is by nature sequential and episodic, making it very different from creativity. When it comes to the actual crafting and production of designs, the manner and order in which things are done make a critical difference. For instance, in order to introduce a designed change into an existing social setting, there is first a displacement of many old structures and processes, ideally followed by a process of letting go of things as they were and opening up to the new. Celebrating and remembering the best of the old defines the provenance of the new design.

To be able to produce a new artifact, whether abstract or concrete, social or physical, necessarily means that the material to be used for the design must be appropriately chosen. To produce a design presupposes instrumental knowledge of the nature of both material and form. Skill-based imperative courses of action must be followed for expected outcomes to be realized. Therefore, there is a necessary temporal order to this process—an *arrow of time.*

Material, as we use the word here, is not limited to physical materials like water, iron, paper, and biologic matter. It also applies to the abstract material used in the composition of a process, or a symbol, or system, such as number, essence, and nature. It applies to people as social, cultural, and spiritual material. Materials are what a designer brings together using structural connections or compositional relationships. Materials are what a designer uses to midwife a design into its existence in the world, to make it appear and be experienced in a real sense.

Materials are not passive in the process of becoming real. Materials in the real world always "speak back" to the designer in response to the instrumental means he or she has chosen to facilitate the designing process. Donald Schön (1983) found in studies that designers frequently use materials in the design process more or less as design partners. A similar reflection on the need to "ask" the material what it wants to be during the design process is found in this famous quote by architect Louis Kahn:

And when you want to give something presence,
you have to consult nature.
And there is where Design comes in.
And if you think of Brick, for instance,
and you say to Brick,
"What do you want Brick?"
And Brick says to you
"I like an Arch."
(Kahn 2003)

When the "material speaks back" it does so by showing the designer its limits and restrictions, as well as possibilities, impossible to imagine without having them voiced in a concrete way. A simple example is what happens when we begin to put our thoughts on paper. Our own words present themselves to us in a way that reveals our less accessible or unformed thoughts. When we read what we have written, we are pressed to rewrite, or even rethink, our ideas. The written text, even though we wrote it ourselves, "speaks back to us" and reveals to us our own thinking through its interactive material agency. Design material speaks to us in a way that our mind cannot anticipate on its own. In this process, carefulness is essential. How conceptual design ideas are crafted and brought into the world will impact how well they can mature developmentally.

The way design ideas are brought into the world, as crafted material, is a critical part of the design process. Producing good designs requires building successful interrelationships and interconnections with the material of the real world. As the world speaks back, joining the designer in a dialogue, we move out of a polarity between objectivity and the subjectivity into a holistic interrelationship. That which is being innovated is a part of the material process itself. When a design is brought into the world, there is no longer a distinction between that-which-is and the not-yet-existing. In this conjunction, we see the real nature of our designs and how they become a part of the world.

Making this holistic relationship as strong and natural as possible is one of the most challenging aspects of design. Through compositional assembly and innovation, designers experiment with this relationship. During the process, a designer has the opportunity to try new ways of realizing an imagined design through prototyping, modeling, simulation, and so on. Prior to these activities, the concepts of excellence or quality are just abstract intentions.

This points out that production related aspects of design are not an addendum to the design process. Indeed, the design process is not over when production specifications are set. Design is not over when something has been created as an addition to the real world. Designing is a process that even extends through the entire time that a design is in use as part of the real world. Sometimes, the design process may even extend beyond the life span of the artifact itself. Instead of seeing design as a time-limited event, it is seen as a constantly evolving or continuous process over extended periods of time. This idea changes the basic relationships between the designer and the clients and end users in the design process. For example, the evolving elements of a design often need to be handled separately when responsibilities in the design are contractual. Computers, airplanes, educational programs and corporations are examples of designed things that continue evolving through generations of particular design instantiations, end users, and stakeholders.

The issues of excellence and quality come into focus as they make their appearance in the production phase of design. Many of the qualities that make a design whole are not apparent until the designer is engaged in crafting materials. There is no way to judge the overall excellence of a design before it has been made real. It is only when the design is placed in its final setting of relations and connections—its apposition—that all of its qualities become apparent and visible.

For the individual designer, questions of excellence and quality can be related to the notion of *connoisseurship*. Eisner (1998) describes connoisseurship as "the art of appreciation." It is the ability to distinguish and name dimensions and qualities of things or experiences. A connoisseur is able to draw upon large and diverse sources of nebulous and complex information. Connoisseurship is an ability that is learned over time. It is an intellectual adroitness that can only be developed through practical training and lived experience.

The canonical example of connoisseurship is the wine expert. It is impossible to become a wine connoisseur by only studying theories of wine and wine making—tasting is crucial and necessary. The same goes for any designer's ability to understand and judge material—direct and intimate contact with the material involved is essential. The process of developing connoisseurship requires attention, time, and devotion (Gladwell 2008).

Being a connoisseur means that you have the ability to assess "objective" qualities of a material. In the wine example, you can distinguish large numbers of colors, flavors, textures, and so on. However, it is an ability that is separated from criticism. Eisner argues that connoisseurship is private while criticism is public. Connoisseurship provides "criticism with its subject matter" (Eisner 1985). Criticism happens when a connoisseur wants to communicate. A designer, in the process of crafting, always engages in connoisseurship, that is, in the intimate handling of materials. In criticism, the designer is dealing with other designers and stakeholders through communication. Criticism is a process whereby connoisseurship enables others to see and discern qualities in something that otherwise they would not have been aware of or able to express. Eisner writes, "effective criticism functions as the midwife to perception." There is a dynamic dialectic relationship between the discovery of qualities—in other words, connoisseurship—and the conceptualization and evaluation of these qualities—criticism—in any design process. It is an integration of mind and hand, of concrete and abstract. Knowing materials therefore is not a matter of technical hands-on experience or an intellectual exercise, but an integration of both.

In a production process, the responsibility for crafting a design can land in the laps of several different design teams. Each team has a time and place where its members have primary responsibility for the design—its evolution and refinement. Team members include designers, clients, end users, managers, and other stakeholders. The design itself may "travel" from one subgroup of a design team to another team, at the appropriate point in the design process. For example, in the case of product design, conceptual designers may hand the design off to prototype designers, who in turn hand off to production designers. In the case of policy design, there can be a similar hand-off process, only with different titles for the custodians.

Throughout this usually complex production process, the design is cared for by people with complex and contradictory needs, not to mention wants, skills, and values. A young design's journey—from its conception as a parti to a final and full presence in the world—is both hazardous and long. For this design to survive and evolve in the best possible way, the design process must be carefully managed. The designer must choose and handle the appropriate materials and maintain the appropriate level of mastery over his or her tools and skill sets in order to transform the imagined design into a real one.

It is important to note at this point that, by definition, production is a transitional phase. By this, we mean that at the end of the production phase there is a transfer of ownership from the design team as a whole to the client. At this point a design is accepted into the client's world and becomes part of it. The design begins to fulfill its purpose and intent. Up until this time, the design team, in its entirety, ideally has been responsible for the design. The design now becomes the responsibility of the client and stakeholders, including the end users. Residual accountability remains for the entire design team, however.

Since innovation is the process of making things a part of the real world, it will always be dependent on the production skills and abilities of the design team. These skills and abilities often are specific to a particular field or client domain within which the design is taking shape. These skills will change over time, as field-specific technology and knowledge continuously develop and new clients emerge. Some aspects of the design process itself are influenced by team members' experiences with field-specific conditions or types of clients.

For example, the content and types of detailed specifications required for the field of organizational design differ significantly from those required for the field of industrial design. Organizational design primarily is people focused, dealing with the details of human relationships, connections, and emergent social behavior; while industrial design primarily is engineering focused, dealing with details of technologic assemblies and industrial processes. As a consequence, it is necessary to acquire the essential skills and experiences inherent in one's particular field-related trade or craft in addition to the ability to work with materials unique to diverse client domains and environments to be a competent designer.

Competent designers devote time and attention to developing a deep understanding of materials as well as crafting skills. However, as we stated earlier, this is not to be undertaken in isolation from the other aspects of designing that have already been discussed, such as imagination, judgment, communication, composition, and so on. The form and appearance envisioned for a particular design determines how its materiality should be shaped and manipulated; however, the materials chosen redefine the design's potential as well as its limitations, and influence what design ultimately can be produced.

Craft and material too often are seen primarily as the concrete and practical aspects of designing and are not included in the broader understanding of design as a tradition of inquiry and action. However, no understanding of design is complete without a deep appreciation of craftsmanship and materials and their place in the essence of designing.

IV METAPHYSICS

Design requires more than a working knowledge of the foundational and fundamental aspects of design. Every designer must also reflect on the substantial metaphysical issues that arise from a design approach to life. Such issues include setting the boundaries of design, determining design excellence, ascertaining the designer's responsibility in the outcome of a design, and confronting the inherent good and evil in design. Understanding the metaphysical aspects of design is not optional in a design approach. Competent designers have an obligation to clients, stakeholders, society at large, and themselves to continuously reflect on the meaning and consequences of these themes.

The subjects we will explore in the next three chapters are the evil of design, the splendor of design, and the guarantor-of-design. The metaphysical considerations presented in these chapters define significant questions found at the edges of design inquiry.

11 The Evil of Design

Design is often paradoxical. Qualities that may appear to be opposites from a single vantage point are actually different dimensions of the same complex set of design relationships. As discussed earlier it is impossible to take in all views of a building at once—you must move around and through its architecture to see all sides of it. In fact, it is impossible to see the whole of anything in a design from just one station point or perspective. In design and designing, when one attribute is revealed as we conceptually move around it, another may suddenly be hidden from sight. But the fact that you are no longer aware of the second attribute does not mean it has disappeared from the architectonic whole of a design or the attending design process. In fact, a wide variety of contradictory design attributes can be present at the same time, as the following list will attest (see figure 11.1).

Paradoxical relationships are more common than we would like to admit. They are, in fact, essential aspects of the human experience. Life is complex and tensional. These tensions between apparent opposites, such as joy and sorrow, are usually perceived as abnormal in the science-steeped Western tradition. This tradition holds that resolved truth, especially objectively resolved truth, is of the highest value. Indeed, from this perspective, resolved truth becomes the only outcome worth seriously pursuing.

Tension is regarded as something to be resolved, rather than valued; paradoxes are looked upon as relationships that must be "fixed" in favor of one or the other member of a tensional pair. But when one side of the pair "wins," tension is released and there is a loss of aesthetic quality, almost a sense of flatness, or lack of depth. It is what we sense when we seriously contemplate utopias and master plans. If everything is in agreement, following a consensual path, the excitement of human differences and diversity—held in breathtaking tension—is lost, along with what is most exciting about engaging in life at its fullest.

- Design is non-attachment and total engagement
- Design is flux and permanence
- Design is knowing and naïveté
- Design is experience and fresh eyes
- Design is collaboration and solitude
- Design is process and structure
- Design is cyclic and episodic
- Design is control and uncontrollable
- Design is unique and universal
- Design is infinite and finite
- Design is timeless and temporal
- Design is splendor and evil

Figure 11.1
Paradoxes

Good design's most interesting paradox is that it is both magnificent and evil. This is not the same pairing of apparent opposites as the more common duality of good and evil. We are not talking about Evil, with a capital E, designating malevolent forces dedicated to the destruction of everything that is good in the world, or counter to the positive presence of God as in many religious traditions. It is true that design has been considered evil in this way. Some designs have been attributed to the work of the devil or the influence of evil spirits. For instance, a European bishop banned the use of rifled barrels on guns, because the resulting superior accuracy over the old, smooth-bore muskets could only be due to the intervention of the devil.

Consideration of the concept of evil in human affairs has not often been the focus of modern thinkers, outside of those associated with religious traditions. But historically evil has been considered from many perspectives—spiritual, social, and political—as well as from the standpoint of dominant religions of the West, which define evil as disobedience to God's authority; as disorder and that which creates disorder; and as abomination, malevolence, sin, and vice. Concepts of evil from secular perspectives have even included willfulness, cruelty, irrationality, waywardness, conflict, immorality, crime, sociopathic behavior, and ultimately the banal cruelty of everyday life (Arendt 1958; Rorty 2001).

A traditional definition of evil concerns that which breaks unity and separates the individuated self from the ultimate prime causal principle of the All, which is a seminal aspect of the "perennial philosophy" (Huxley 1944). Within this framework, evil in a large number of spiritual traditions has been identified with a separation from the one, absolute and supreme

Nature. Aldous Huxley points out that spiritual traditions throughout time consider evil as any division of this unity, beginning with the concept of duality, the first step in the deconstruction of the ultimate whole. This separation can be detected in the removal of "self" from the whole through reasoning, will, and feeling.

These attributes are manifest in our definition of evil in design. Design is evil when that which is not desired nevertheless is made manifest because of design activity—whether by chance, necessity, or intention—and becomes part of the world. To a lesser degree, evil in design is something that disrupts balance, harmony, order, and other meaning-making qualities of human existence. Design can be considered evil even by some of the earliest definitions of evil, such as breaking a taboo, or going beyond the territorial boundaries of the tribe. The modern creative imperative to "break out of the box" is an example of how this form of evil has in many cases become banal. In every case, evil is not merely the absence of something desired but also the presence of something immensely unsettling and undesirable.

Even when the splendor of a particular design is clearly apparent and bears witness to the best of human potential, that design often has aberrant effects, in addition to those desired and expected. Unintended, systemic consequences of an innovated design make themselves visible in both the near and long term. These consequences arise out of not knowing enough about the complexity of the design context prior to designing, and not understanding enough about the dynamics of introducing a new set of relationships or variables into a complex environment.

Designers, in their rational persona, imagine that this situation can be improved by just learning more about the nature of complex realities. However, there are some outcomes that cannot be mitigated through more knowledge or more information. It is impossible to be comprehensive in the acquisition of knowledge, particularly design knowledge concerning how to guarantee outcomes that are only good. Judgments are always made in the absence of perfect knowledge, and there are always surprises in the form of unintended consequences when changes are made to the real world. It is impossible to predict and control every outcome of a design intervention made in the context of a complex, particular situation.

There are certain qualities or effects of design that can only be considered as evil in light of all the variety of ways that evil has been defined throughout the ages. It's also true that some of these evil outcomes are considered to be inevitable, necessary, or unavoidable. We now briefly discuss three categories of evil that can be the consequence of any design.

Necessity—natural evil

- Going beyond boundaries
- Natural order of life—survival at any cost
- Lost opportunities
- Lost alternatives
- Point of view
- Natural force

Chance—accidental evil

- Power without understanding
- Cause without connection
- Misfortune and accidents
- Breakdown of natural order

Intension—willful evil

- Destroying life and life-giving essence
- Power without charity
- Agency without community
- Destroy other's selfhood
- Using others as a means only
- Separation from unity

Figure 11.2
Categories of evil in design

This classification schema builds a conceptual framework for reflective consideration in any design approach (see figure 11.2).

Our first category is *natural evil*, which is always an integral part of the process of change, including the types of changes wrought by design. This is a form of evil that is an unavoidable part of all life. In any creative act, something new is brought into the world at the expense of the old—which is then destroyed. There may be good and necessary reasons for the change brought on by design, but that does not deny the real and painful experience of grief and emptiness, brought by the loss of that which has been replaced.

By definition, any design is an act going beyond established boundaries—in other words, "thinking outside the box." This is also one of the oldest definitions of evil. In most cases, everyday designing isn't considered boundary crossing or breaking because those boundaries that such designs do cross or break are too weak to be thought of as strong norms in the same sense as a taboo, for example. Moreover, these boundaries usually are not even visible as boundaries for behavior.

Those designs and designers that are seen as causing changes affecting the normal routine of life, however, often are treated with a certain amount of irritation, if not outright hostility. This is because they have crossed a boundary maintaining the defined limits of normal or typical everyday activity. This form of design evil can be perilous to the designer, because even if the change is for the benefit of those affected, the designer is still cast as an enemy of people's peace of mind and their routine existence.

New designs always bring shadows with them. There are always unintended consequences associated with new designs, many of which can be quite negative. This is related to another, more obvious natural evil—the loss of opportunities. When a design is brought into the world and made real, its very presence excludes other opportunities. The substantial investment of money, energy, material, and time in a new design directly prohibits other attempts to make alternative designs and realities because of lack of resources. This also holds true for more abstract investments, such as pride and status. This is because identity and self-image become invested in a commitment to the new reality emerging as a consequence of the new design's meaningful presence. This form of evil is closely related to the "survival-at-any-cost" strategy of evolution. Even though it appears this strategy is the essence of nature, in our human vocabulary it carries the suspicion of being an evil that seriously needs to be redeemed.

New designs also bring with them specific points of view that define them as evil because of our human frame of reference. The material, corporeal world forms the substance of design, yet this realm is considered evil and base in many spiritual traditions. Humans are encouraged to avoid focusing on this aspect of life, yet it is the very material from which a designer assembles his or her design palette.

Associated with this perspective of evil is the old and enduring notion that evil is a natural and eminent force in the affairs of people: one must continually balance and compensate for the effect of this unrelenting evil energy that's always at work in the natural order of things.

Our second category is *accidental evil*. This type of design evil can be thought of as avoidable. Some examples are: power without understanding, agency without interrelationship (i.e., acting without personal connection to consequences), and the misfortune of being in the wrong place at the wrong time as a matter of mischance, bad luck, or tragedy. This form of evil happens out of ignorance, carelessness, or inattention and is not the outcome of an intention to do harm. For example, the design of toys that are actually dangerous for children is the consequence of inattention to those being served. Accidental evil can be modified, or mitigated, by becoming more fully informed and aware when engaging in design.

Good design judgments are dependent on having the right design knowledge, but that's not all. Design knowledge cannot be separated from the "knower." Therefore, in design, character counts. This is similar to the way that good character counts in making wise decisions, in the absence of a predetermined outcome. Good design is dependent on good designers as much as on the best information or know-how.

Finally, there is the category of *willful evil*. In a design context, this includes power without charity and agency without community—in other words, acting on people's behalf without their contractual consent to do so. It also includes dominance over others such as collective dominance over the individual, individual dominance over the collective, and individual dominance over another individual. The Kantian form of willful evil involves the use of people as a means only rather than an end. Finally, it includes the destruction of life, especially human life and life-giving essence.

These are just a few examples of intentional evil that can become a part of design. The history of human affairs is filled with designs that were evil by intention, such as those of Albert Speer, the German architect, who among other things created organizational designs based on slave labor for the Nazis during World War II. A more recent example is the design of Web-based technology that intrudes on unsuspecting users of the World Wide Web. This design also shields the identity of all those involved in the creation and use of child pornography websites, for example. Powerful design theories and approaches can be used in the creation of things, concrete or abstract, that history will hold as evil in the most literal sense, such as the design of nuclear weapons, which were considered defensible in their time.

Becoming good at design, or helping others to become good at design, does not assure that good design will be the outcome. The theories and practices of design are still subject to human willfulness. As human beings we are not bound to proscriptions of character that guarantee our good intentions as well as magnificent designs. That challenge is well beyond the scope of this book, but it is an essential consideration for designers and design stakeholders.

How is it possible to become a designer and accept design as a legitimate and sensible human activity that ought to be supported and developed by the larger human enterprise when evil is intimate to the whole enterprise? A wise next step would be to embrace the essential nature of design and prepare accordingly. This includes resolutely accepting design's most uncertain, contradictory, dangerous, and promising summons (see figure 11.3).

ACCEPT CHALLENGE OF DESIGN
- no right answers
- no givens
- not comprehensive

ACCEPT POWER OF DESIGN
- create real world

ACCEPT RESPONSIBILITY OF DESIGN
- service to other

ACCEPT ACCOUNTABILITY OF DESIGN
- evil of design
- guarantor-of-design
- artifact evokes own reality

ACCEPT PARADOXES OF DESIGN
- both/all and none

ACCEPT DISCIPLINE OF DESIGN
- skill
- authentic engagement
- focus
- limits

ACCEPT POTENTIAL OF DESIGN
- change human evolution
- fulfill human desire
- evoke the sublime
- create the beautiful
- cause new reality to come into being
- secure the ethical and just
- take a wise action from infinite possibilities
- meet basic functional needs and expectations

Figure 11.3
Acceptance in design

While focusing on the evil of design, it is good to remember that the splendor of design reaches beyond the grasp of the potential and actual consequences of evil. We truly can create the sublime, despite imperfect designers and an unpredictable, dangerous world. Design can accommodate the hopes and aspirations of every human being, even given strict limits and imperfections of design situations and designers. Human nature is such that it is completely natural—not unnatural—to take on the challenge of co-creating the world. And human designers must do this by fully participating in the tension that results from the struggle between doing good or evil in our all too real world. This is why it is so important that we create a design culture to act as a crucible for this intense and demanding work.

We live in a world of designed artifacts, some concrete and others abstract. Together with the natural world, these designs—whether things, systems, processes, or symbols—make up the whole of our reality. It is a reality populated by the beautiful and the ugly, the good and bad, and sometimes even the dangerous. Every day, we use—or struggle with—designs of every type of influence, shape, and size. Some of them we love, some we endure, others we hate, but most of them we never even notice. They just exist as a natural part of our lives.

But sometimes a design becomes the conveyor of *soul*. Soul is an animating essence, an essential quality of a holistic, architectonic design. We are struck by the emotional power of such a design—by its beauty, integrity, and usefulness. We marvel at the way it bestows meaning and value on itself, on the lives it touches and in its environment. As a designer, measuring our own steps along the design path, this is what we are, in our more noble moments, striving to create—designs that emanate soul, that are part of something unbounded by time, place, and material.

How do we distinguish those shallower designs that are superficially stylish or fashionable from those that express levels of excellence that reach down into the realm of soul? What is the process by which we experience, evaluate, and judge our designs? What is it that makes us experience designs as inferior and meaningless, or superior and soulful? These are some of the questions we will reflect upon in this chapter.

Consciously or unconsciously, we are in constant evaluative relationships with the designs making up our reality. The forms these types of discerning judgment take are not always obvious. Given the importance of this mindfulness, we will spend some time trying to understand how we connect appreciatively to the world, specifically the artificial world that we ourselves are responsible for having created.

One way to broker an understanding is to entertain the idea that our environments—physical, social, and cultural—include all the attending material forms that are, or can be, conveyors of soul (Hillman 1996). They can be *ensouled*. Such a view has crucial consequences for anybody who wishes to be a complete designer. First, how is it possible, for an all-too-human designer, to ensoul a design? Second, why is it important to judge design in this way, using such loaded concepts as "soul" and "ensoulment"? Isn't it sufficient to evaluate designs in the context of efficiency, functionality, quality, experience, or at least excellence?

We don't think so. Quality is not robust enough as a scale of measurement against which to judge "good" design. At least, this holds if the ambition is to create designs that will have a positive and lasting impact on our reality, including how we affirmatively occupy that reality—an ambition to create designs that are of consequence in the emergent course of human destiny that extend, augment, and ennoble our human "being."

Functionality, efficiency, cleverness, usefulness, or whatever other pragmatic measurement we can come up with, doesn't capture, in totality, the way people relate to a design. A design must also be valued and judged by the experience it evokes—how it "moves" people, and by the aesthetic nature of the design as a whole (Dewey 1934). This has to do with relations and connections, with balance and the other aesthetic relationships connecting all possible aspects of the design (Janlert and Stolterman 1997).

The meaning and value of a design is taken in as a feeling of being deeply moved and, as a consequence, of being significantly and meaningfully changed. When we encounter a design's essence or soul, our basic assumptions and worldviews are most likely to be challenged. Something profound happens to us as a consequence of our encountering a design at the level of its ensoulment. Our understanding of the world, of our own place in it and our core judgments, all are changed.

For instance, when we encounter a building that has survived over centuries and has become symbolic of culture and civilization, we may, if we give our full attention, become overwhelmed by the depth and strength of its design. Or, we might find ourselves in an organization so well designed that we take immense pleasure from just being part of it. Or, we touch the fine work of a skilled craftsperson and feel the delicate balance between form and material that leads to exquisite beauty. Sometimes, in situations like this, we get the feeling that such a design could not have been different. We might even feel that it is nearly a perfect design. When we are in the presence of a design bearing soul, we glimpse the splendor of design. We are captured by the realization that design is about the creation of a "soul-full" world.

What a remarkable challenge—to aid in the ensoulment of the world! But, given this as the Holy Grail, we have to accept that it is certain that most of the time we will not reach this ideal. In most instances, we are designing for everyday use, hoping to achieve everyday utility and adequate quality. We are under the pressure of restrictions, such as time, material, resources, and, as always, money. Still, we know that even in the most circumscribed and restricted design situation, there might be a design that will turn out to have all the qualities and attributes of excellence we strive for. In our thousands of endeavors, there just might arise a composition, a choice of material, a never-used organizational assembly, a combination of human skills and nonhuman artifacts that will reveal a fundamental new understanding, an emergence of soulfulness, breaking open any previous restrictions.

What is it that gives a design that special character of wholeness and integrity? It is frequently assumed that quality is something entirely subjective—in other words, "beauty is in the eye of the beholder." It is just as often agreed that taste cannot be judged or defined in any general way. However, there are others who propose the opposite: that quality can be defined without any reference to a specific subject of evaluation. In some aesthetic and art traditions, general definitions of what constitutes both acceptable quality and good taste are asserted. This hangs the discussion concerning quality on a very old and engaging question: Where does quality reside—in the object or in the subject or in the "in between"?

For a designer, the philosophical situation is even more complicated, since we not only have to consider our own appraisal and valuation approaches to quality, but also those of our clients. As designers, we do not stand in isolation from the reality we hope to design. We do our work in close relationship with other people, who may have completely different values and preferences.

Therefore our examination of ensoulment begins with the concepts of *value* and *meaning*. These concepts define two of a myriad of dimensions that can denote the quality of a design—the intrinsic value of the design itself—value or worth—and the value of the design in relation to something larger—meaning (Nozick 1989). It is important to note that from a philosophical viewpoint distinguishing value from meaning in this way is fairly controversial. We will still use this distinction, however, not for a philosophical purpose but as a good way to help designers think about the nature of design.

Let's jump into our discussion of value by noting that all designs have their own intrinsic value or worth. This intrinsic value is what you are taught to recognize and evaluate in an art appreciation class, or a literature class, or during a wine tasting. When we are shown how different components are interrelated, how structure, form, material, texture, smell, taste, and so on fit into the overall theme or purpose of the thing we are evaluating, we learn to see and appreciate the intrinsic value of the design itself. We can become a *connoisseur*. To be a connoisseur of something means that you can discern, understand, and appreciate subtleties in a design (we discussed connoisseurship further in chapter 10).

The intrinsic value is captured in an integrated, unified, and emergent whole, which Nozick (1989) termed the *organic unity*. The intrinsic value is one reason why we may actually appreciate a specific building, or organization, even though we do not like what the building or organization stands for, or what its purpose and use are.

Just as creating a soulful design takes time and energy, so does the process of sincere valuing. To value something means to stand in close relation to it. This is why people react strongly against those who dismiss their favorite design (be it a book, music, food, building, or game) without paying the design enough respect through close examination and attention.

Value does not have to be defined as necessarily dependent on a context or larger system. In reality, however, this is not the typical situation. In fact, it is quite often the opposite. We as individuals typically are quite bad at evaluating things that make up our reality based solely on their intrinsic value. More often, we take a much more intentional, or purpose-oriented, approach in our process of evaluating designs. We expect them not only to have intrinsic value but also to be useful, to be relevant—that is, to be meaningful. We want our lives to have meaning because of such designs.

A design has *meaning* when we can see how it is connected to other things that we *value*. This may lead to an infinite regression, as it is always possible to ask what the meaning is of that which we connect to the design in order to evaluate its meaningfulness.

However, we can also see this as a consequence of value and meaning being closely intertwined. For instance, the meaning of an object can be ascertained by linking it with something of value, and something of value can gain meaning by being linked to something else of value. What really makes the difference is the nature of the linkages—the relationships and connections.

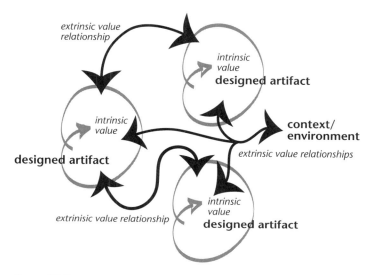

Figure 12.1
Value and meaning making in design

This examination of value and meaning gives us a chance to see the difficulty of evaluating designs. We cannot evaluate a design only through its intrinsic value, or only through its extrinsic meaning—there is also the interrelationship or interconnection between the two that must be taken into account (see figure 12.1). It is important—at this juncture—to understand that the way these concepts are defined earlier in this chapter presupposes a static reality. In real life our perception of reality and our understanding of reality constantly change. This changes our preconditions for evaluating the value and meaning of a design, as the conditions for making such judgments likewise constantly change.

A design with a strong interdependence between value and meaning entertains the necessary conditions for our recognition of it as a conveyor of a soul. In this sense, soul is the animating essence of the original unifying design parti. It denotes a design that has both *intrinsic value* and *relational meaning*. We experience this form of soul when we encounter a design with a unified coherence, in relationship to something giving it meaning. Such a design is sometimes described as having "integrity" and "wholeness", or of being "rich," "deep," and "authentic." All of these words point to the fact that such a design has a depth and complexity that are not easily discerned.

Even if a design possesses value and meaning in some measure, this will not necessarily assure the presence of soul. If the design does not fit effortlessly into its specific situation, we will not be able to experience its soul. If the design is "ahead of its time," or doesn't make its debut at the right place and the right time, we will—despite its value and meaning—not be able to appreciate it fully. We might be able to appreciate its value and, separately, its meaning, but if it is not a unified whole it will lack the valence for the habitation of soul. In addition, it must be in resonance with its context.

Value and meaning, as defined earlier, do not fully account for, or illustrate, what it is that makes a design soulful. Widening our discussion with more abstract conceptualizations would bring us closer to a full understanding of ensoulment, but at the same time, would carry us too far away from the integrative thinking about design that we have tried to focus on in this book. Rather, we will stop here and define the appearance of soul in a design as an emergent phenomenon that is made possible when value and meaning in a design are in *resonance with a particular situation*—in other words, when it is a holistic compositional assembly.

A compositional assembly is about details and relations, connections and systemics, wholeness and integrity—in effect, it is about giving presence to those things that evoke soul. Composition is very much the emergent quality of a system's unifying essence, in the same way that soul and character are emergent qualities of composition. Therefore, it is not made visible without effort. Every detail in the system contributes to its overall composition, but the composition transcends the details. The connective structures, functions, and forms constituting a design, in compositional relationships with the appropriate context and purpose, set the stage for the emergence of transcendent qualities and attributes. How a designer combines and proportions all of these elements determines whether the composition is strong or weak; and whether it will, to a greater or lesser degree, succeed or fail.

It is not easy to find universal concepts that fully capture the qualities of architectonic designs. But when a design evokes a sense of unity and integrity, it is felt to be a holistic composition: it holds together in oneness, with a purpose and intention.

Another aspect of ensoulment that is sometimes used as a measure of quality is apparent *timelessness*. Given that, with the passage of enough time, everything is temporary, timelessness is not about time-based considerations. A timeless design can be understood as a design that is not only appreciated at a specific time and in a specific place, for a specific purpose, but also is valued by people in different times and places because it represents enduring and commonly held human values (Alexander 1979). Timeless designs are evaluated for qualities of abiding excellence and virtue. Such designs are not valued for timely appearance in the world. They are not examples of the latest fashion or style or movement in—to give only a few examples—clothes, cars, music, or art. They do not become "old fashioned" with the passage of time. Designs with soul stand outside of the realm of time. In this way they express the enduring qualities that spiritual traditions seek through religious experience.

How is this timeless quality possible, if we have defined the expression of soul in a design to be the manifestation of a resonance between its value and meaning, in a specific situation? One answer could be that soul is evoked in a timeless design not merely because it resonates with a particular situation, but because it resonates with something more enduring, more constant, and more eternal. What could this larger, eternal reference be? There are several possibilities. A traditional option could, of course, be found in religion. If a design can be understood in relationship to the structure or content of religious beliefs, it will have some of the stability of the religion itself. In today's society, we can also imagine using cultural heritage as a general reference. However, the most powerful reference today, which evokes timelessness, is the notion of the natural or nature.

Timeless design, in this context, can be seen as a design that has values and meaning, which relate to things in our society that are very stable over time or are outside of time—in other words, it is sustainable. Given this prerequisite, timeless designs are immensely difficult to realize. A designer is typically too preoccupied or influenced by contemporary styles, fashions, fads, and "the latest" theories (flavors of the month). To be able to grasp contemporary ideals, as well as relate them to something that is less temporal, may be a task too difficult to be done as an intentional act by the average designer. The timelessness that we see in some designs is, perhaps, more often a result of luck rather than exceptional skills.

In a society like our own, which depends so heavily on its designs, we need both that which is timeless and that which is meant only for the presently desired yet sustainable end. We need timeless designs to remind us of those values that are unchanging, common, and eternal. We need temporal designs to serve immediate pressing needs. Timeless designs bear witness to our common humanity, from which we form our cultures and other diverse expressions of valued creations. Temporal designs exhibit our ability to react and adapt to the moment. The design approach is a lifelong challenge to create designs that some day might be appreciated as timeless.

To ensoul a design in a way that serves people now and far into the future is something worth striving for.

So, an ensouled design appears to be a complex combination of knowledge, skill, circumstances, and luck. But, what happens when we encounter a design that is already in existence? How do we recognize or experience the soul in it? Does it matter how we approach a design? Do we need any special knowledge, skill, procedures, or preconditions to be able to divine the soul of that design?

The answer is yes. But a purely analytical approach is not the best way to perceive a design's soul. Such souls are ephemeral creatures, not easily analyzed into constituent parts and functions. Instead each design has to be understood as a whole, as one unified experience. According to a popular view of the late nineteenth-century artistic and intellectual movement, romanticism, there is only one means for accessing original unity and that is through the instrumentality of *immediate experience.*

For some people, the immediate experience is believed to be a way to reach the almost magical, hidden dimensions of our everyday world. To see the world holistically, as a sacred wholeness, where every single aspect of the totality of experience is also seen as a member of, or even the same thing as, "the" divine. Still, there are many other ways of interpreting immediate experience. For instance, it could be thought of as a different form of rationality or intuitive knowledge. Whatever it is, the immediate experience of a design is not a question of total subjectivism, or relativism. A design carries something that strongly influences us, something that affects our imagination. It is not about the superficial surface of the design, or is it about its depth. The surface and the depth create an emergent totality or image. We experience an artifact as ensouled when its image shows a sufficient complexity. "An object bears witness to itself in the image it offers, and its depth lies in the complexities of this image" (Hillman 1992). It is in this complexity that we can see and experience the carefulness and concern that have been devoted to the composition and the production of the design.

The idea of immediate experience tells us that designs have to be approached as a whole. They must be experienced as creators of complex and rich images. This does not mean that we just wait around for a design to jump out of its seat and grab our full attention. To be able to read and appreciate the soul of a design, we must pay the same kind of full attention in our examination of it as the designer did in the design process.

Carefulness and concern for both the details and overall compositional order and organization are things we look for in good designs. It is, in part, how we recognize ensouled artifacts. To make an artifact soulful requires time and effort. We have to "put our own soul" into the design. But what is also needed is a similar devotion from the beholder or user. There is symmetry between the carefulness required from the designer and the user. Such careful attention and examination of artifacts can be seen as a manifestation of notitia.

As designers, we're all familiar with the situation in which we have designed something, really putting our hearts and our souls into the work, but when introduced into the world the work is not taken seriously. Even complimentary critiques, such as, "that looks good," or "that is a nice design," are basically worthless to us, if we suspect that it is not based on a careful examination or full engagement. What we are looking for from those evaluating our design is statements that show that they have devoted authentic attention, notitia, to our design.

Another aspect of ensouled designs is related to the notion of *caring*. As designers we design for the entire life span of the designs we create. We need stakeholders to be drawn to take accountability, to be responsible, for the well-being of the design throughout its life. The designer can facilitate this by creating ensouled designs. To do this requires that the designer strive to create a sensibility of the whole—the internal unified coherence of how the design relates to a specific situation—for this is what makes it feel as if it were timeless. When we ensoul our work, we also make it into something loved and precious; when something is precious to us, we want to care for it. Beloved artifacts give us pleasure when we use them. They even bring pleasure when we are simply in close proximity to them. This is true for all manner of designs—the soulful experience, organization, car, cup, toy, or learning process. We find them soulful. We want to protect them. Thus, by ensouling our designs, we create a desire in others to care for their future use and development.

We live in a world of designed, artificial environments. Within this artificial world, we have created organizations, work processes, procedures, and rules. To live in such environments, especially if they are constantly changing, takes time and energy. If these environments are without soul, they drain us of energy. An ensouled environment, on the other hand, *evokes life*. When we encounter ensouled designs and environments, we are energized. We feel that our own souls are filled. To take part in the ongoing design of reality is therefore a task of ever-greater responsibility. It's not just a question of creating a functioning, ethical, and aesthetic environment, but also involves creating a reality that can either give people energy and hope, or make their lives poorer in spirit.

The creation of ensouled designs not only affects the user, but also the designer. The act of creating ensouled compositions infuses life-enhancing energy into the designer, as much as it does the client. On the one hand, to be given the opportunity to discharge design intentions in a manner that assures a soulful outcome is one of the designer's most satisfying rewards. It feels great! On the other hand, to not be able to work in a soulful way drains the designer's energy and the splendor inherent in designing disappears. What remains is merely a process of adapting and compromising to given conditions and predetermined outcomes. The deeper meaning of being a designer vanishes.

Let's recap what we understand about the ensoulment process. It is abundantly clear that there are no guidelines, no techniques, and no straightforward methods on how to ensoul our designs. The entire process presupposes the utilization of much energy, time, and careful attention. In addition, it is not enough to focus on the surface appearance of designs, the visual shape or sensual presence of the artifact. There must be more.

Ensoulment is about wholeness and architectonic composition, as well as value and meaning. It is about carefulness when attending to details and relationships. To ensoul a design—in a way that attracts attention and appreciation—demands a respect for the materials, the structure, the shape and its social dimensions. To ensoul a design is to evoke energy and life.

When we start to understand design as a process of ensoulment, when we become aware that every design process and composition ultimately contributes to a larger whole, we—as designers—begin to realize more fully our responsibility to the planet as a whole. We become aware that every design process, every composition, contributes to a larger design. To be a part of this endlessly unfolding process is both wonderful and terrifying, as every design—no matter how small or presumably insignificant—either contributes to that wholeness or diminishes it. The responsibility is there. The challenge is clear—expedient lifelessness or splendor.

13 The Guarantor-of-Design (g.o.d.)

Design is an act of world creation. As such it can be experienced both as inspiring and intimidating. As a world creator, a designer can be overwhelmed by questions such as: Do I have the right to cause such significant change in the world? What is the right approach to take when making such changes? What kind of changes are good, or just, and for whom? As a designer, am I fully responsible and accountable for my designs and to whom? Can I be relieved of responsibility in some way? If not, how can I prepare for this responsibility and assume the liability of being fully accountable for my design judgments and actions?

Today we understand that our designs can dramatically change the conditions of reality experienced by ordinary people. The world is becoming more and more a human artifact, a designed place. Some scientists have even applied a new term to the present era, calling it the Anthropocene age—in other words, the human age. Nowhere is the globe untouched by human activity. To be a designer is therefore to be the co-creator of a new world. It is a calling of enormous responsibility, with its concomitant accountability. This is true even if each individual designer is only involved in a very small design act, playing merely a minor part in the totality of the redesign of an emerging new reality. Our individual designs will always be contributing causes to an overall composition that is an emergent new world.

Given this fact, what is the nature of this ever-renewing world—one that each designer is consciously or unconsciously midwifing into existence through her or his designed contribution? Is it possible to discern the attributes of good design and to be intentional about evoking their presence in such a complex environment? The only thing we know for sure is that it is impossible to predict with certainty whether a realized design will result in the betterment of human life. We can hope for this to be the case, but nothing is certain before it becomes real and begins to

have its effect. Also, we can never know what the unintended consequences of a design will be and whom they will affect. So, with this state
of affairs in mind, what are the limitations to our responsibility, as designers, in co-creating this new world, and what are our fiduciary duties? Can
we accept unlimited responsibility for our part in world making? If we do
accept this responsibility, what does that mean for our accountability and
liability? How can we become competent designers in the face of so much
uncertainty and unpredictability?

Most designers would probably answer that they don't really have any
responsibility for the whole—that they can only take responsibility for
their small piece of reality. Often, designers feel they are merely agents
working for a client, doing what they are told to do in exchange for fair
compensation and professional recognition. But are these valid answers?
Are there valid arguments for making the case that, as a designer, you do
not have responsibility for your design in the context of the whole? This
thorny question is the focus of this chapter.

For most of us, it would be truly comforting to know with certainty that
we are doing good things for the right reasons—that our imagination and
creativity lead us to the right conclusions, solutions, ideas, and designs
within clearly delineated bounds of responsibility. But how can this
happen? Is it even possible for a designer to learn how "to know" in that
way? Is there a guarantor of good, dependable design judgments, whether
designing a life, an experience, an artifact, a system, or an organization?

These are difficult questions to answer. We will begin our response by
distinguishing between two kinds of *guarantors* that are involved in design.
C. West Churchman used the concept of guarantor as the ninth category
in the formulation of his twelve "categories for planning" (Churchman
1971, 1979). Churchman stated: "I was reminded of Descartes' 'Dangerous
voyage' of doubt, and his search for a guarantor, and of Kant's vision, in
the second Critique of humanity's gradually reconciling virtue and happi-
ness, and the need to postulate a guarantor of this endless search" (1979).

At an annual meeting for the Operations Research Society of America,
Churchman presented his formulation of the guarantor category, which
resulted in an arresting response to the concept by one of the attendees.
Recalled Churchman: "I gave my luncheon address, which fell unheeded
into the pool, except for one ripple. The ripple was Wroe Alderson, who
delighted, suggested a slight addition, 'guarantor of destiny'—or, in these
days when everything has its acronym, GOD" (Churchman 1979).

Building on this seminal idea, we first consider the *guarantor-of-destiny*
(G.O.D.) in relation to design. This is the challenge of discerning the guar-

antor of human intentions. It is the expected guarantee that choosing to engage in the complex and challenging process of design is a good decision, one that will secure the desired improvement in the lives of everyone touched by design. The locus and character of the guarantor-of-destiny is the fundamental concern of the clients and other stakeholders who are being served in the design process. It is the foundation upon which they can place their belief that they serve their best interests by choosing to initiate and participate in a design process.

The purpose of trying to gain some instrumental understanding of the guarantor-of-destiny is to find enough certainty and security in humankind's ability to deal intentionally, and successfully, with the deeper issues of life—issues that have been the focus of philosophic and religious discourse through the ages. These issues are only obliquely confronted in any design process. For example, what does it mean to be human? What is the purpose of our individual and collective lives, to what end? Is the cosmos indifferent to humans, or do we have significance? Is the world an accident of physics, or is it designed? Can there be change by intention, or only as the consequences of chance and necessity? Do we have the right to expect to gain any deeper understanding of others or ourselves? Although they may not be conscious of it, destiny is the foremost implicit issue for clients of design. The guarantor-of-destiny—G.O.D—is an implied contract among all of us, given the unknowns, the unknowable and the uncertainties in the human condition; that what we ought to do is ascertainable, what we try to do is possible and what we can do counts.

Next, we consider the allied idea of a guarantor-of-design (g.o.d.) that is focused on the legitimacy and certainty of the designer's actions and accountability. In our day-to-day lives as designers, we rarely spend time pondering questions of human destiny. Instead, we tend to deal with particular design situations, involving a particular design process that occurs at a particular place and time, with particular people and resources. Regardless of whether we choose to be aware of them or not, questions of responsibility for outcomes in design decisions, and actions in the particular design situation, create difficult challenges for designers. They also have significant consequences for clients and other stakeholders. These difficulties lead to the designer's wish for some kind of guarantor, someone or something that can guarantee that the decisions and judgments made are the right ones and that they can be achieved in the real world. This frames the longing search for a guarantor-of-design.

It seems common for designers, even at the limited level of the particular project or program, to be unwilling to accept full responsibility for the consequences of their designs. This is, in many ways, not surprising, as taking on responsibility can be not only challenging, but also quite dangerous morally, socially, and politically. To bring this issue of design responsibility to greater light and open it up to reflective dialogue, we will present some common ways designers relieve themselves of account-ability for their design decisions. We will argue that these attempts by designers to divorce themselves from responsibility for the ultimate out-comes of their designs cannot be justified and are unacceptable, given the accumulating effect of small designs on the emergent design of social reality.

One of the main ways designers avoid responsibility is by cloaking their actions within the tradition of "truth telling." In this tradition, we do not have to take on any responsibility for unintended outcomes, or for the larger emergent whole, since we are only obeying principles that transcend our individual volition. The only thing we have to be concerned with is whether or not we possess true knowledge and how we came to acquire it. In this "truth-telling" tradition, our focus is on appropriate methods of inquiry, controlled techniques of observation and record keeping, which guide us with certainty in our search for reliable truth. This design approach to avoidance is strikingly similar to the Western tradition of scientific inquiry used to prescribe action.

Design, however, does not reside restrictively in the realm of the true. It lives in the world of the real and ideal as well. Within the context of the real and the ultimate particular, we will never be able to find absolute truths that can guide us in our design actions. This is because, as we said earlier, description and explanation do not prescribe action. Moreover, predication and control do not justify action. As designers, we cannot depend on a source of wisdom outside of ourselves for guidance that will relieve us of our ultimate responsibility. Design decisions are based on judgment and judgment is both personal and situational. In the end, design is always an act of faith in our abilities and ourselves.

Sometimes the nature of the real situation can be difficult to handle. It provides the designer with a potential for power and authority, which can be both overwhelming and frightening. It is overwhelming when you realize that you can act on the world in such a way as to create significant and irreversible change in other people's lives. It is frightening when people hold you responsible for these changes. Or, more perversely, when not held responsible, you may feel disinclined to take responsibility on your own and become accountable for getting better at what you do, thus possibly perpetuating poor habits of judgment.

There are several additional routes designers use to escape responsibility. These strategies are not necessarily chosen in a conscious and intentional way. They are not tactics used solely by designers who lack courage or ethics. These approaches are quite likely very natural reactions to situations where a designer comes face to face with mind-numbing complexity and uncertainty, or when the designer is not in possession of enough resources, knowledge, or skill to fulfill the task at hand.

All of these strategies attempt to find some solid and dependable base for justifying design actions. This yearning can be labeled as the search for a guarantor-of-design. It is a search that takes on many disguises and can be found in every design field. The search for a guarantor-of-design can be understood as a way to reduce the designers' feeling of isolation, which can occur as a result of their assuming sole or primary responsibility for a design. A guarantor-of-design constructs a means of measuring design judgments and decisions against some standard of "good" or "bad." This allows the designer to move with confidence through the design process, lending legitimacy to the outcome at the same time.

We are not arguing that every designer is trying consciously to escape responsibility. There are designers who embrace responsibility, not only as something necessary (although problematic), but also as a challenge that gives design a special quality, character, and attraction. Responsibility means to be accountable for how one employs power. To be able to use your power skillfully and appropriately to change the world is one of the real wonders of design competency. But even for those who already embrace responsibility, we believe it is important to reflect on the source, place, and nature of responsibility in design.

Often within design teams, communication around the issue of responsibility remains foggy at best. Most of us have met with statements like: "I don't think we have to do that, it's not our responsibility," or "We can't do that, no one told us to." This is why everyone on the design team needs to actively reflect on what the concept of the guarantor-of-design means to them, as well as how it relates to colleagues, employers, clients, and society as a whole.

There are at least three reasons why designers search for a guarantor-of-design, each involving a different approach. The first approach involves designers who are trying to move responsibility, the second motive is an attempt to hide responsibility, and finally some designers hope to remove responsibility entirely.

The most common way of avoiding responsibility is to try to restrict the degrees of freedom in the design process, by moving responsibility to something outside the control of the designer. This can be done in many different ways. You can move responsibility to the design process itself, or to other people, or to some other guiding principle.

For instance, a designer can use a prescriptive method that guides him or her lockstep through the entire design process. The more detailed and rigid the method, the fewer degrees of freedom the designer has. A completely controlled and comprehensive method restricts the designer's freedom fully. It means that the method is the sole bearer of responsibility. If a designer rigorously follows the method, he or she cannot be blamed for not being rational, or logical, or competent. The designer can show that the method was followed and if something is to be judged critically, it is the method, not the designer. By following this route, the role of the designer is transformed into something more along the lines of a simple operant.

Another way to move responsibility is to turn to other people for help. A designer can always argue that he or she is only trying to satisfy someone else. It could be a client, a decision maker, a customer, a stakeholder, or an end user. The designer can ask any one of these people for help in the process, in a way that relieves the designer of responsibility. If the designer always lets other people decide on choices and solutions, responsibility will by default be removed from his or her shoulders. Unfortunately, at the same time, the designer's skill and specific knowledge disappears, since the designer has stopped being the person creating the new and the unexpected architectonic composition. When a designer only produces what other people want or decide, that designer simply becomes a facilitator.

Shifting responsibility by any of the means described is not, necessarily, problematic or bad if a good outcome still emerges. It is not ideal, however. In no case is it possible to practice design—as an authentically competent designer—if responsibility has been removed by any of these options. The point we would like to make about shifting responsibility is that it still leaves a situation where responsibility is apparent and open to judgments: the only change is that the designer is no longer the focal point for accountability.

Another approach is to hide responsibility, or at least to hide it from inspection. This approach can happen in any number of ways. We will discuss a few here. We call these forms of hiding responsibility internal, external, or administrative *slough-off*.

Like an artist, a designer can argue that the design is a result of an internal force, such as intuition, or a feeling that is beyond the control of the designer—the internal slough-off. A designer who uses this approach often trusts this nebulous internal stimulus as a reliable source and uses it as a guarantor-of-design. Expressions such as "I trust my intuition," "Let your feelings guide your way," or "Just follow your heart," are common. These internal sources of inspiration cannot, by definition, be inspected by the designer—or by anyone else. Using this platform, the designer argues that he or she only did what had to be done in response to these internal sources. Since these sources are situated beyond the reach of our conscious, reflective mind, we cannot analyze, inspect, or influence them and, therefore, cannot judge them. The designer acts only as a conduit, a spokesperson, or a messenger, for his or her inner inspiration.

By looking to the spiritual, the designer can find external sources of guidance—the external or spiritual slough-off. A spiritual source can be used as a guarantor-of-design for almost any kind of design process. We can count on this source to provide us with insights, ideas, and guidance, and, as a soothing consequence—peace of mind. A spiritual approach is used in order to see things in a different way, or to interpret reality in a more true or ideal way. To let yourself be a channel for a spiritual mandate shields you from responsibility as a designer, which makes the rationale behind your design actions very difficult for anyone else to inspect, analyze, or challenge. This can be the whispering of the muses, the demands of selfish genes, the commands of a personal God, or the manipulations of evil spirits—in other words, "the devil made me do it." In extreme cases, this can lead to situations where the designer ceases to be an individual, or independent entity, and becomes essentially part of something transcendent of the human realm—something impossible to hold accountable to mere human agency.

One of the easiest ways to hide responsibility is to imbed all actions in a complex, administrative web of responsibilities and authority relationships—the administrative slough-off. When this web becomes convoluted enough, it's practically impenetrable; it is impossible to tell what consequence resulted from what cause and which decisions affected what actions. This effectively stops anyone from knowing whose ideas are actually being manifested in the design. The administrative approach is often more accidental than it is intentional. In many design processes, we end up in an administrative situation no one really wanted or planned for and responsibility just seems to evaporate into a web of contorted relations. With this slough-off, the individual designer may still act as a piecemeal designer, but—in relationship to the overall design process—it is now impossible to know who is responsible.

As was the case with moving responsibility, hiding responsibility is not necessarily problematic or bad if the outcomes are acceptable. Although the strategy of moving responsibility is often deliberate, the hiding process seems to be more unintentional. Frequently, it is simply a consequence of many decisions being made in a helter-skelter fashion, or out of embedded habit regarding how the design process should be carried out.

When a designer can convincingly show that the result of a design process is based on something that is not negotiable, or subjective, but is, instead, something truly universal, then responsibility has been effectively removed. This can be done in a number of ways, but some approaches are more common than others.

A popular approach is the scientific method. Scientifically derived truth, as the guarantor-of-design, is one way to say that the process cannot end in any way other than the one prescribed by the universal laws of logic and reason. When the design process is guided by scientific truths, the correct design will always be determined in relation to nature and natural laws. Nature is the container of all answers; if we obey the rules dictated by nature, we cannot be accused of making the wrong kind of design decisions.

Another approach is to use the principle of ecological sustainability as the most appropriate guide for decision making. If nature's design is taken as a given—and we assume that humans have no right to question or change the natural order of things—then, everything we design has to be in full accord with the way nature requires things to be. The only responsibility the designer has is to maintain, or preserve, nature's naturally ordered design.

Even in the absence of universal, scientific truths, or some template of nature's own design, one can find belief systems that provide the means to remove responsibility. In these cases, the designer only acts in accordance with something larger, truer, or nobler than any set of criteria that may emerge from a specific client's expressed needs.

When all else fails, designers can simply use the logic of harsh, everyday reality as an argument for not assuming responsibility. "I can only do so much!" a designer might wail. In this case, he or she feels constrained by a concrete, real-world situation and, therefore, claims that his or her design outcome is not a matter of choice or volition. Here, we're letting chance or fate be our guarantor-of-design.

All of these choices generally can be seen as attempts to restrict the degrees of freedom in a design practice. But they differ significantly in how they operate in practice and the types of assumptions they make about the role of the designer. There are no simple answers to the questions: Who should have responsibility in design? How should this responsibility be put in operation? Answers to these questions will continue to elude us, just as we will never know the exact difference between the particular and the true. We will never find an absolute, or universally correct, answer. But we believe it's possible to argue that based on our definition of what good design is, if you want to be a good designer there are no justifiable ways to move, hide, or remove responsibility for your own actions.

Given our very busy lives, we often want to minimize our efforts and the energy necessary to accomplish things we need done. We try to find ways to make things happen without our complete attention. This is also true in design. Since design is very demanding and basically very personal, it takes a lot of intellectual energy. If we are afraid of doing the wrong thing in a design process, it is only natural that we search for ways to reduce the need for expending energy and personal engagement while attending to this concern.

But there is no guarantor-of-design "out there" that allows us to conserve personal energy and minimize focused attention. None of the approaches described in this chapter are valid candidates for such a guarantor. Design is about creating a new reality, and there are no givens in that process. There are no theories, methods, techniques, or tools that can calculate, predict, or envision the truly best future reality. The true future does not exist as a predetermined, objective fact. As human beings, we have the capacity to create a different future—restricted only by our present reality and our imagination.

So, given that responsibility can never be escaped, where does this leave us? Can we find a guarantor-of-design anywhere? We argue that, in fact, it is possible only through the development of one's own design character.

A designer's character is his or her core. No judgment made by a designer can be made solely based on comprehensive knowledge. Judgments always depend on the designer's core values as introduced in chapter 8. Design judgment, in this sense, is an act of faith in one's core values and beliefs. The designer has to believe in his or her capacity to make good judgments. In design, we find many kinds of judgments, all with their roots grounded in the character of the designer. It is a question of a designer's whole "human-being." As a consequence, this leaves us in a place where we must consider the designer to be a self-reflective individual, with a fully developed character. This character manifests itself through design tasks, illuminating the designer's values, beliefs, skills, sensibility, reason, ethics, and aesthetics.

Thus, designers must learn to accept design responsibility as something integral to each designer's character. But how can we reduce the stress and worry designers invariably feel regarding this responsibility? We think that the more a designer understands the real nature of design, the better he or she can deal with the responsibility of design. This, in turn, actually enhances the joy of creating new designs. When a designer truly realizes his or her ability and skills, as well as shortcomings, he or she can deal with the dilemmas of responsibility in the only way that works: by learning to live with them.

This is in line with the reasoning of Martha Nussbaum, when she argues that we need education that liberates students. When this is done, we get students that "have looked into themselves and developed the ability to separate mere habit and convention from what they can defend by argument" (Nussbaum 1997). Not only will this help students to become more personally accountable in their creative work, it also allows them to "have ownership of their own thought and speech, and this imparts to them a dignity that is far beyond the outer dignity of class and rank." Nussbaum argues that this is the only way to cultivate students who will not be uncritical, moral relativists. For her, ownership of one's own mind yields understanding that "some things are good and some bad, some defensible and others indefensible."

The same is true for designers. We must nourish our own dignity of mind in order to develop the necessary ability to make advanced design judgments, at our own skill level, within any unique situation. In order for this to happen, designers need to develop a strong character. We agree with Nussbaum when she writes about students that it is possible to "teach them how to argue, rigorously and critically, so that they can call their minds their own."

Robert Nozick (1989) states that in order to create character we have to live the examined life. Like Nussbaum he seems to argue against the idea of an external guarantor. He writes: "When we guide our lives by our own pondered thoughts, it is our life that we are living, not someone else's." To be good designers, we must base our design actions and judgments on our own developed core character.

Now, how does one learn to trust, or even know, one's core character? We can do this by constantly examining our practice and our thoughts. Donald Schön describes this examination as two types of reflection: *reflection-in-action* and *reflection-on-action* (Schön 1983). Reflection-in-action is a first-order reflective process that focuses on each judgment or action taken in the process of our designing something in the particular. Reflection-on-action is a second-order reflective process that involves stepping back from any immediate judgment making that takes place within a specific design process, in order to focus reflectively on the process of our design behavior in general.

It is an approach in line with the ideas of James Hillman, when he discusses character and calling (Hillman 1996). He argues that a person's character has a calling. In order to fully live, you have to live in accordance with your calling. In design terms, we interpret this to mean that each individual is developing into a unique designer and has to form his or her design character in line with his or her design calling. This can't be done if character development is neglected, in the hope of discovering an external guarantor.

So, once again, we are led to the conclusion that there is no justification for an external guarantor-of-design, even if there is a felt need. Designers must accept responsibility for all they design. This accountability must be an integral part of their character. Designers should be relied on to fulfill obligations, not only to their clients, but also to a higher authority, one that is concerned for the sake of others and the environment in which we all live.

This added requirement is not meant to restrain a designer's ability to design, but to improve the designer's capacity to create better designs that will, in turn, have fewer unintended or undesirable outcomes. Any negative consequences the designer incurs by accepting her or his design responsibilities can be mitigated in part through better education, professional training, and ongoing self-reflection.

In terms of education, there is a big difference between *knowledge in design* and *knowledge about design*. To know how to design does not necessarily mean that the designer has a well-developed understanding of the role of being a designer. To have a good understanding of design is the first step toward developing a mature design character.

Reflecting on responsibility, as we have done in this chapter, is one way of better understanding design. If this is taken seriously, it will provide the designer with the intellectual tools needed to make visible in design the issues of responsibility, thus triggering further dialogue and reflective thought.

Knowing how people move, hide, or remove responsibility, we can start to evaluate our own habits and preferences. Students or professional designers can easily do this while they engage in design on different projects. A close analysis of how responsibility is accounted for will show not only the complexity of the issue, but may also reveal outlets through which we can deal with responsibility in open and constructive ways. This increased willingness to accept responsibility, on the part of the designer, requires that society also step up to the plate, by not wielding vindictive, fault-based responses, but instead, by sharing in the ultimate responsibility for design outcomes.

Now, more than ever, there is a need for serious dialogue on design responsibility; especially given the speed with which we are designing new hard and soft technologies that radically change the foundations, structure, and dynamics of our social reality, as we know it. Even if each individual designer's creation is not primarily responsible for the totality of the changes brought by new designs, that totality is an emergent consequence of each small design's contribution. Therefore, every designer plays an important and significant part in the designed world in which we all live.

V   A DRAWING TOGETHER

Now is a good time to think about how to bring some convergence to the divergent and immersive journey we have been on in this book—to begin to draw things together. Much of what has been introduced in this book, in addition to any questions and insights formed by the reader, will be revisited again, in greater detail, with greater relevance, during the actual processes of learning to become a designer and in practicing as a designer.

There are two distinct ways in which things can be drawn together systemically. The first is through relations—namely, comparing similarities and differences. The second is through connections—namely, binding or joining things together. Thus a drawing together is about what identifies anything as similar and what binds the differences together.

In addition, things can be drawn together by maintaining multiple levels of resolution or resolving multiple options at the same time (Martin 2007). This is the ability to keep the big picture and details in perspective simultaneously, or to understand the individual and the collective in conjunctive unity. It involves the ability to integrate competing perspectives by dissolving them into a common mix. It also involves integrating the traditions of inquiry into an organized whole so that design, art, science and spiritual traditions, for example, are drawn together into a grand strategy. This sort of drawing together is not a type of summation or aggregation but is a process of "sweeping in" (Singer 1959), relating or forming things into compositions and connecting things into emergent wholes.

The promise of design cannot be realized on its own. Design thinking and design action takes place within a milieu of history, tradition, and natural forces. It resides next to other traditions of inquiry that assist in providing insight into and understanding of the human condition. Design's reemergence places it as a third culture, next to science and the humanities and arts in the academic traditions of inquiry. In order for design to successfully mature as an equivalent tradition, it needs to be nurtured within a supportive design culture, bolstered and advanced by the synergistic behavior of a culture of designers.

Becoming a designer is a process of integrating the development of the whole person—namely, mind, body, and spirit—with the development of professional expertise. This can be characterized as the development of the inner life of the designer concomitant with the progression of a novice to levels of routine, adaptive, and design expertise. The process of combining preparation—becoming a designer—and praxis—being a designer—is a good example of how diverse concepts and experiences can be drawn together into a unified whole. Learning and praxis in design depends on one paying full attention to personal and collective progress in comprehension (understanding) and competence (skills). It means learning how to engage in inquiry for action and taking action with care and competence.

No one begins his or her design career *being* a designer—emerging as a full-fledged designer at birth. Instead, each of us engages in the processes of *becoming* someone in particular from the beginning of our existence. To *become* a designer, it is necessary to engage in learning processes that lead to our development as skillful individuals—to master the requisite elements comprising adequate design competence. Becoming a designer also means maturing as a whole person within larger webs of life—natural, social, and cultural. It means moving from being a novice to becoming an expert—becoming an adept *routine expert*, *adaptive expert*, and finally, *design expert*. It means serving the best interests of a *value expert*. It means listening to the inner guidance of the *seed* of character pushing for full expression in a well-lived life.

No one comes into the world fully equipped intellectually and physically to navigate and intervene in the turbulent courses of one's life. Luckily, human beings are advantaged for gaining design competence from inception by the existence of a priori expertise. We are born with intellectual strengths and preferences that make it possible to engage in early educational experiences as protodesigners. For anyone desiring to become a designer, it is necessary to strengthen the weak or missing areas and further refine those primal strengths or inborn competencies that are already in place.

It is generally agreed that humans come into the world hardwired for some things, including the ability to learn all the important and necessary stuff that was not provided from the beginning by nature. One of the most fundamental hardwired abilities is the ability to formulate schemas (see the "Prelude" in this book)—from *grand schemas* of all-encompassing significance such as cosmologies and philosophies to *tactical schemas* on how to do things in a concrete and practical manner. These schemas negotiate between our personal experiences of the exterior world—the perceived world—and our conscious and subconscious minds in action.

Although everyone comes into the world with designerly potential, and engages in design-related activities in their everyday lives, it is important to remember that individuals, born with different strengths and preferences, intellectually and physically, are tasked with being intentional about how they manage the processes of becoming fully competent designers. Individuals may have a predetermined trajectory that guides their development over time as exemplified by the Greek concept of *entelechy* (the vital principle that guides the development and functioning of an individual or living system). The life choices individuals make as a result of what they learn and experience may be biased in one direction or another by the influence of a deep predisposition, what James Hillman calls the *souls code* (Hillman 1996)—an individual's daemon. However, the responsibility to be intentional in the management of becoming a designer resides with the individual's a priori possession of free will.

This means that individuals can and will develop different relations with design. Some will become dedicated, exceptional designers, some will become dilettante designers, and some will become champions of design, while others will learn to engage with designers collaboratively. People may choose not to take any of these paths but no one is excluded—by nature—from traveling any of them. Anyone can become a designer or design connected.

If one chooses the path to become a designer there are many demanding, yet doable challenges to face. One challenge relates to the need to balance gaining one's competence in designing or design praxis with developing one's personal character as a designer. The designer's character is as important to one's success as any design skill or expertise.

It is difficult, if not impossible, to know all the elements required in the composition of a competent designer, and to know how to go about composing the complex mixture of attributes. Despite such uncertainty, one can gain enough understanding to move forward. It is possible to evaluate the development of design abilities by a *reflective utilization of useful schemas*, from the all-encompassing (the universal) to the specific (the particular) as guides through an uncharted landscape.

To become a designer, a person must struggle with several aspects and schemas of knowledge that are particular to design, and are discussed in this chapter. We also examine the notions of design philosophy, metadesign, design epistemology, design scholarship, and design inquiry—all foundational to any understanding of design and of what constitutes design expertise. We will devote this chapter primarily to the discussion of these high level schemas related to becoming a designer.

We begin the exploration with our first grand schema—*design philosophy*. A philosophy of design is different from a philosophy of science and other formulations of philosophy for scholarly inquiry. A philosophy of design has a different aim in that it focuses on what distinguishes design from other forms of inquiry and action—for example, to intentionally create change. Answering the question of what philosophy is in general, or in any definitive way, is of course difficult and beyond the scope of this book. However, we do want to make some comments on the notion of what would constitute a philosophy of design from the perspective of supporting and influencing an individual's ambition to become a designer.

The traditional understanding of philosophy favors abstract thinking over concrete actions and "doing." This imbalance is what is mentioned in part I as a consequence of the division of sophia. A design philosophy approaches the love of wisdom as a devotion to the *reconstitution of sophia*— in other words, the reunification of *inquiry* and *action*, or more specifically, inquiry *for* action. Actions creating the right thing, for the right people, at the right time, in the right place, in the right way, for the right reasons is design wisdom. A schema that frames and guides such an inquiry at this highest level—leading to an understanding of the means and ends for wise action—becomes part and parcel of design philosophy.

A solid philosophy of design can and should be engaged with diverse purposes and activities (see figure 14.1).

As an example, any deeper understanding of design rests on a foundation of philosophical *assumptions* about the nature of inquiry and the possibility for meaningful, intentional change (see figure 14.2).

It is obvious one can formulate universal or particular assumptions for many other core ideas as well. A design philosophy can be measured in how well it covers the scope of design and how deeply it explores the meaning and consequences of each assumption. Any aspiring designer goes through either an intentional or an unconscious process of formulating a basic philosophy of design. How well one manages the process of becoming a designer depends partly on how carefully and consciously one attends to this process. It depends on how much attention is given to exploring fully the underlying nature of design and how well the person is able to frame and formulate those considerations and reflections into some form of a personal, coherent philosophy of design. We are not arguing that becoming a designer means having to subscribe to a prescribed design philosophy, instead it is a matter of constantly struggling

~ connecting design philosophy to metaconcerns—metadesign, metaphysics, ethics, aesthetics, etc.

~ identifying design postulates and axioms that are fundamental and foundational

~ opening accesses to the means for formulating strategic and tactical schema

~ framing design inquiry as a compound form of inquiry that unifies knowing

~ defining the specifications for the design of the designer

~ formulating the means to see and value the particular or the ultimate particular

~ determining the nature of making judgments

~ creating knowledge for action

~ attending to the conjunction of ideas, concepts, and experiences

~ enabling the ability to hold paradoxes without paralysis

~ defining acceptance of the limits, responsibilities, and accountabilities of design

~ determining the nature and activities of design scholarship

Figure 14.1
Philosophy of design

with the question, of exploring what makes sense depending on one's own predispositions and desires.

The next type of schema is on the level of *metadesign*. Many types of situations arise that call for change both in the lives of individuals and in the lives of social systems of various types and scales. Not all situations are best approached with design. The question to be asked in each case: Is design the best approach to apply here? If yes, why? If not, why not?

At the level of metadesign, deliberations and decisions concerning strategic approaches are not in the hands of the designer. Instead it is a client, or other decision maker, who determines whether design is the approach to pick in a particular situation. This means that an understanding of design is needed not only on the level that design actually takes place, but on a metalevel as well. This broader culture of design is needed to inform and guide clients and stakeholders on when to turn to design to realize the change intended, and when to turn to a different approach. Anyone becoming a designer needs to engage in metadesign issues, to understand the larger context within which design is practiced. Becoming a designer means learning to recognize when design is or is not the appropriate

~ design will is free will

~ guarantors of design and guarantors of destiny underwrite design

~ the ideal (design inquiry) is an expression of desiderata

~ design is the reconstitution of sophia

~ conjunctions, dilemmas, and acceptance are required "buy ins"

~ the real (ontological inquiry) is revealed through systemic inquiry

~ systemics is the logic of design

~ particular and ultimate particular are real

~ the true (scientific inquiry) confirms design concepts

~ service determines agency

~ design postulates and axioms are particular to design

~ schemas (grand, strategic, and tactical) are seminal to design inquiry

~ unconscious judgments form design partis

Figure 14.2
Design assumptions

approach to an interventional change in a particular situation. Only someone who thoroughly understands the limitations of design as well as its potential can determine whether or not an undesirable or problematic situation can be "solved" using a design approach. Becoming a designer, therefore, involves becoming a thoughtful advocate for design when it is the appropriate approach to take, and an honest advocate against design when it is not. Any practicing designer will be part of a broader culture of design, and as such will function as a spokesperson for that culture in other domains of interest, while also charged with engaging in the ongoing development of a design culture. Such advocacy requires a deep understanding of design philosophy and design as inquiry for action.

Epistemology is the reflective study of inquiry. Among the many forms of inquiry that are in use, *design inquiry* is a distinct form that deserves its own close examination. First, it is important to understand some aspects concerning the "design" of inquiry in general. To begin, there is always an underlying epistemology for any design of inquiry—in other words, anyone who engages in any form of inquiry does so based on some fundamental ideas about what knowledge is, how it can be captured or created, and what determines valid and reliable knowledge. Based on these fundamental assumptions, an inquirer engages in a process of designing a form of inquiry suitable to his or her purposes, the specific situation, and the needs of the stakeholders involved.

Many thinkers have devoted considerable time exploring what the best designs of inquiry might be. For instance, C. West Churchman's *designs of inquiry* (Churchman 1971) are examples of epistemologies, based on historical philosophical schools of thought, designed to reveal "trustworthy" truths—in other words, that-which-is-true. The same approach can be taken for designing epistemologies meant to reveal that-which-is-real and that-which-is-ideal, influenced by contemporary schools of philosophic thought.

A design epistemology is a form of inquiry that has been designed to support a design approach. Such an epistemology can be seen as a strategic schema based on the reflective study of how to gain knowledge for action in relationship to methods, validity, and scope. Such a schema also becomes the basis for formulating what determines a justified belief in the outcomes of design inquiry. Design epistemology asks: What can be known about design inquiry? How can it be trusted to lead to good design arguments, actions, and outcomes? And: What does it mean to "know" as a designer?

How design epistemology is formulated or schematized by design thinkers or practicing designers determines the strategy for designing learning processes and for defining academic content suitable for guidance in how to become a designer. If design education is assumed to be an outgrowth of a scientific epistemology, then design scholarship and academic programs in design will take a particular scientized format. If design learning is assumed, more correctly, to be a congruent formulation of a design-based epistemology, then scholarship and pedagogy will be practiced accordingly. A schema based on the idea of *centers* might help to explain this (see figure 14.3). Each type of center in this schema reveals how different fundamental principles, or foundational epistemologies, lead to specific outcomes.

Scholars sometimes assume that knowledge is generated through greater and greater reductive analysis, further specialization, and greater divergence from any shared or common center of understanding. This leads to an *abandoned-center*. This results in scholarly institutions, such as universities, that have no unifying center and are without common ground or shared purpose. It results in academic and professional programs, and ever more specialized disciplines that are isolated from one another. It also

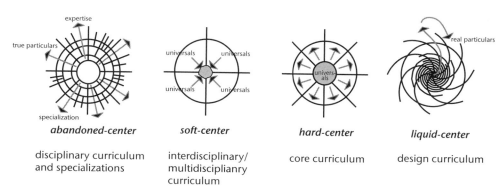

Figure 14.3
Centers

results in businesses or institutions that don't know what is at the heart of their enterprise—what their center of gravity is.

Scholars may also assume that the universal and generalizable truths of divergent disciplines can be clumped together in a *soft-center* of interdisciplinarity or multidisciplinarity. The idea is that someone will in some way be able to create an aggregate summation, a collective understanding from this accretion.

Other scholars may assume that all universal or contingent truths emerge from a common, fundamental center of shared principles and laws—a *hard-center* of consilience. Based on this assumption universities create core curricula common to all disciplinary and professional offerings across campus. These assumptions all arise from a shared scientific epistemology and all seem reasonable, though quite different in approach and outcome, in the context of producing scientific knowledge and outcomes.

For design scholars the assumptions are different. Designers need to know everything that is reasonably possible to know about a situation from a systemics perspective. It is not possible in design to use reductionist approaches that only take certain aspects into consideration while neglecting others. It is impossible to use a hard-center approach since each design situation is an ultimate particular and requires its own unique understanding. It is impossible to use a soft center approach since this primarily leads to multiple interpretations from a multitude of perspectives and thus does not provide an integrative basis for design.

The assumption can be made, from a design perspective, that the center of a design inquiry system is a *liquid-center*, that is mixed and enriched with inputs from a diversity of sources leading to supersaturated solutions that crystallize with a slight perturbation into unified understandings in particular situations.

Different epistemologies lead to radically different environments that may be more or less suitable for supporting design learning. Unfortunately there are very few educational or professional environments today built on a design epistemology that reflects design in an adequate way. This explains why becoming a designer may be a struggle or challenge in many existing educational institutions. When there is no well-developed design epistemology in the learning environment it becomes the responsibility of the individual, who is in the process of becoming a designer, to determine how and what to "know" as a designer. A personal understanding of design epistemology becomes an instrument to use in navigating through learning environments and processes.

Epistemology is naturally and closely related to the notion of *scholarship*. Traditional forms of scholarship are usually brought into question during discussions on how to improve the practice of educators, the structure of academic programs, and the measures of learning. Such times of reflection also allow an opportunity to reconsider the value of education to society more generally. Scholarship is an important concept that is not easily defined. However, the Carnegie Foundation for Higher Education (Boyer 1970) made the case for replacing existing measures of scholarship with four new types of scholarship (see figure 14.4).

Typically, scholars are considered to be academics who conduct research, publish, and convey their knowledge to students or apply what they have learned as experts. This profile usually defines the purpose of Ph.D.s and the structure of Ph.D. programs. There are today other types of advanced doctoral degrees designed to serve professions and related fields that have borrowed and adapted the means and ends from this Ph.D. template.

The Carnegie Foundation for Higher Education's report makes a case for changing the normative priorities of the professorate to the four listed in

• scholarship of discovery
• scholarship of integration
• scholarship of application
• scholarship of teaching

Figure 14.4
Scholarship redefined

• scholarship of design inquiry for action (re: discovery)

• scholarship of systemics (re: integration)

• scholarship of service and agency (re: application)

• scholarship of learning and training (re: teaching)

Figure 14.5
Design scholarship

figure 14.4. This has been taken as an opportunity for many universities and colleges to explore conceptually if not concretely new forms of scholarship among the professorate.

So, what would a new approach to *design scholarship* look like, taking a cue from Boyer's list but remembering that design scholarship is based on design epistemology and not scientific epistemology? Design scholarship might be divided into four related forms in a symmetrical schema (see figure 14.5).

However, there is obviously more to design scholarship than these four candidates. What does it mean to be fully engaged in design scholarship? For one thing, it means there is a focus on asking questions—the right kind of questions. Design is fundamentally a divergent process—a quest, a search—unlike scientific inquiry, which is predominantly a convergent research process leading, if successful, toward a logically deterministic outcome. Design scholarship is concerned with how best to ask well-formed questions. How can the right questions be identified? How are questions best answered when the outcomes are a result of value judgments and sudden insights—unconscious judgments—rather than purely rational algorithms? How can this be learned? How does one learn how to go about answering design questions—What's real? What would be ideal? What ought to be made real?—in addition to the fundamental scientific question, What's true?

Design scholars must also reflect on how it is possible to create *well-formed* schemas and to evaluate their commodity since they cannot be proven in the way a scientific hypothesis is proven and becomes accepted as a full-blown theory. There are scholarly questions about different types of schemas, hierarchies of schemas, and the durability of schemas. There are questions such as: Are there universal design schemas as well as situational schemas? What is the process for establishing the relevance and trustworthiness of schemas? Can design schema be tested, compared, and evaluated? How can schemas best be taught and learned?

Design scholarship must be inclusive of reason, imagination, emotion, and experience. It is possible to distinguish design scholarship as essentially a scholarship of inclusion, diversity, relationships, and connections; one that engages questions that involve the abstract and concrete at the same time. It is a form of scholarship that formulates and applies schemas of learning that unify reflection and action, thinking and doing, imagining and making, plus confronting indeterminate responsibility and accountability. It is a scholarship that deals with overwhelming complexity, insufficient but overwhelming information and knowledge, and contradictory and constantly changing conditions and dilemmas, needs and wants. Design scholarship also investigates the interdependency of individuals and collective social structures, the conjunction of one-of-a-kind and the commonly found and other paradoxes. What all this points to is that design scholarship is about *sweeping in* and *integrating* and not about *parsing out* and *separating.*

Design scholarship is the continuous exploration, creation, development and refinement of schemas of design inquiry and action that are based on a well-thought-out design philosophy and epistemology. Taken seriously as being foundational, these conceptual schemas give guidance to what design scholarship could and should be. As such they can guide design educators and those who are becoming designers in their respective aims to succeed in design mentoring and learning.

Becoming a designer does not mean only learning to use and apply "correct" or even existing schemas produced by design scholars and professionals. It also means constantly engaging in the creation, application, and critique of ones own schemas. It means, as an individual designer, engaging in design scholarship by developing a personal design philosophy that leads to a carefully considered design epistemology to guide design inquiry for wise action. This might sound ambitious, achievable only for experienced design philosophers and thinkers. It is clear, however, that every designer expresses his or her philosophy, epistemology, and scholarship in every design process, even if they are not explicit and externalized. Becoming a designer means that the engagement with practical issues, such as developing hands-on skills and techniques, has to be complemented with the intellectual activities addressed earlier. To become a well-rounded designer means understanding design as a tradition, as a philosophy, with a sense of what constitutes design epistemology and inquiry as well as a concrete practice.

The process of becoming a designer is not a solitary, individual undertaking. It always takes place within a *design milieu.* This milieu or setting influences, facilitates, or limits what an emerging designer can deal with, in relation to and in connection with becoming a designer. Practicing designers are always working in contexts and environments that involve other people, other systems, and other purposes. Their design milieu includes the history of events leading up to a design project's formulation. It includes the larger system within which the design project is embedded. The same is true for the learning environments and activities an emerging designer engages in.

The intellectual tradition within which design takes place is part of a very old tradition. Throughout history humans have developed institutions, protocols, and habits of thought that make up the contextual tradition within which human inquiry for action—design—takes place. Even though we claim that design is the first tradition of inquiry and meaning making, it is still not well established as a formal intellectual tradition and does not always provide the stable and supportive intellectual foundation that designers need. Any design endeavor takes place in relation to a cultural environment, and the more that environment accepts design as a valid approach for intentional change, the better it provides support for design and for the designer.

At the more concrete level it is possible to see the *context* for becoming a designer as residing within a third tradition—a *tertium quid*—among the other more familiar and better established traditions of the sciences and the arts (see figure 14.6). This nascent contextual tradition forms a container, a protector, for design learning and eventual design praxis. It forms the crucible that holds the superheated liquid form of inquiry at the center of design learning as well as design praxis.

So, what is it that a person who wants to become a designer will become? What is it that they are learning to be? The list that follows (see figure 14.7) presents some qualities that constitute what a potential designer needs to develop. This is not a comprehensive list by any stretch— merely a sampling. It is certain that the list can and will continue to grow through scholarly attention.

Among the items on the list that are extremely significant when it comes to becoming a designer is *expertise*. This is the unfolding process of moving from novice to expert, from neophyte to master, which echoes a very long tradition of learning that extends well beyond the history of modern academic institutions. Recent scholarship and research have pointed out important differentiations to be made when it comes to expertise (see figure 14.8). For instance, there has been seminal work on the difference between *routine expertise* and *adaptive expertise* (Lin, Schwartz,

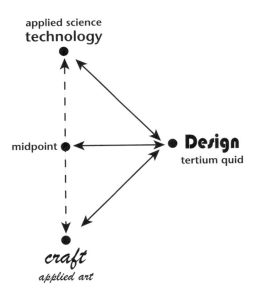

Figure 14.6
Tertium quid—the third way

- character

- scholarship

- systemic thinking

- connoisseurship

- craftsmanship

- creative and innovative competence

- design, adaptive, routine expertise

Figure 14.7
Designer qualities

Figure 14.8
Bransford's routine to adaptive expertise

and Bransford 2007; Bransford et al. 2010). Almost all formal learning environments are designed to produce routine experts. The problems that routine expertise is focused on are the kind for which the answers are readily at hand or easily accessible, drawn from a data bank of correct responses paired with consistent and stable contexts and environments. The assumption behind routine expertise, or "technical rationality" (Schön 1987), is that nothing fundamental changes in the background or foreground of design situations, and that these situations can be approached as if they are members in predetermined categories. It is believed that the answer to any particular design issue will be equally valid for the next issue in any place at any time. Routine expertise is of course essential for everyone to have, whether in complex technical situations or in everyday routines. However, when it comes to design, situations are unique, undergoing change continuously.

When things have fundamentally changed in the background or foreground, or both, of a design issue, routine responses no longer work. There is a need to be able to adapt to situations that are overwhelming, complex, and confusing. We need to be able to respond as adaptive experts so that we can reactively formulate new cognitive models and make new meaning from which to take action. There is, for instance, a repeated plea for people who can "connect the dots" after catastrophic events. The call is for individuals who can respond to a crisis in a disciplined fashion such that it leads to desirable outcomes. However there are very few formal learning environments that support the development of adaptive expertise.

• design expertise   create change

• value expertise   direct change

• adaptive expertise   react to change

• routine expertise   no change

Figure 14.9
Expertise and change

Adaptive expertise, or *artistry* in Schön's (1983) vocabulary, is essential to good design practice and human well-being, but merely reacting or adapting to change is not always the best long-term strategy. We can improve situations by reacting to the way situations are changing, but often we need to *create change*, the kind of change that is desirable. Thus there is a third and fourth kind of expertise that competent designers need to acquire or access that is essential to good design practice: *design expertise* and *value expertise* (see figure 14.9). The two must be connected with other forms of expertise in order to assure that experts are heading in the right directions when called upon for their services. Designers, value experts in their own right, need to be able to accommodate and work with other value experts who are not designers.

All four forms of expertise are important, but unfortunately, routine expertise receives the bulk of attention in both formal and informal educational settings—especially troubling for how designers are educated.

In most educational programs the expected learning outcome, generally speaking, is knowledge that is logically predictable from the input made into the learning process, or more accurately a training process. It is knowledge that can be confirmed through standard tests—in other words, *routine knowing*. But as John Bransford and others have pointed out in their work on adaptive expertise (Bransford et al. 2010), there is a different kind of learning that is focused on the ability to make sense of emergent change in a particular moment under particular circumstances. Such knowledge cannot be tested in abstract isolation, only in application—in other words, *adaptive knowing*. There also is a realm of learning that facilitates the ability to create desired change. Designers as professionals need to have both training and learning experiences in order to develop the multiple forms of expertise needed to create desired change in the complexity and uncertainty of today's world (see figure 14.10).

Knowledge that is the outcome of educational experiences, either training or learning, is often contextualized in knowledge hierarchies of one

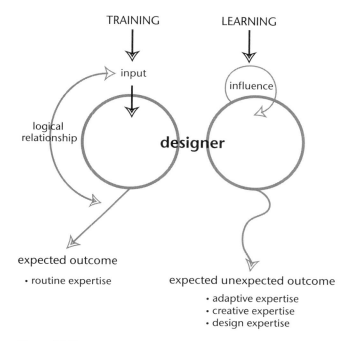

Figure 14.10
Training and learning

kind or another. Russell Ackoff's (1989) hierarchy is a typical example (see figure 14.11). But design knowledge and, in particular, design knowing is different in that *wise action* and not just evaluated understanding is a demonstration of design wisdom.

Design learning can be addressed in four domains: (1) design character, (2) design thinking, (3) design knowing, and (4) design action or praxis (see figure 14.12). These domains can be expressed as sets. The outcome

1. Data: symbols
2. Information: data that are processed to be useful; provides answers to "who," "what," "where," and "when" questions
3. Knowledge: application of data and information; answers "how" questions
4. Understanding: appreciation of "why"
5. Wisdom: evaluated understanding

Figure 14.11
Ackoff's knowledge hierarchy

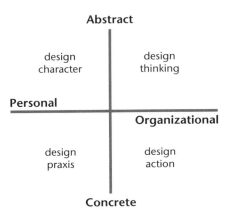

Figure 14.12
Design learning domains

of design learning or inquiry can be seen as a process of managing *competency sets* that are interrelated among the quadrants formed by the crossing axis of familiar dichotomies such as *concrete reality* and *abstract thinking*, and the *individual* contrasted to *social collectives*. These sets—mindsets, knowledge sets, skill sets, and tool sets—must be established and filled, in the process of becoming a designer (see figure 14.13).

There is a connection between the design domains and competency sets. Design character and design thinking are expressed through *mindsets* and *knowledge sets*. Design knowing and design action are expressed through *skill sets* and *tools sets* (see figure 14.14).

In addition, it is necessary to be able to mediate among the sets such that their utility is integrated into a holistic and synergistic resource in support of designing (see figure 14.15).

The ongoing responsibility in learning to be a designer, as well as in the practice of designing, is the challenge of maintaining the sets over time—discarding and renewing content as needed (see figure 14.16). Learning to become a designer entails learning how to be a learner as well as absorbing what a designer needs to know in order to practice design.

The meditated sets are distributed between design knowledge, which is separable from the knower, and design knowing, which is inseparable from the knower (see figure 14.17). Separable knowledge is inclusive of the knowledge set and tool set. Inseparable knowledge involves access to the skill set and mindset.

What constitutes the core of a designer's knowledge is revealed in the management of the different competency sets internal to the learner. In

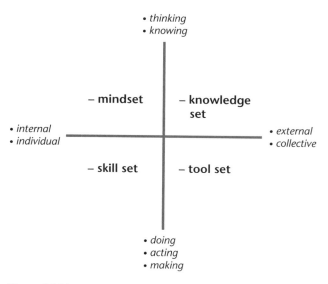

Figure 14.13
Design competency "sets"

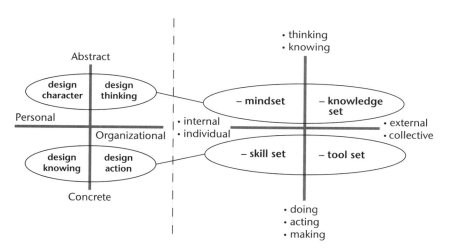

Figure 14.14
Interconnections of domains and sets

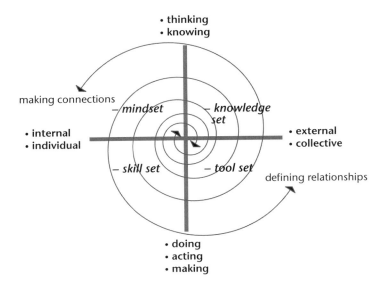

Figure 14.15
Mediation of sets

becoming a designer

- Establishing and Maintaining Sets - learning
  - update
  - remove
  - add

abstract
epistemological

- thinking
- knowing

being a designer

- Applying Sets - designing, etc.
  - why
  - where
  - what
  - when
  - how
  - who

– mindset   – knowledge
                    set

- internal
- individual

- external
- collective

– skill set   – tool set

- doing
- acting
- making

ontological
concrete

Figure 14.16
Establishing and maintaining sets

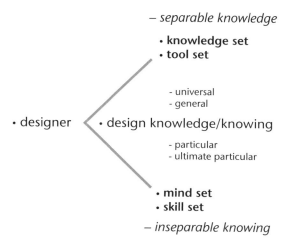

Figure 14.17
Design knowledge and knowing

addition, what a designer needs to know is defined or influenced by many external forces. The designer has his or her own intention of what to become, and also predispositions and talents that influence what can and should be aimed for as goals. However, at the same time, society, clients, and other stakeholders have expectations for what a learner needs to know. Further, norms, laws, and professional expectations are all necessary, influential elements in a designer's education and praxis. This means that the expected outcomes of design learning are defined both subjectively and objectively.

What a design learner needs to master is not entirely or even sufficiently explained through taxonomic elements such as the sets or schemas presented in this chapter. Such sets and schemas are valuable and necessary but are not adequate for a full understanding of what goes into the development of design expertise. We have so far discussed learning outcomes as different categories at the same level of resolution. However, learning outcomes are differentiated hierarchically as well as categorically. The hierarchy of design-learning outcomes shows the interrelationship of the different types of expertise to levels of outcomes (see figure 14.18).

A hierarchy is based on the understanding that the things in a lower level are given significance, meaning, and value by the next higher level. For example, for design *capacity*, facts and skills are valuable only in the context of the *confidence* to take action or to do things. The *competence* to

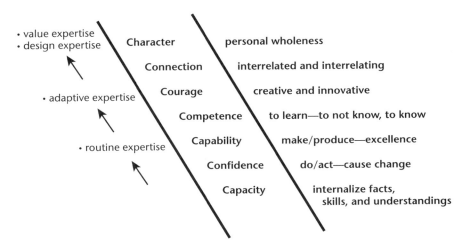

Figure 14.18
Hierarchy of design-learning outcomes

learn is only valuable in designing if there is the *courage* to be creative and innovative, to take risks with the full understanding of responsibility and accountability which is the next higher level in the hierarchy—that of *connection*.

The hierarchy of learning outcomes is necessary and crucial to understand since it makes it clear that some outcomes are not possible to achieve if others at a lower level are not already achieved. It also shows that at the end of the day, to become a designer is a process that deepens over time and becomes more personal as you move up the hierarchy.

A different way of ordering design learning outcomes can be seen in a schema of *orders of learning* (which is distinct from a hierarchy) that delineates levels of learning different in kind and not just degree (see figure 14.19). Each order of learning must be approached with categorically different means and methods. The design of learning activities and ancillary environments is distinct and unique to each level.

Becoming a designer is not something one does on one's own. It is in most cases a process that you engage in as a student in a more formal educational process, in addition to any informal learning that may be taken advantage of. It is important that any educational process you engage in is designed to provide the structure and activities needed to support the process of becoming a competent designer as we have discussed it. An example of a formal design studies program would need to

first order—truth and reality
data/information/knowledge

facts/theories
norms
universals/generalities/particulars

second order—systemics
finding meaning

systems approach/systems thinking
systems theory
systems analysis, synthesis, critique, restoration
systems mileu

third order—schemata
making meaning

protocols/heuristics
designed inquiry
frames/limits/foreground/background
containers, crucibles

fourth order—composition/assembly
creating value

connections/functional assemblies
relations/compositions
wholes
orders of change

fifth order—guarantor-of-destination/design
How/Why/When/for Whom is it possible?

g.o.d.

sixth order—guarantor-of-direction/destiny
What is desirable?
What is valuable?
Where do you stand?

G.O.D.

Figure 14.19
Orders of design learning

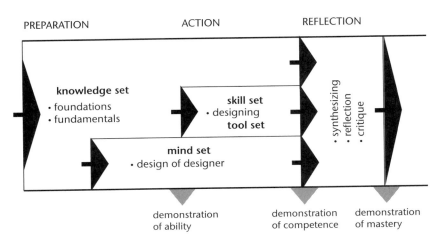

Figure 14.20
Design learning

take into account different categories, different hierarchies, and different orders of learning and how to achieve each of the desired outcomes. Such a formal framework would need to be designed—scored—as a process, flowing along an irreversible *arrow of time* that progresses through distinct phases and stages organized around the different types of learning experiences involved in design education. An example of a score of such a learning process can be seen in figure 14.20. Depending on what desired outcomes are emphasized, the proportional allocation of time and effort may vary among the different elements and sections, but there needs to be an overall design of the process in place to ensure that expectations are met.

Designing the learning for a prospective designer involves creating a complex composition of elements, structure, and processes. Too often design curricula are treated as if they were merely a matter of curriculum and pedagogy (K–12) or androgogy, rather than the design of a whole learning experience whether to complete a grade, degree, certificate, or any other structured learning event. This is mistaking the cake for the ingredients. A cake comes into being because of ingredients that are measured, blended, and baked into a final emergent form. Neither the ingredients, nor the bowl and mixer, nor the oven, nor the extended time in a heated environment, nor the presence of a cook, call a cake into existence. It is all of these things coming together at the right time in the right proportion in the right environment managed by the right people that becomes an interconnected temporal whole. A design curriculum (or any curriculum for that matter) ought to include courses and other learning resources, context, and process in an appropriately proportioned mix processed skillfully into an emergent whole—a competent design professional.

The truth is that learning to become a designer is a process of never-ending "becoming." One doesn't stop becoming a designer when one turns to "being" a designer in practice. Designers engaged in design inquiry in the praxis of design are still and will always be learners, as we will show in chapter 15. "Being" a designer is the threshold in the process of "becoming" where the judgment is made that the novice is now expert enough to begin practice—but not to end learning. Interestingly, the individual practices design throughout the process of becoming a designer. There are many design projects the learner engages in while becoming a designer, including the design of oneself as a designer. Becoming and being are entangled from the beginning, and continue to be so.

15 Being a Designer

Designing is the means by which desired ends *become* real. This is strikingly different from the purpose of scientific inquiry, which is focused on describing and explaining things that already exist—that are already *being* something. If someone is practicing as a designer they are *being* designers who are experts in the process of facilitating intentional *becoming*.

In chapter 14 we discussed what becoming a designer requires. Now the question needs to be asked: How is it possible to know when someone is ready to begin practicing design? In the historical traditions of craft design, a novice or apprentice passed successfully through distinct stages of professional development that marked the progression from learner to master for the public to see. In some traditions, the development of a level of accomplishment in a concrete skill marked a concomitant level of development in character. Thus a craftsperson who was considered to be "on the level" demonstrated he had mastered a set of tools and skills, which included construction competency levels used in carpentry and masonry, in parallel with a matured development of character.

Design praxis can be considered to be a similar progressive integration of the designer's personal and professional development and refinement, which are displayed in their approach to designing. To be considered sufficiently developed in skill and character to engage successfully in real-world design projects means that there is an adequate balance between the two domains of professionalism, that is, the *design of the designer* and the *design of designing* (see figure 15.1).

Designers practice in a manner that is reflective of *who* they are as individuals and professionals. The design process results in artifacts that "are what they are" based on *why* they were desired in the first place. To be a practicing designer therefore is not only a matter of skill and knowledge. Design praxis also requires personal integrity and proficiency,

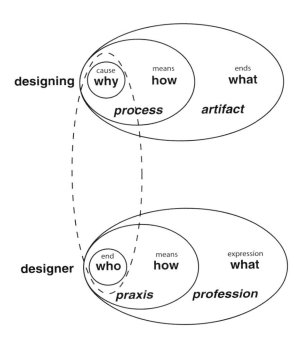

Figure 15.1
Designers and designing

in conjunction with a design process that is compatible with and reflective of the designer's character and competence.

Designers in the past have often been identified as experts in applied science or applied art, or both in some cases. But as we discussed in chapter 14, in today's expanding domain of design practice, designers need to be design experts—with deference to value experts—with competence in routine expertise and adaptive expertise, but more than a mere aggregation of the two.

For designers, individually and collectively, it is important to be able to both understand and participate in designing. The process of designing is highly complex and extraordinarily dynamic. Apart from designers being adequately qualified as designers, it is also crucial for a designer to be able to manage the design process skillfully and responsibly. In this chapter we further examine the design process, explore how it is possible to understand and describe such a process with any degree of comprehensibility, and consider what a reflective designer needs to be aware of, in order to understand something so elusive and complex.

We will neither try to describe the process in detail nor discuss it in any prescriptive way. Instead we will offer some general observations about the nature of the design process and how it is unique in relation to other processes.

The design process is not an algorithm, not a heuristic search pattern, and not a list of prescriptive steps. It is an approach to dealing with the uncertainties and complexities of reality that a designer is thrown into at the beginning of each new project, which continue for the duration of the designer's involvement. It is an alternative to the default mode of being or becoming reductionist and simplistic. It is an integration of the three forms of expertise (routine, adaptive, and design), with the primary focus on design expertise.

Like any other intentional and disciplined process, designing involves preparation (see figure 15.2). As preparation for a design project gets under way, an essential consideration is to determine and legitimize the designer's *agency*. This involves the process of *contracting*, either explicitly or implicitly. In some cases designers are able to sign a contract with clients and others establishing formal agency. But in many other cases those who will be served by the design process are not able to engage in explicit contracting (see chapter 2).

Figure 15.2
Letting go

When stakeholders are not available for contracting, other means must be found for establishing and justifying agency, such as identifying legitimate surrogates or design ombudsmen. The clients may be too young, too sick, too large in number, or not yet born to participate competently and directly in a design process. This requires that a means for establishing agency must be found. The issue of agency is obscured in the special case of designers who are contracted by companies or agencies to design things for their markets or constituencies. However, this ought not mitigate the designers' responsibilities, as professionals, to serve the interests of those most effected by their designs. This challenge becomes even more consequential as designers assume greater reach in their work.

Contracting is the part of design process preparation that reveals not only practical responsibilities but also ethical issues concerning "who" the designer is to serve and in what capacity other stakeholders are to appear contractually. Contracting in design is crucial since the issues of responsibility and agency are impossible to avoid. If these issues are not dealt with in the beginning, those who believe they should have been contracted with as clients or stakeholders will reveal themselves after the design process is in motion, when the process reaches critical stages, causing serious unwanted disruptions leading to undesirable consequences. However, when contracting and agency are handled and finalized at the preparation stage, the designer is freed up to finish other preparation tasks and move on to the rest of the design process.

Every design process is a process of inquiry, and every inquiry is unique. Design inquiry is therefore a process that begins with unlearning old answers and starting with a *new mind* or *beginner's mind* open to new learning, exciting new possibilities, and rewarding new insights—in other words, starting with a *letting go*. Designers, clients, and stakeholders who will benefit from the design and who initiated the design process in the beginning subjectively experience this letting go, this heightened readiness for change, as highly desirable. Letting go means that everyone involved from the beginning commits to the specific conditions of a particular situation, and opens their minds to new understandings and interpretations of what lies in store for them. They are called to open up to new ideas, new ways of seeing things, altered directions and surprising outcomes, by letting go of their previous experiences and design solutions. This early letting go is not to be confused with a later letting go (see figure 15.2).

For other stakeholders who are not to be served intentionally as clients by the new design, but who will nevertheless be affected by the new design, there is a letting go that is forced on them by a designed, nonnegotiable change. These stakeholders' existing reality will be modified, distorted, or even destroyed by a new design. The new design may be both desired and needed, but at the same time can be experienced after the fact as both frightening and destructive. Such an experience will lead to a letting go that too often is experienced as loss, and can only be mitigated, if at all, by healing through grieving. This later form of letting go can lead to accepting what turns out to be a beneficial adaptive change, but may also result in adapting to a change that is potentially harmful or destructive. Designers have a duty to try to make the former the case, and not the latter.

The beginning of design inquiry also requires actively preparing to pay full attention to an ultimate particular situation, and having the courage to step into the unknown. This means that the design process deals with reality in its ultimate uniqueness in a way that has consequences for the performance requirements of the process. It is important to remember that when we talk about process here, we do not mean a specific method or a prescribed sequence of actions. Instead we look at the primary relationship between a process and its outcomes—a relationship that is different in a design process from other approaches to inquiry. For instance, an important distinction between science and design, or art and design, involves the relationships between processes and outcomes that are defined by the focus or purpose of each approach (see figure 15.3).

Scientists are not invested in reaching a predetermined outcome using the scientific process, but are extremely invested in making sure that their process is precise, accurate, and valid so that whatever does appear as an outcome can be trusted as being true. In a scientific approach the outcome is not what is desired from the outset, but what is logical and necessary as a consequence of the process. In contrast, artists are not necessarily vested in any particular process but instead are extremely invested in reaching a particular outcome—expressed through the art itself.

Designers are heavily invested in developing and using good design processes and in realizing desired outcomes. In design inquiry, process is aimed by design intention—desiderata. The right process going in the right direction will reach the right outcome. Desired outcomes—in other words, ends—are made visible and are successfully achieved with mindful, intentional aiming. Process and outcome are entwined and equally important to the designer. A good process, properly aimed in the right direction, reveals the answer to the question: What design is desired to be made real?

In order to fully appreciate the situation at hand (see figure 15.4), it is crucial that all involved understand the importance of paying attention

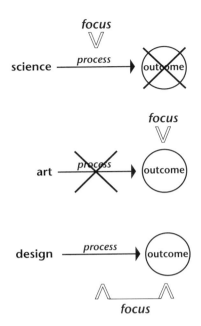

Figure 15.3
Process and outcome relationships

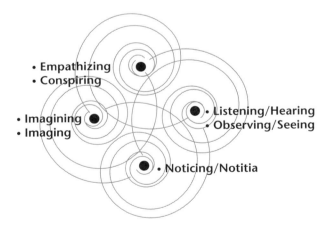

Figure 15.4
Design attention

deeply and holistically to the particular situation. Participants in the design process need to know how to establish and maintain this level of attention. The designers, clients, and other key players must engage in a form of *conspiracy*, based on shared intention and mutual empathy. Everyone involved must *hear* and *see* what is pressing for expression in the design process, including input from those individuals or entities that cannot give voice to their own expectations, such as future generations and the natural environment.

It is essential that everything of importance is *noticed* in the whole and taken into account in scale and completeness rather than totality alone. Finally, as full attention is given to "objective" realities, a systemic connection is made with the "subjective" processes of *imagining* the forms in which all this hearing, seeing, empathizing, and noticing come together in congruent images of understanding and meaning.

Asking questions, or more important, asking the right questions, is essential in any form of design inquiry into the particular and ultimate particular. Questioning provides direction to the process of designing. Too often processes are seen as merely unfolding through ordered, unidirectional steps. It is also often assumed that such processes are recursive, and can bend back on themselves, repeating phases or stages of the process at any intervention point chosen. These assumptions cannot be made concerning design processes.

First, any design process can unfold in an infinite number of directions unlike scientific processes, which commonly have predetermined trajectories. Aiming a design process carefully from the beginning is essential, however. Such things as *first intentions* and initial design questions send the design process in a unique direction particular to these initial considerations. These first judgments in conjunction with a systemic assessment of the design situation codetermine the stance of the designers in relationship to that which is being designed.

First intentions and initial questions set the stage. They lay out the direction the process will take. Without direction, a designer is lost and the process becomes aimless. Since a design process can unfold in an infinite number of ways, it is not possible to reach a desired outcome without using a navigational process like design and the notion of desiderata. The design process is not about approaching the design situation with the ambition to "uncover" the right problem or "discover" the right solution. Nothing is there a priori to be bumped into. Things will be made to become real because of the path the design journey sets out on. The possibilities are infinite until the first step is taken.

Second, there is the challenge of working in real situations, with real materials and real people moving along an arrow of time. One cannot un-light a match. One can recapitulate an earlier phase or stage in a design process, but one does not experience the same reality. The material elements have undergone a history of change that cannot be undone. Ideas cannot be thought again as new; they are influenced by the earlier contexts from which they initially emerged. The output of one part of the design process becomes the input for the next. The transformations are irreversible and there are consequences to returning to earlier steps. As Heraclitus reminds us, we cannot step into the same river twice, for the water has flowed on and is not the same river and time has passed and the waders are no longer the same people.

There is a category of questions that involves asking: What are the essential, overarching first intentions of any design process? (See figure 15.5.) Designers, clients, and other stakeholders already are up to something prior to or at the beginning of each design project. It is not possible to enter a project with a completely open mind. Too often these first

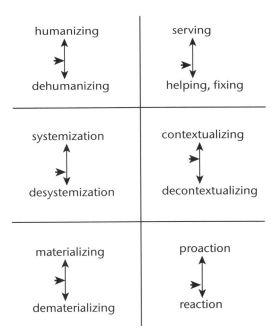

Figure 15.5
First intentions

intentions are invisible to those individuals involved in a project, even to the individuals themselves. This means they don't realize why a particular process is going in the direction that it is. It is important, of course, for all involved to know what the first intentions are and to make assumptions and judgments explicit about what they would like the first intentions to be.

For example, in the design of technologies, it may be assumed from the beginning that, on the one hand, human activity is to be replaced by computerization or, on the other hand, technology is to enhance or augment human activity only. It may be the case that a first intention is to augment the strongest aspects of human behavior and to replace humans only where their natural abilities are weakest. In any case, wherever the pointer aims, this first intention will set the course for all subsequent design activity.

The types of questions focused on first intentions are not typically at the same level of questioning associated with the creativity and innovation of designers working for business interests. Questions on how to challenge the status quo, identify the next market niche, or "break out of the box" may alter the direction a design process takes, but they do not *set the course* in the same fundamental way that the initial first intentions do.

Many aspects of design and first intentions are complex and bring in different ethical and value issues. For instance, there is an ongoing critique of material designs in the "developed" countries of the world, particularly in the United States and the West in general, concerning issues of sustainability. The questions in particular relate to product innovations that use energy and natural resources in their production and that become waste once they are no longer in use, which are the consequences of material design. Is the intention to be opportunistic or concerned with sustainability?

Innovation is the integration of artifacts or concepts—designed or otherwise—into people's lives. There are several ways to think about innovations in relation to basic or first intentions. We can, for instance, order innovations, meaning technologies, into three categories that in different ways reflect a variety of first intentions. The categories are (1) stuff, (2) things, and (3) junk. The three denote ways we can define and make sense of new innovations and new designs that are added to our shared reality. Each category represents a particular type of first intention.

The concern over too much *stuff* has received a lot of attention academically, politically, and economically, both in the present and in the past. "Green" or "sustainable" labels are staples in the marketing of anything:

ideas, products, projects, and so forth. The concern that we have too much stuff is twofold: first, certain types of innovated stuff too often lead to personal overconsumption; second, too much stuff consumes limited resources and pollutes limited space.

As designers we also need to be concerned about *things*: the concepts, artifacts, and technologies that extend and amplify our humanity—the things that redefine what it means to be human in the best sense (Borgmann 1984). Things become a part of who people identify themselves as. Things expand and amplify the power of individuals and their concomitant networks, making them into prosthetic gods. Things add or amplify people's competencies and abilities, extend their identities as individuals, and bind them through real connections into larger networks of technology and essential others. People's interconnections with things define their evolutionary path.

As for the second category of innovation, designers need to be concerned about the *junk* that diminishes us as humans. These are the innovations—social and material—that dehumanize us. Junk can be the technological interface that removes personal responsibility for consequences of actions. This kind of junk removes the burden of being held responsible for one's judgments and decisions. Junk diminishes the influence of personal agency because it diminishes the potential for individuals to face the consequences of their own (mis)behaviors, or transfers power to those who believe they are better able to control the behavior of others through innovative designs. Interestingly, there is a trend in design schools and design professions focused on creating things that "change behavior." The confluence of those who like to tell people what to do and those who like to be told what to do seems to be growing.

Unfortunately, too little is being done to enable people to understand and accept the challenge of being human—in other words, "lame gods"—possessing the skills to make almost anything happen, but lacking the competency to discern which among all the possibilities actually ought to be done. As designers we have the freedom to choose whether we create *stuff, things,* or *junk.* Our responsibility of course is to better understand how best to bring the right things into existence, for the right reasons, for the right people, at the right time and place.

This is why first intentions are crucial when it comes to design and the design process. Engaging with the question of first intentions forces designers to reflect on their overall responsibility, as well as on the fundamental purpose or intention of the process—is it to produce more stuff, things, or junk? Being aware of first intentions is part of the preparation *before* the design process begins. First intentions influence every other step and activity during the process. Deciding what the list of first intentions ought to be is directly linked or rooted to the designer's own character and ability to see his or her role in a larger context.

When designers first become engaged in a design situation or project they are thrown into an existing milieu. Things are already happening. Things are going on in people's lives in contexts affected by their environments and provenance. The situation is always a dynamic and evolving ultimate particular. The changes under way, and the influences and pressures in play, have histories as well as trajectories. Designing is like laying track for a moving train while on board. So, even when preparation, contracting, and first intentions are in place the question remains: How do designers maintain balance and keep their feet under them while encountering the inertia of change?

Good designers do not accept any situation as given; instead they always begin by asking challenging questions to better understand the true nature of what they are dealing with. They never settle for the "problem" as presented to them by clients, users, or stakeholders. They do not accept the initial ideas for "solutions" given to them, not even by people who live and work in the situation and who see themselves as experts in the environment. Designers always need to expose the underlying forces of change that their design intervention is expected to successfully confront, modify, and use. They try to become aware of problematic symptoms, and they try to expose underlying forces and root causes that need to be taken into account when attempting to actualize expressions of desiderata for the particular situation at hand.

Designers begin by making assessments of the design situation. Working from well-developed assessments, they can confidently take courses of action that will enable an appropriate design to be conceptualized and innovated with the greatest chance for full success. A systemic assessment starts with three undertakings—apposition, analysis, and synthesis.

As discussed earlier in chapter 3, the first task in assessing a situation involves *looking around* to see what the environment is that the project needs to fit into—in other words, determining the *apposition* of the situation. A second task involves *looking into* the situation to determine what constituent elements are in play—that is, making an *analysis*. A third task involves *looking out of* the situation to discern the larger systemic context within which the project is embedded—creating a *synthesis* of the aggregated elements of the project in relationship to external influences and limits. Throughout the assessment process the designer is deeply engaged in the activities of interpretation and communication with the purpose of establishing a solid foundation for revealing desiderata.

This assessment process is culminated in a fourth task—a *critique* of the design situation. This involves both determining what aspects of the situation are *satisfactory* and what things seem to be *problematic*. The problematic conditions determine the nature of the problems at hand, if any, and what type of strategic action is most appropriate.

The critique that emerges from the initial assessment process leads to a judgment concerning which strategic path to take to best serve the clients' and stakeholders' interests. Choices of directions to take based on the critique include whether to *fix* or *restore* a situation by repairing or replacing elements and connections. Another choice is whether to *redesign* the means—in other words, reform a situation—for getting something done, or whether as part of a redesign, to redefine the ends—transform a situation—for which something is done. Finally, the choice can be whether to design something new—to form something that does not yet exist (see figure 15.6).

Beyond initial preparations and assessment, what does a holistic design process look like? Design processes are intentional experiences—temporal objects that are complex and multidimensional. Designs—the results of design processes—are experiences as well as things. Designed experiences as temporal "objects" are often thought through and communicated using a category of schematization called *scoring*. The most familiar type of scoring for people is music notation, but there are many forms of scoring in use including for dance and other forms of artistic performances. Scoring schemas can include recipes for cooking, algorithms in software design, and processes formalized as methods.

There are many station points from which to score the complex process of designing. Multiple perspectives, worldviews, and all the other cognitive frames we employ provide vastly different images and representations of temporal objects or scores of the design process. They all seem to hold some truth and utility for designers and the diversity among the many images seems to offer fleeting glimpses of the deep, complex nature of the beast. Efforts to resolve the many, often conflicting, images of what the process of designing looks like, into one accurate and comprehensive image, is not time well spent. It is better to examine the nature of the design process using multiple schemas that are each pragmatically useful and intellectually helpful (see figure 15.7). That makes it also possible to synthesize multiple schemas of the design process by using integrative schemas—a schema of schemas if you will.

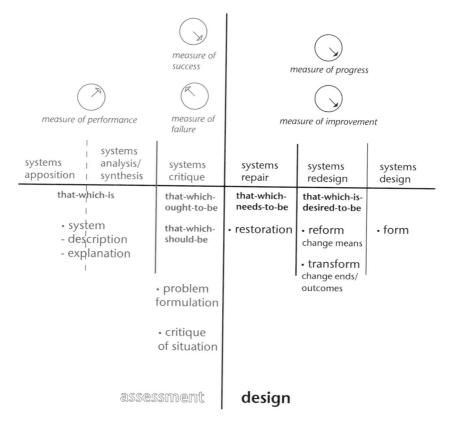

Figure 15.6
Design

In figure 15.7 a common design process (based on schemas of creativity inclusive of these steps: preparation, immersion, divergence, convergence, and emersion) is related to two other concepts or scores of the design process. The first is a *deep design* schema beginning with centering, then moving on to intention, purpose, and finally the particular. The next example is a schema of *greater granularity*, with more detail concerning specific activities in each phase of the process. Neither schema is particularly better than the other; they just focus on different qualities. Each is good for gaining an understanding of the general process of designing from specific vantage points. Taken together they give one a sense of what the whole process entails.

Similar to the way that light can be understood scientifically as having attributes of either particles or waves depending on which of two different

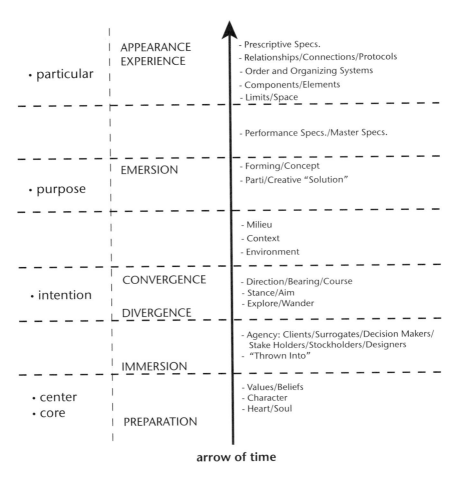

Figure 15.7
Design scores

points of view is used, the design process can be regarded as a compound of different processes, each with dramatically different apparent qualities as well (see figure 15.8).

As shown in figure 15.9, the best designers synthesize these two very different processes and are able to manage the design process in a very disciplined way, bringing a project in on time within budget and within specifications while not sacrificing the open flow of a free and fluid creatively dynamic process.

The stages and phases that are common to both the crystalline and the liquid processes are complex activities that may reflect the qualities of one

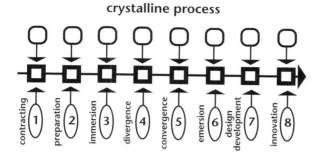

Figure 15.8
Liquid and crystal design process

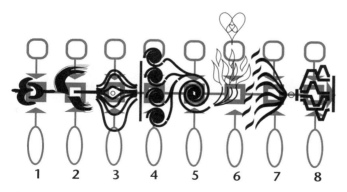

Figure 15.9
Liquid–crystal design process compound

or the other dimensions of the process but that remain entangled with each other as a compound (see figure 15.10). In the same way that colors change one another conceptually when put into relationships with one another, rational activities and creative activities influence each other in the design process, creating emergent qualities rather than attenuating or canceling each other out.

Another aspect of design processes that need careful attention is the necessity to pay full attention to details and the whole at the same time. During any design process a good designer must stay focused on the overall design, how it relates to the client's desiderata, the stakeholder's interests, the social context, and the natural environment. This requires an ability to monitor how the emerging whole reflects the first intentions and how the details are coming together as an integrated whole. At the same time the designer has to pay full attention to each and every detail since they must be adequately developed in every aspect in order to contribute effectively to the whole design. Good designers have the ability to shift focus from the overall big picture to the particular details of the process without losing control of the process (Löwgren and Stolterman 2004).

The fact the design process can be represented with such radically different images does not mean that it is a fruitless attempt to describe the process. Every designer has to find ways to represent the process, to think about the process, and to communicate that understanding and representation of the process to others. Any design process is a socially dynamic process involving many actors with different understandings of the process based on their experiences and perspectives. Therefore, before a design process can begin, there is a need to *design the design process* in order to establish a common understanding of the process, its stages, its flow, and its management in a fashion that can support collaboration on a particular project. It is not a question of finding the perfect or correct model, score, or schema. It is about having a common understanding of the process, what is expected, when it is expected, and by whom. A well-developed image of the process helps designers and stakeholders to understand their roles, relationships, and responsibilities.

From another viewpoint the design process can be seen as a quest—a process of seeking the attainment of conditions that establish necessary states from which the process can continue unfolding (see figure 15.11). For example, it is essential to establish agency and mark out intention in order to create the context for engaging in the process of preparation, such as creating a new mindset for the particular project.

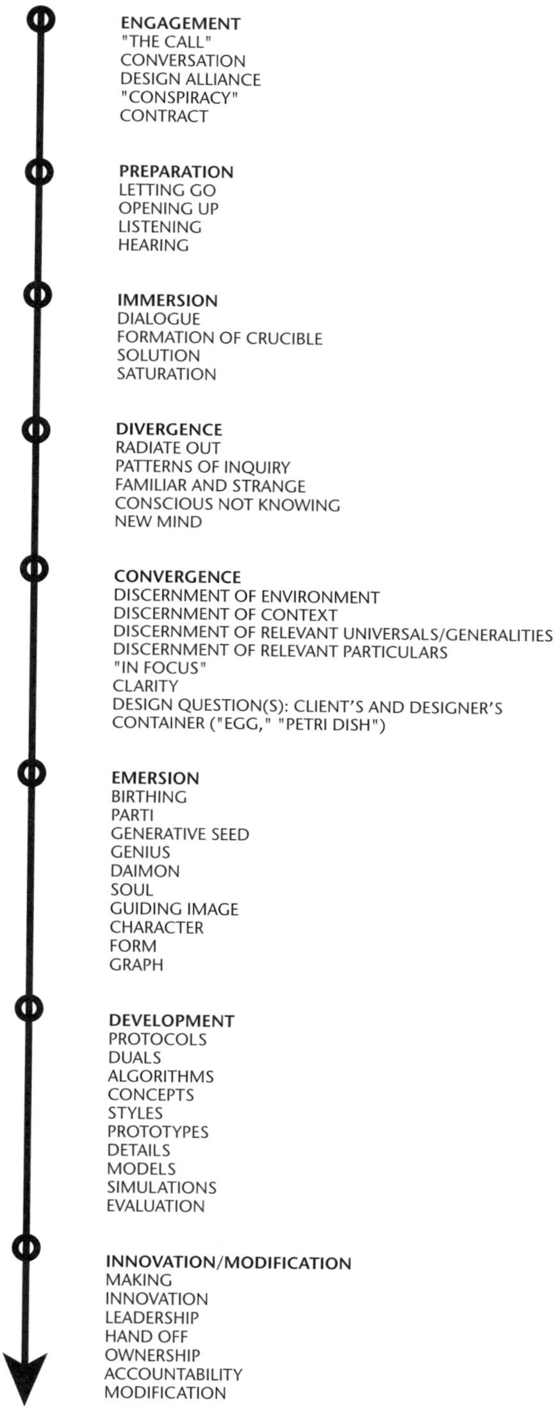

ENGAGEMENT
"THE CALL"
CONVERSATION
DESIGN ALLIANCE
"CONSPIRACY"
CONTRACT

PREPARATION
LETTING GO
OPENING UP
LISTENING
HEARING

IMMERSION
DIALOGUE
FORMATION OF CRUCIBLE
SOLUTION
SATURATION

DIVERGENCE
RADIATE OUT
PATTERNS OF INQUIRY
FAMILIAR AND STRANGE
CONSCIOUS NOT KNOWING
NEW MIND

CONVERGENCE
DISCERNMENT OF ENVIRONMENT
DISCERNMENT OF CONTEXT
DISCERNMENT OF RELEVANT UNIVERSALS/GENERALITIES
DISCERNMENT OF RELEVANT PARTICULARS
"IN FOCUS"
CLARITY
DESIGN QUESTION(S): CLIENT'S AND DESIGNER'S
CONTAINER ("EGG," "PETRI DISH")

EMERSION
BIRTHING
PARTI
GENERATIVE SEED
GENIUS
DAIMON
SOUL
GUIDING IMAGE
CHARACTER
FORM
GRAPH

DEVELOPMENT
PROTOCOLS
DUALS
ALGORITHMS
CONCEPTS
STYLES
PROTOTYPES
DETAILS
MODELS
SIMULATIONS
EVALUATION

INNOVATION/MODIFICATION
MAKING
INNOVATION
LEADERSHIP
HAND OFF
OWNERSHIP
ACCOUNTABILITY
MODIFICATION

Figure 15.10
Design stages and phases

1. seeking intention

2. seeking agency

3. seeking complexity

4. seeking limits

5. seeking unity

6. seeking form

7. seeking realization

Figure 15.11
Seeking

As was stated earlier, the design process is personal; immeasurably complex, it cannot be fully comprehended from any one vantage point, or captured in any one image. Every new schema allows some part of the whole to be seen while obscuring other aspects. Improvements in how the process is structured and managed are enabled by the insights gained through each glimpse into the process afforded by experience of the process in action. So far we have made the argument that being a designer involves reflecting on the overall nature of the design process in relation to the particular project at hand. Being a designer is not about following a predetermined process, it is instead about designing a process.

What does it mean for an individual designer to develop a more personal understanding of these ideas—to think and practice in a designerly way? The single most important guarantee of design excellence is the attendance of good *design character*. Someone who is in the process of becoming a competent designer can rattle off basic design tenets from memory without hesitation. However, not until design's core values have begun to reside within—to be embodied in—the designer's character will he or she be able to competently practice authentic design—especially design that is soul-full.

Design takes place where there are no universal truths, no generalized solutions. Design resides in the realm of creating the ultimate particular. Designing is about handling complexity and richness, tensions and contradictions, possibilities and limits, all of which require design to be a process of making good judgments where, as stated earlier, judgment is defined as "knowing," based on knowledge inseparable from the "knower."

Also, design is about forming compositions, and compositions never emerge from prescriptive rules or principles. They are always the result of acts of judgment.

All in all, design, as described in this book, emanates from and depends for success on the individual designer's core of being—his or her character. In design, character counts. This doesn't mean that design is such an individualistic process that it emulates the heroic tradition of the lone wolf. Design has always been and will continue to be collaborative at its core, even if that collaboration only involves one designer and one client. Design activities are typically carried out collectively, with people playing many diverse roles, all involved in complex interrelationships. Still, the bearer of cultural norms and values, and the source of design imagination and agency is the individual. It is the individual designer who is a design catalyst, who carries the responsibility to act in a design-driven way to initiate and develop a design culture; foster design behavior in other stakeholders and in society at large; mentor design colleagues; and form design contexts in the particular.

This leads us straight to the big question concerning the designer and his or her character: How is it possible to develop one's design character—in other words, design a designer? The first step, of course, is to take the question seriously. Design learning not only is an objective process focused on learning external facts and methods, it also involves the subjective process of developing mindsets and skill sets as well. It involves developing personal attributes that make up what would be considered excellent character—that is, personal *arête* (the Greek word for "excellence"). Therefore design learning is the same thing as designing the designer. The question then becomes: How does one design an excellent design learning process?

A designer's character evolves at a snail-like pace, staying remarkably recognizable over time. That is why its development demands ongoing attention. Character is not something that can be changed quickly nor should it be. A person's character is shaped by his or her *daemon*—the essence of the "soul" with which one is born. It is this soul that evokes our "calling" in life. The daemon determines who we are and who we will become from the very beginning of our lives (Hillman 1996).

Hillman presents a way to understand the complex connection between who we are when we are born, and how we change and develop over time. He explains that to carefully reflect on who we are, in our soul, is a lifelong exercise. It is an exercise that is both painful and rewarding. It is through such continuous reflection—on who we are, what our calling is, what we can do with our life—that we create the basis of our character. For Hillman, our character (even when stable and deeply rooted) is open to change in intentional ways. As designers, we have an obligation to continuously examine, challenge, and influence our design character. To act in this way is not simply a matter of going about one's design activities, but also involves reflecting proactively on the development of the connection between design character and design competence.

As we have stated many times, to design is to intentionally change the world and ourselves. Thus, every designer is a leader in the truest and fullest sense of the word, because every design process is about leading the world into a new reality—a place we have never seen or been to before. Design is always moving toward the unknown and unknowable. Because of this, design creates unintended outcomes along with the intended ones. We can never really "undo" a design. Even if the specific artifact or design is removed, the design has already made a residual imprint on the world as an idea or experience. It has caused things to change through complex causal entanglements. People have been changed in both their thinking and their actions. Materials and energy have been used in a way that is never recoverable. Therefore, to be a designer requires an intrepid nature. Such a person opens up portals to new realities and prods the world into a new present. This type of person is a leader in the most profound sense.

Conversely, a leader is always a designer, since a leader's role is, by definition, guiding or—less fulfilling—leading, people into new realities. Good leaders are good designers and vice versa. This reciprocal relationship holds true even when a designer acts in service to a client. The designer still has the obligation to make available new ideas, new realities, all triggered by the desiderata of the client. As there is no guarantor-of-design—except the character of the designer—there is no way to diminish this leadership role. This added responsibility of leadership may sometimes be difficult for designers to embrace, but it is a very real part of the designer's calling.

Being a designer means to be someone who engages in design activity, obviously, but in addition it means reflecting and improving on one's character and role as designer-leader. Of course, the most visible aspects of being a designer are the visible design activities—the acts of creativity and imagination; the forming of concepts, artifacts, and systems; the collaborations with clients and stakeholders, and so on. But being a designer and, even more important, continually developing as a designer requires attending to the less visible activities introduced in this chapter. This includes gaining a deeper understanding of the nature of the design process and a developed sense of how each personalized and particular design process should be designed.

Being a designer is about doing design. It is about being involved in design inquiry and action. It is about developing a sensibility to the particular while drawing from past reflective experience. It is about developing one's core values and character as a designer and applying those in appropriate ways to the situations at hand.

The Way Forward

The Design Way is focused on making the case for a design culture and a design-driven approach to the world. Design thinking and design activity need to be held in a cultural container—a social crucible—that provides perspective while nurturing, supporting, and protecting the work of designers and all those who benefit from design activities. This crucible—as a container for creative and innovative work—is not something that occurs naturally. It needs to be developed, continuously renewed, and eventually superseded. Within a healthy design culture, designers, their champions, clients, and other stakeholders accept their respective responsibilities for bringing this crucible into being.

It is important to remember that design as an approach driven by desiderata is a choice, one among many triggers of change that drive intentional behavior (see figure 16.1). Depending on how this choice is made, the outcomes and consequences will vary significantly. The choice will also have a major influence on what actually can be accomplished in the end. If a design approach is chosen from among the many avenues for change, there is a concomitant requirement that a context and environment—congruent with design behavior—be in place. In other words, a design crucible must first be formed. Within this container, which defines the limits and possibilities of design activity, design competence can become fully realized.

One of the benefits of intentionally choosing a design approach is that all parties will have "bought into" design as its own tradition. With an awareness of this initial precondition, any creative or innovative actions taken in the world will include the accountability that comes with a design contract because of the fundamental service relationship it codifies. When designers are socially and culturally legitimized, design becomes a recognized and valued approach to change by society at large. In other words, there exists a design culture.

Figure 16.1
Drivers of action

In the absence of a design tradition nested within a design culture, designers are redirected into other traditions of intentional action, in order to find the necessary support for their work. However, there is a growing understanding that this "borrowing" does not serve or fit the essential nature of design and that the core activities of the design process are not efficiently or effectively supported under such conditions. Design and its design-driven behavior are fatally restricted because the borrowed approaches, such as science or art, do not match the challenges of a design undertaking and critical elements are missing in the process. Of those elements that are present, many are unsuitable for design-related tasks. Designing must be supported by a design tradition composed of design-favorable activities.

A well-nourished design culture allows us to become self-consciously reflective world creators. The implications of such a culture extend well beyond the confines of this book. Among such implications is the recognition of a new form of democracy, based on design-inspired relationships of service. Another implication is the concept of inclusiveness, which embraces differences, diversity, and complexity with all their contradictions. The design tradition is, by nature, inclusive of other modes of inquiry and action. In design, there are no "science wars" or "cultural wars." When there are conflicts of this nature it means that the true rather than the real and ideal has become the foundation for inquiry and action. This means that design is no longer the focus. Design deals with the real and ideal, which by definition include all possible aspects of reality and that which will become reality.

Design competence allows individuals to become causal agents in the real world. This competence is an embodiment of the foundations and fundamentals presented in this book, which are enacted using the values and principles of a design culture. Anyone who so chooses can become design competent, as can any collective of like-minded individuals. Design competency asserts the capacity to create a design crucible—through the positive presence of a design culture—unleashing the potential for cross-catalytic cause-and-effect functionality.

Design touches nearly every aspect of our real world. This is something that we can't ignore, or pretend isn't the case. We must come to terms with our own ingenuity, authority, and responsibility. In *The Design Way*, we hope we have presented you with an introduction to a powerful and important way of working and being in the world. Design has done great service for humanity, as well as great harm. Possessing design competence, the ability to engage so significantly with the world, is the essence of being a designer and a human being. Pursuing the design intentions and purposes presented in this book is a lifelong commitment to one of the most important design processes you can engage in—the design of your own life.

References

Ackoff, Russell L. 1978. *The Art of Problem Solving*. New York: John Wiley & Sons.

Ackoff, Russell L. 1989. From Data to Wisdom. *Journal of Applied Systems Analysis* 16 (1): 3–9.

Ackoff, Russell L., and Fred E. Emery. 1972. *On Purposeful Systems*. Seaside, CA: Intersystems Publications.

Ackoff, Russell L., and J. Pourdehnad. 2001. On Misdirected Systems. *Systems Research and Behavioral Science* 18: 199–205.

Alexander, Christopher. 1979. *The Timeless Way of Building*. Oxford, UK: Oxford University Press.

Arendt, Hannah. 1958. *The Human Condition*. Chicago: University of Chicago Press.

Arnheim, Rudolph. 1995. Sketching and the Psychology of Design. In *The Idea of Design*, ed. Victor Margolin and Richard Buchanan, 70–75. Cambridge, MA: MIT Press.

Banathy, Bela H. 1996. *Designing Social Systems in a Changing World*. New York: Plenum Press.

Bertalanffy, Ludvig von. 1968. *General Systems Theory: Foundations, Development, Applications*. New York: George Braziller.

Boland, Richard J., Jr., and Fred Collopy. 2004. Toward a Design Vocabulary for Management. In *Managing as Designing*, ed. R. J. Boland Jr. and F. Collopy, 265–276. Stanford: Stanford University Press.

Borgmann, Albert. 1984. *Technology and the Character of Contemporary Life: A Philosophical Inquiry*. Chicago: The University of Chicago Press.

Boulding, Kenneth. 1956. General Systems Theory—The Skeleton of Science. *Management Science* 2 (3): 197–208.

Boyer, Ernest L. 1990. *Scholarship Reconsidered: Priorities of the Professoriate*. Published by the Carnegie Foundation for the Advancement of Teaching and Association of American Colleges and Universities. Stanford, CA: AAC&U.

Bransford, John, Susan Mosberg, Michael Copland, Meredith Honig, Harold Nelson, Drue Gawel, Rachel Phillips, and Nancy Vye. 2010. Adaptive People and Adaptive Systems: Issues of Learning and Design. In *Second International Handbook of Educational Change*, ed. A. Hargreaves, A. Lieberman, M. Fullan, and D. Hopkins, 825–856. Springer International Handbooks of Education, vol. 23. The Netherlands: Springer Science + Business Media.

Campbell, J. 1968. *The Hero with a Thousand Faces*. Princeton, NJ: Princeton University Press.

Churchman, C. West. 1961. *Prediction and Optimal Decision: Philosophical Issues of a Science of Values*. Englewood Cliffs, NJ: Prentice-Hall.

Churchman, C. West. 1971. *The Design of Inquiring Systems: Basic Concepts of Systems and Organization*. New York: Basic Books.

Churchman, C. West. 1979. *The Systems Approach and Its Enemies*. New York: Basic Books.

Collingwood, R. G. 1939. *An Autobiography*. Oxford, UK: Clarendon Press.

Crosby, A. W. 1997. *The Measure of Reality: Quantification and Western Society, 1250–1600*. New York: Cambridge University Press.

Cross, Nigel. 2001. Designerly Ways of Knowing: Design Discipline versus Design Science. *Design Studies* 17 (3) (Summer): 49–55.

Cross, Nigel. 2011. *Design Thinking*. Oxford, UK: Berg.

Csikszentmihalyi, Mihaly. 1990. *Flow: The Psychology of Optimal Experience; Steps toward Enhancing the Quality of Life*. New York: Harper & Row.

Dewey, James. 1910. *How We Think*. Amherst, NY: Prometheus Books.

Dewey, James. 1934. *Art as Experience*. New York: Perigee Books.

Dunne, Joseph. 1993. *Back to the Rough Ground: "Phronesis" and "Techné" in Modern Philosophy and in Aristotle*. Notre Dame, IN: University of Notre Dame Press.

Dunne, Joseph. 1999. Professional Judgment. *European Journal of Marketing* 33 (7/8): 707–719.

Eisner, Elliot W. 1985. *The Art of Educational Evaluation: A Personal View*. London: Falmer Press.

Eisner, Elliot W. 1998. *The Enlightened Eye: Qualitative Inquiry and the Enhancement of Educational Practice*. Upper Saddle River, NJ: Merrill.

Follett, Mary Parker. 1930. *Creative Experience*. New York: Longmans, Green and Co.

Gharajedaghi, Jamshid. 1999. *Systems Thinking: Managing Chaos and Complexity; A Platform for Designing Business Architecture*. Boston: Butterworth Heinmann.

Gladwell, Malcolm. 2005. *Blink—The Power of Thinking without Thinking*. New York: Little, Brown and Company.

Gladwell, Malcolm. 2008. *Outliers: The Story of Success*. New York: Little, Brown and Company.

Herrigel, Eugen. 1953. *Zen in the Art of Archery*. New York: Pantheon Books/Random House.

Hillman, James. 1992. *The Thought of the Heart and the Soul of the World*. Dallas, TX: Spring Publications.

Hillman, James. 1996. *The Soul's Code: In Search of Character and Calling*. New York: Random House.

Hillman, James. 1999. *The Force of Character and the Lasting Life*. New York: Random House.

Huxley, Aldous. 1944. *The Perennial Philosophy*. New York: Harper and Row.

Isaacs, William. 1999. *Dialogue and the Art of Thinking Together: A Pioneering Approach to Communicating in Business and in Life*. New York: Currency Doubleday.

James, William. 1975. *Pragmatism: A New Name for Some Old Ways of Thinking, and The Meaning of Truth: A Sequel to Pragmatism*. Cambridge, MA: Harvard University Press.

Janlert, Lars-Erik, and Erik Stolterman. 1997. The Character of Things. *Design Studies* 18 (3): 297–314.

Jantsch, Erich. 1975. *Design for Evolution: Self-Organization and Planning in the Life of Human Systems*. New York: George Braziller.

Jullien, François. 2004. *A Treatise on Efficacy: Between Western and Chinese Thinking*. Trans. Janet Lloyd. Honolulu: University of Hawaii Press.

Kahn, Nathaniel. 2003. Quotes from the documentary film *My Architect: A Son's Journey* about Louis Kahn.

Kahneman, Daniel, and Frederick Shane. 2002. Representativeness Revisited: Attribute Substitution in Intuitive Judgment. In *Heuristics and Biases: The Psychology of Intuitive Judgment*, ed. Thomas Gilovich, Dale Griffin, and Daniel Kahneman, 49–81. Cambridge, UK: Cambridge University Press.

Kant, Imanuel. 1790/1987. *Critique of Judgement*. Trans. W. Pluhar. Indianapolis, IN: Hackett Publishing Company.

Krippendorff, Klaus. 2006. *The Semantic Turn: A New Foundation for Design*. Boca Raton, FL: Taylor & Francis.

Kuhn, Thomas. 1962. *The Structure of Scientific Revolutions*. Chicago: University of Chicago Press.

Lin, Xiaodong, Daniel L. Schwartz, and John Bransford. 2007. Intercultural Adaptive Expertise: Explicit and Implicit Lessons from Dr. Hatano. *Human Development* 50 (1): 65–72.

Linstone, Harold. 1984. *Multiple Perspectives for Decision Making: Bridging the Gap between Analysis and Action*. Amsterdam: Elsevier Science Pub. Co.

Löwgren, J., and E. Stolterman. 2004. *Thoughtful Interaction Design: A Design Perspective on Information Technology*. Cambridge, MA: MIT Press.

Makkreel, Rudolf A. 1990. *Imagination and Interpretation in Kant: The Hermeneutical Import of the Critique of Judgment*. Chicago: The University of Chicago Press.

Margolin, Victor, and Richard Buchanan, eds. 1995. *The Idea of Design*. Cambridge, MA: MIT Press.

Martin, Roger. 2007. *The Opposable Mind: How Successful Leaders Win through Integrative Thinking*. Cambridge, MA: Harvard Business School Press.

Martin, Roger. 2009. *The Design of Business: Why Design Thinking Is the Next Competitive Advantage*. Cambridge, MA: Harvard Business School Press.

May, Rollo. 1975. *The Courage to Create*. New York: W. W. Norton & Co., Inc.

McEwen, Indra Kagis. 1993. *Socrates' Ancestor: An Essay on Architectural Beginnings*. Cambridge, MA: MIT Press.

Nelson, Harold G. 1987. Other Than Chance and Necessity: Intention and Purpose by Design. *European Journal of Operational Research* 30 (3): 356–358.

Nelson, Harold G. 1994. The Necessity of Being "Undisciplined" and "Out-of-Control": Design Action and Systems Thinking. *Performance Improvement Quarterly* 7 (3): 22–29.

Nelson, Harold G. 2007. Simply Complex by Design. *Performance Improvement Quarterly* 20 (2): 97–115.

Norman, Donald. 1993. *Things That Make Us Smart: Defending Human Attributes in the Age of the Machine*. New York: Addison-Wesley.

Nozick, Robert. 1989. *The Examined Life—Philosophical Meditations*. New York: Touchstone Book.

Nussbaum, Martha C. 1990. *Love's Knowledge: Essays on Philosophy and Literature*. New York: Oxford University Press.

Nussbaum, Martha C. 1997. *Cultivating Humanity: A Classical Defense of Reform in Liberal Education*. Cambridge, MA: Harvard University Press.

Pink, Daniel. 2009. *Drive: The Surprising Truth about What Motivates Us*. New York: Riverhead Books, Penguin Group.

Platts, M. Jim. 1997. "Competence: The Virtue of Maturity." In *Automated Systems Based on Human Skill*. Proceedings from the 6th IFAC Symposium, Kranjska Gora, Slovenia, September 17–19, pp. 231–234.

Remen, Rachel N. 1996. In the Service of Life. *Noetic Sciences Review*, no. 37 (Spring): 24.

Rittel, Horst. 1972. On the Planning Crisis: Systems Analysis of the "First and Second Generations." *Bedrifts Okonomen*, no. 8: 390–396.

Rittel, Horst. 1988. "The Reasoning of Designers." Republished in Jean-Pierre Protzen and David J. Harris, *The Universe of Design: Horst Rittel's Theories of Design* and *Planning*. New York: Routledge, 2010.

Rittel, Horst W. J., and Melvin M. Webber. 1974. Dilemmas in a General Theory of Planning. *Design Research and Methods* 8 (1): 31–39.

Rorty, Amelie. 2001. *The Many Faces of Evil—Historical Perspectives*. London: Routledge.

Schön, Donald A. 1983. *The Reflective Practitioner*. New York: Basic Books.

Schön, Donald. 1987. *Educating the Reflective Practitioner*. San Francisco: Jossey-Bass.

Schön, Donald A., and Martin Rein. 1994. *Frame Reflection—Towards the Resolution of Intractable Policy Controversies*. New York: Basic Books.

Searle, John R. 1983. *Intentionality: An Essay in the Philosophy of Mind*. New York: Cambridge University Press.

Simon, Herbert. 1969. *The Sciences of the Artificial*. Cambridge, MA: MIT Press.

Singer, Edgar A. Jr. 1959. *Experience and Reflection*, ed. C. W. Churchman. Philadelphia: University of Pennsylvania Press.

Snow, C. P. 1959. *The Two Cultures*. Cambridge, UK: Cambridge University Press.

Stolterman, Erik. 1999. The Design of Information Systems—Parti, Formats and Sketching. *Information Systems Journal* 9 (1): 3–20.

Stolterman, Erik. 2008. The Nature of Design Practice and Implications for Interaction Design Research. *International Journal of Design* 2 (1): 55–65.

Sunstein, Carl R. 2001. *Designing Democracy—What Constitutions Do*. Oxford, UK: Oxford University Press.

Taleb, Nassim Nicholas. 2007. *The Black Swan: The Impact of the Highly Improbable*. New York: Random House.

Toynbee, Arnold J. 1948. *A Study of History*, vol. 1–12. Oxford, UK: Oxford University Press.

Trainor, Rosaline. 2001. "Befriending Our Desires." Lecture presented at Seattle University, Seattle, WA, May 1.

Tufte, Edvard R. 1983. *The Visual Display of Quantitative Information*. Cheshire, CT: Graphics Press.

Tufte, Edvard R. 1990. *Envisioning Information*. Cheshire, CT: Graphics Press.

Vickers, Geoffrey. 1995. *The Art of Judgment: A Study of Policy Making*. Thousand Oaks, CA: Sage Publications.

Weber, Max. 1904/2007. "Objectivity" in Social Science. In *Classical Sociological Theory*, 2nd ed., ed. C. Calhoun, J. Gerteis, J. Moody, S. Pfaff, and I. Virk. Malden, MA: Blackwell Publishing.

Wittgenstein, Ludwig. 1963. *Philosophical Investigations*. Trans. G. E. M. Anscombe. Oxford, UK: Basil Blackwell.

Ziman, John. 2000. *Real Science, What It Is, and What It Means*. Cambridge, UK: Cambridge University Press.

Zsambok, C. E., and G. Klein, eds. 1997. *Naturalistic Decision Making*. Mahwah, NJ: Lawrence Erlbaum Associates.

Index